COLLEGE CREDIT FOR WITHDRAWN
WRITING IN HIGH SCHOOL

College Credit for Writing in High School

The "Taking Care of" Business

Edited by

Kristine Hansen
Brigham Young University

Christine R. Farris
Indiana University

National Council of Teachers of English
1111 W. Kenyon Road, Urbana, Illinois 61801-1096

Copy Editor: Jane M. Curran
Production Editor: Carol Roehm
Interior Design: Jenny Jensen Greenleaf
Cover Design: Pat Mayer
Cover Image: iStockphoto.com/ugurkoban

NCTE Stock Number: 07225

It is the policy of NCTE in its journals and other publications to provide a
forum for the open discussion of ideas concerning the content and the teaching of English and the language arts. Publicity accorded to any particular
point of view does not imply endorsement by the Executive Committee, the
Board of Directors, or the membership at large, except in announcements
of policy, where such endorsement is clearly specified.

Every effort has been made to provide current URLs and email addresses,
but because of the rapidly changing nature of the Web, some sites and
addresses may no longer be accessible.

Library of Congress Cataloging-in-Publication Data

Hansen, Kristine.
    College credit for writing in high school : the "taking-care-of"
business / edited by Kristine Hansen, Christine R. Farris.
        p. cm.
    Includes bibliographical references and index.
    ISBN 978-0-8141-0722-5 (pbk.)
    1. English language—Rhetoric—Study and teaching—United States.
2. High school students—Education (Higher)—United States. 3. Dual
enrollment—United States. 4. College credits—United States. I. Farris,
Christine, 1949– II. Title.
    PE1405.U6H36 2010
    808'.0420711—dc22
                                                    2009050591

Contents

FOREWORD

Tough Questions for Thoughtful Educators

DAVID A. JOLLIFFE
University of Arkansas

College Credit for Writing in High School: The "Taking Care of" Business is a book about thorny questions, and that's why it's a superb book for anyone interested in joining the conversation about high school–college articulation in English and the language arts, ratcheting up the rigor and relevance of high school reading and writing instruction, and making sure that college and university courses appropriately meet the needs of all incoming students—developmental, mainstream, and advanced alike.

What are the questions? First of all, should high school students even be encouraged or allowed to accelerate and earn college credit in composition via Advanced Placement (AP), International Baccalaureate (IB), early college (EC), or concurrent enrollment (CE) programs? Isn't there something developmentally appropriate about learning how to read critically and write effectively all along the way—from preschool through college—with the instruction becoming more rigorous as the intellectual work facing the students becomes more demanding? This question, of course, raises another, one about dividing lines: What reading and writing abilities and skills distinguish student performance at the primary, elementary, secondary, and postsecondary levels? And this question prompts even more: What's the difference between "ability" and "skill" in reading and writing? Or what about this one: How is the new national Common Core State Standards Initiative (www.ccsso.org) defining levels of student performance and achievement in high school English and language arts? Finally, if students are encouraged or allowed to accelerate, how can all the stakeholders in the acceleration process—parents, educators, legislators, and, lest we forget, the students themselves—be certain that the acceleration, whether it's through AP, IB, EC, or CE, is legitimate and appropriate?

I'm not sure I know the answers to these questions after having read *College Credit for Writing in High School: The "Taking Care of" Business*, but I do know that I am—as other readers of the book will be—in a better position to enter informed discussions about them. Let me chew on two of them, the first and the last, as an entrée into the intellectual ferment that readers will enjoy in the book.

Should students be encouraged or even allowed to accelerate? Lest I hear cries of "that's the pot calling the kettle black" as I begin this rumination, let me begin with two confessions. First, I finished my PhD—course work, languages, exams, and dissertation—in three years. I was a fool to do so. When I was just beginning my breakneck gallop through the degree—I was twenty-nine years old, had been teaching for five years at the high school and college level, and was eager to get on with my life—the late Steve Witte asked me, in his well-meaning, laconic way, "Why don't you slow down and learn something?" I've done okay with a degree earned in three years, but I should have listened to Steve. Second, I spent fifteen years, from 1992 through 2007, in increasingly important positions—reader, table leader, question leader, test developer, and chief reader—for the AP English Language and Composition Program. In those capacities, I probably helped several hundred thousand high school students accelerate and get first-year composition "out of the way," even though I have stated publicly that the reason I supported AP English Language and Composition (and still do) was not that its test exempted students from any course but that its curriculum is better than most students get in high school English (Jolliffe and Phelan).

So I am no blushing novice in this "ratchet-up-the-pace" business in education. But when reading the chapters in this collection, I finished the second paragraph of Barbara Schneider's piece on the early college high school program at the University of Toledo and learned that the six "test cases" she interviewed will "if all goes as planned . . . be ready for work or graduate school by the time they are twenty," I had to scribble in the margin, "Good god, what's the hurry?"

Since I didn't actually start my own personal ratcheting up until I was twenty-nine, I look back fondly on my own even-paced experiences with literacy, both curricular and co-curricular, in high school and college. I recollect how much I learned about reading and writing in high school from being in plays and writing for, and later editing, the monthly student newspaper. I call to mind not only the excellent classes I had in writing, literature, and language at my undergraduate alma mater but also the enriching literacy experiences I had over those four years by participating in student government, competing on the intercollegiate debate team, and, once again, acting in and directing for the theater. If someone had actually asked me if I was interested in being "ready for work or graduate school" when I was twenty, I would have considered him or her certifiably insane. I wonder, as I read the chapters in this collection, how frequently anyone asks the high school students themselves whether they are eager to "be ready for work or graduate school" when they reach twenty. I wonder who makes the bulk of decisions and who influences the decisions about participating in early-college initiatives—the students, their parents, the program administrators?

If a student's high school experiences with reading and writing, both curricular and co-curricular, are truly quotidian, excessively humdrum, just plain uninspiring, then that student probably should look for courses and activities that are more challenging and rewarding. If those courses and activities should happen to place him or her into more advanced college courses, all well and good. I simply hope that some wise soul will say two things to this high school student: (a) slow down and learn something, and (b) realize that, if you're fortunate, the years from fourteen to twenty-two will be overflowing with wonderful opportunities to know your world, to know yourself, to know friends and family, through reading and writing. And I hope the student listens better than I did to Steve Witte. What's the hurry?

But despite my latter-day misgivings about racing through literacy education, I should probably acknowledge, now that American youth and their parents have tasted the fruit of early credit for college, that there's no turning back, so that's why the final question, about how we can assure rigor, relevance, standards, and accountability in AP, IB, EC, and CE, comes into play. In a book chapter I wrote with Bernie Phelan, we acknowledged that neither AP nor college composition is probably ever going to go away. Neither are IB, EC, and CE. We quoted Rodney King then, and I reiterate his rhetorical question now: Can't we all get along? Can't college-level instruction co-exist with AP, IB, EC, and CE? Can't we figure out ways to capitalize on the energy of all these programs and improve reading and writing instruction on both sides of the "divide"?

We can, but to do so I think all parties involved with literacy education on both sides ought to embrace two ideas. First, high school and college literacy advocates need to look skeptically at two propositions that seem to support tacitly not only AP, IB, EC, and CE but also articulation agreements that permit transfer of composition credit from one postsecondary institution to another: first, the notion that literacy is literacy is literacy, no matter what the context; and, second, the idea that once you've "got" literacy, then you've "got" it for life. Second, if colleges and universities are going to award waivers or credits for AP, IB, EC, and CE, the colleges and universities ought to have some kind of advanced course—or at least an orientation experience—in university-level academic literacy for students to become grounded in the actual reading and writing practices of their new institutional home.

Because precollege literacy programs are such an attractive option, financially and logistically, I fear that most of their advocates have not interrogated theoretically two ideas that underlie them: literacy is literacy is literacy, and once you've got it, you've got it. The scholarly field known as the New Literacy Studies, a term coined by Brian Street (see Street, *Literacy*; Street, *Social*; Barton; and Gee), draws a distinction between what Street calls the "autonomous" and the "ideological" model of literacy. The former holds that literacy consists of a fixed set of skills that are "neutral" and "universal" and that introducing literacy to people "will have the effect of enhancing their cognitive skills, improving their educational prospects, making them better citizens, regardless of the social and economic conditions that accounted for their 'illiteracy' in the first place" (Street, "What's New" 77). In contrast, the ideological model sees literacy as "not simply a technical and neutral skill," but instead as a "social practice" (77). Street elaborates:

> It is about knowledge: the ways in which people address reading and writing are themselves rooted in conceptions of knowledge, identity, and being. It is also always embedded in social practices, such as those of a particular job market or a particular educational context and the effects of learning that particular literacy will be dependent on those particular contexts. (77–78)

In other words, literacy is not literacy is not literacy. Doesn't the same principle apply to the *teaching* of literacy, to the *teaching* of reading and writing? If so, how can a precollege program teach students thoroughly about reading and writing in postsecondary settings when the two sets of contexts are different?

Moreover, a fundamental tenet of adult intellectual development is that most adults are capable of substantial learning in activities that call for critical reflection. The prominent adult education expert Stephen Brookfield describes four activities as central to critical reflection: analyzing assumptions upon which any argument is built, realizing the historical and cultural context-embeddedness of our thinking, speculating imaginatively about alternative ways of thinking about phenomena, and developing a reflective skepticism about supposedly universal truth claims. These sound to me an awful lot like the abilities of critical reading and analysis that students should be learning and practicing throughout their school years, from at least late elementary or middle school through college. Given the prominent role that critical reflection plays in learning to read and write, doesn't it make sense that most young adults will continue to improve as readers and writers as they proceed through college and into their careers? What are the consequences of tacitly ignoring the potential of this development by offering sixteen-, seventeen-, and eighteen-year-olds the chance to complete their formal study of reading and writing prior to even going to college?

I don't mean these questions to insinuate that we ought to do away with AP, IB, EC, and CE. I am suggesting, however, that colleges and universities need to do more than most of them currently do to acknowledge that (a) they have an entering population of students who have already developed some admirable reading and writing abilities, (b) the contexts of literate intellectual activity at the college or university are different from high school, and (c) they expect the students to continue learning to read more thoroughly and critically and write more effectively. Phelan and I put forward the idea that colleges and universities might place students who earn AP English Language and Composition credit into a more advanced reading and writing course, rather than simply exempting them from one or more mainstream first-year composition requirements. Let me extend and alter this line of thinking a bit: perhaps students don't need an entire course; perhaps they (and their parents) would balk at such a requirement, thinking that this is what the AP, IB, EC, or CE course "got out of the way." So, if not a complete course, why not require students entering with credits or waivers to participate in an intensive workshop—a long weekend, a handful of two-hour blocks, or whatever configuration seems reasonable—so they can learn about the culture of reading and writing that successful students inhabit at the college or university? And why not work through college advising or institutional research offices to get these students to reflect in journals or portfolios about how their perceptions of what it means to read and write successfully in college develop over the years of their baccalaureate education? The advanced course or intensive workshop would counter (ideally in a relatively painless way) the notion of literacy is literacy is literacy, whether you get it in high school, a two-year college, or a four-year college. The reflective journals or portfolios would offer not only to the students but also to faculties and administrators on both sides of the high school–college divide tremendous insights into young adults' literacy development.

The question of AP, IB, EC, or CE versus traditional college composition doesn't have to be an either/or question. There's rich soil for literacy work, for literacy growth, on both sides of the fence.

Works Cited

Barton, David. *Literacy: An Introduction to the Ecology of Written Language.* Oxford: Blackwell, 1994. Print.

Brookfield, Stephen. *Becoming a Critically Reflective Teacher.* San Francisco: Jossey-Bass, 1995. Print.

Gee, James Paul. *Social Linguistics and Literacies: Ideologies in Discourse.* 2nd ed. London: Taylor and Francis, 1996. Print.

Jolliffe, David A., and Bernard Phelan. "Advanced Placement, Not Advanced Exemption: Challenges for High Schools, Colleges, and Universities." *Delivering College Composition: The Fifth Canon.* Ed. Kathleen Blake Yancey. Portsmouth: Boynton/Cook, 2006. 89–103. Print.

Street, Brian. *Literacy in Theory and Practice.* Cambridge: Cambridge UP, 1994. Print.

———. *Social Literacies: Critical Approaches to Literacy in Development, Ethnography, and Education.* London: Longman, 1995. Print.

———. "What's 'New' in New Literacy Studies? Critical Approaches to Literacy in Theory and Practice." *Current Issues in Comparative Education* 52.2 (2003): 77–91. Print.

ACKNOWLEDGMENTS

The editors would like to thank the family, friends, and colleagues who helped make this book possible. Kristine thanks her two dedicated editorial assistants, Jon Ogden and Kim Allen, for their tireless and painstaking efforts. Christine particularly thanks her former and current colleagues Barry Kroll, Sharon Sperry, Ted Leahey, and John Schilb, whose beliefs, research, and practices regarding college English courses in high school have shaped her own. She would also like to thank the high school teachers in IU's Advance College Project and their counterparts in other such programs, whose commitment to teaching writing, however it is branded and marketed, inspired this project. We are also grateful for the generous and honest reflection of the contributors to this volume and the equally generous and thoughtful appraisals of the anonymous reviewers. Finally, we thank Kurt Austin of NCTE, not only for his support and patience during the long months required to complete the book but also for his willingness to give our ideas full and fair consideration in the first place.

INTRODUCTION

The "Taking Care of" Business

KRISTINE HANSEN
Brigham Young University

CHRISTINE R. FARRIS
Indiana University

In late 2007 Harvard Education Press published a book called *Minding the Gap* with the intriguing subtitle *Why Integrating High School with College Makes Sense and How to Do It* (Hoffman et al.). The book is a collection of forty-two essays written by people interested in public education policy. Eleven of the authors are from universities, either professors or administrators. Four others are directly employed in formulating or carrying out public educational policies in federal or state education agencies. Of the remaining twenty-seven authors, twenty-two represent nonprofit groups such as the following :

- The American Youth Policy Forum, a "professional development organization" that provides "learning opportunities for policy leaders, practitioners, and researchers working on youth and education issues at the national, state, and local levels." This entity receives grants from a long list of foundations, including the following: Bill and Melinda Gates, Carnegie, Eli Lilly, Ford, General Electric, and Kellogg.
- The Institute for Educational Leadership, a Washington-based nonprofit organization founded in 1971 to "build the capacity of individuals and organizations in education and related fields to work together—across policies, programs, and sectors." It receives funding from Lockheed Martin, J. P. Morgan, and UPS, as well as Atlantic Philanthropies, the Carnegie Corpo-

ration, the Ford Foundation, and the Bill and Melinda Gates
Foundation, among others.

◆ Jobs for the Future, a nonprofit research, consulting, and advocacy agency, founded in 1983 to influence "major national
policies on education, welfare, job training, and unemploy-
ment." It has been or is now funded by businesses such as
IBM, Fidelity Investments, and McGraw-Hill, as well as by
private foundations, including Ford, Wal-Mart, and Bill and
Melinda Gates Foundation.

◆ Achieve, a bipartisan, nonprofit organization created by state
governors and business leaders in 1996 to help "states raise
academic standards, improve assessments and strengthen
accountability to prepare all young people for postsecondary education, work and citizenship." Among the companies
and foundations that help support its efforts are Boeing, IBM,
State Farm, the Carnegie Corporation, the Bill and Melinda
Gates Foundation, the Intel Foundation, and the Prudential
Foundation.

◆ The National Center for Educational Accountability, an arm
of the Education Commission of the States (ECS), organized
in 1965 to help "states develop effective policy and practice
for public education by providing data, research, analysis and
leadership; and by facilitating collaboration, the exchange of
ideas among the states, and long-range strategic thinking."
Home of the prototype of the National Assessment of Educational Progress (NAEP), the ECS was funded by federal grants
until 1983, when the federal government took away its $10
million a year and gave the private Educational Testing Services management of the NAEP program. ECS has struggled
financially since then but has managed to stay alive with revenue from state membership fees, contracts, grants from private
foundations, and sponsorship by Microsoft, Pearson Education and its National Evaluation Systems, College Board, ETS,
and Measured Progress.

◆ The National Center for Public Policy and Higher Education, founded in 1998, which "promotes public policies that
enhance Americans' opportunities to pursue and achieve
high-quality education and training beyond high school" and
"prepares action-oriented analyses of pressing policy issues
facing the states and the nation regarding opportunity and
achievement in higher education—including two- and four-
year, public and private, for-profit and nonprofit institutions."
(Its sources of funding are not publicized on its website, and
our requests for information were ignored.)

From this roll call of nonprofit organizations that most Americans have likely never heard of, it is clear that public educational policy is being subjected to concerted influence from private groups supported by the private foundations of private businesses. But it's not just centers, institutes, and forums that are bidding to help formulate policy: three of the authors in *Minding the Gap* are independent researchers who consult with state agencies on educational policy. Two are from the Oregon Business Council—and one of those wears a second hat as a member of the Oregon State Board of Education. The biographical profiles of many of the authors, printed at the back of the book, suggest how intensely their interests in education and economics are intertwined.

Not surprisingly, then, the gap that the authors of *Minding the Gap* have in mind is an education gap that results from and perpetuates an earnings gap. It is the earnings gap that many students fall into after high school when they fail to complete or even to begin any postsecondary education. The editors observe that "young people from the middle and upper ends of the socioeconomic spectrum are almost five times more likely to earn a two- or four-year college degree than those from low-income families." Low-income students with test scores in the top quartile, who apparently have the ability to succeed in postsecondary education, are no more likely to attend college than high-income students with test scores in the lowest range. African American and Latino students are at even greater risk of not seeking higher education, as their likelihood of even completing high school is "a 50:50 proposition at best" (Hoffman et al. 1). But in order for the United States to stay competitive in a global economy, the editors argue, "our postsecondary systems must produce millions of additional college degree holders" to fill the jobs that will require college degrees—jobs that will be the only sure avenue to an adequate standard of living. To help more students from low-income and minority groups leap safely across the gap, they propose "an integrated secondary/postsecondary system, one in which a post-high school credential is the default end point, and in which the transition between sectors is eliminated to the greatest extent possible." Because so many "low-income students disappear in the transition between high school and postsecondary," the United States must "rethink and restructure the transition and build the structures needed for a seamless system" (2).

In their view, such an integrated educational system would require that K–12 and postsecondary systems (1) assume joint responsibility for defining standards, curricula, expectations, and assessments; (2) share seamless accountability, finance, and governance systems; and (3) create multiple pathways to a postsecondary credential (Hoffman et al. 2–3). As evidence that some states are already beginning to create the integrated systems needed, the editors point to state programs that offer to pay part or all of the college tuition for students who complete the requirements for an associate's degree while still in high school, as well as to programs that allow students to fill high school requirements with "equally or more challenging college courses at no cost" (3). Although they don't name names, the editors apparently have in mind such things as Advanced Placement and International Baccalaureate courses, which are generally considered to be as challenging as college courses, as well as early college high schools and concurrent enrollment programs—most of which many states are now either encouraging or mandating and even giving students financial incentives to enroll in. However, the editors of *Minding the Gap* add that the momentum toward this type of integration "remains under the radar and is not yet seen as the backbone of a K–16 or 9–14 system" (3).

We have sketched at length this evolving national context because it is undoubtedly spurring some of the developments analyzed and evaluated in the essays collected here. Our aim in this book is to bring fully onto the radar screen a picture of what we see happening across the nation as educational institutions and state governments pay growing heed to the businesses and private foundations urging the integration of high school and college. However, we have limited our focus in this volume to just the ways in which high school students are offered instruction in college composition. Virtually everyone acknowledges that the ability to write competently contributes to success in college and beyond, so writing courses are usually required for graduation. Despite its professed importance, however, writing—as a course of study in itself—has a minimal and marginal presence in the postsecondary curriculum. Usually only one or two courses are required. While many of these required courses are taught by full-time, permanent faculty, more often they are taught by adjunct faculty occupying tenuous positions or by a constantly changing cadre of graduate students, many with little teaching experience and meager formal course work preparing them for their teaching roles.

Given these circumstances, it seems fair to ask whether there are compelling reasons to continue the practice of having most students enroll in a first-year writing course once they arrive on a college campus. Perhaps there are better reasons to facilitate students' receiving what we call college writing instruction and credit for it before they even set foot on a college campus. The rationale for college composition, as Sharon Crowley reminds us, "did not emanate from some subject matter, discipline, or field of study, as most university courses do" (6). Instead, composition came into existence in the nineteenth century because of literacy deficiencies college faculty perceived in students and in their high school English instruction. While entrance examinations to determine whether students were ready for college work may have redirected high school teachers' emphases and reshaped their practices, more often they indicated that students were not prepared (67). "Not ready for college work" is, not surprisingly, a conclusion routinely arrived at to this day by standardized testing services, like the ETS, whose raison d'être is to predict, if not determine, college readiness along with placement, curriculum, and credits accrued. Over the course of one hundred years, freshman composition, first created to remedy supposed deficiencies, became a requirement—sometimes the only requirement—of college students at all skill levels, as well as an industry fraught with questionable labor practices and disrespect from the scholarly wing of the English departments it supports through credit hours in composition instruction.

Why, then, vulnerable as composition is to criticism and institutional practices that may have little to do with the improvement of student writing, would we not want to return this preparation to the secondary level, where, it has long been argued, writing skills should have been addressed in the first place? One answer, of course, as Crowley and others maintain, is that we like the idea of a universal requirement in college, and we repackage its historical gatekeeping and acculturation function to keep it in place. We invent and reinvent a need in order to fill it and maintain the managed economy of funding graduate students who teach writing while seeking their degrees. A less cynical answer might be that composition studies over the last thirty years has made more of the first-year gatekeeping function, evolving the study of writing into a multifaceted discipline, with an expertise to be nurtured, researched, and taught in the university setting. Claims like David W. Smit's that the fragmented field of composition can and should do more to reach "consensus" (12) and "put into practice what we know about how people learn to write" often include calls like his for all disciplines to teach writing and for the training of writing specialists conversant with the discourse practices in the communities they are preparing students to join (13). Smit also notes that where once an acceptable basic definition of "literacy" was reading and writing well enough to get along in everyday life, today we commonly speak of "literacies," and "we expect the general population to achieve levels of literacy that in the past were achieved only by a limited elite" (37–38). Add to that the proliferation of technologies that people can now use for communicating in writing, and the educational picture becomes much more complex. Smit argues that universities should broaden the notion of research in composition studies to include promoting literacy generally, not just in the first year of college (199).

In today's global economy—with its more complex understandings of literacy, higher standards expected of students and employees, and quickly evolving technologies and practices—it is perhaps not surprising that the nearly universal first-year writing course should be one of the first that policymakers would identify as appropriate to move into the high school to speed up student development and make room in college for other kinds of learning. The authors of *Minding the Gap*, referred to earlier, apparently assume that early instruction in college writing will give high school students a foundation for further success once they enter college. If it doesn't speed their progress through college and get them into the workplace sooner, they may think, at least it should prepare them for higher achievement in college, which will lead to the all-important postsecondary certification now requisite for earning a decent living.

These assumptions are part of what we analyze in the essays collected here. We offer analyses from on the ground, at the level where the courses are offered, from places where the fabrics of college and high school are even now being blind-stitched together to make the seamless transition envisioned by the movers and shakers in the centers, institutes, and forums that want to influence education policy. Some of our analyses examine another assumption as well, the belief that private entities that are not a part of state-supported educational systems should contribute their own fabric and thread to help create this seamless transition. Just as private corporations and their philanthropic foundations are funding much of the thinking that propels educational policymaking, nonprofit corporations and business-style thinking also play an increasingly larger role in offering students alternate pathways to college credit in high school. The two most prominent avenues for early completion of college requirements are taking an Advanced Placement (AP) test or enrolling in a concurrent enrollment (CE) course that might be offered at a high school, on a college campus, or via distance learning. However, a growing third option is the International Baccalaureate (IB) diploma, completed in high school and then accepted by some universities for a varying number of credit hours. A fourth option is enrolling in an early college (EC) high school, where students are accelerated through the final years of secondary school and the first years of postsecondary learning simultaneously, beginning college as young as age fourteen and completing it as early as age twenty.

Of these four options, two—Advanced Placement and International Baccalaureate—are not businesses seeking profits, but they are sponsored by organizations that, in effect, sell educational products and services and that are clearly interested in increasing the size of their market. Although the College Board is a nonprofit organization, it is heavily involved in the marketing of tests of all kinds—not only more than 35 AP tests, but also the well-known SAT and CLEP exams. It has trademarked the AP name—you can see the little ® next to the name on its website, where it declares its mission is to "connect students to college success and opportunity." Its aim with AP is to help students "gain the edge in college preparation" and "stand out in the college admissions process." The IB initials are apparently not trademarked, but the International Baccalaureate Organization acknowledges that to achieve its mission of developing "inquiring, knowledgeable and caring young people who help to create a better and more peaceful world through intercultural understanding and respect," its main strategic goal in the twenty-first century must be sustainable growth. This goal requires ever-increasing access to IB educational programs, particularly for students whose socioeconomic and geographic circumstances currently hinder their participation. Both AP and IB present statistics on their websites documenting the growth of their share of the educational market that offers to provide access to college credit.

The CE option is also not exactly a business, but it is susceptible to the increasingly competitive atmosphere in which educational services are now being offered. For example, as one or more colleges in a given region begin to offer CE courses, other colleges in the same region may feel they need to offer such courses as well in order not only to generate enough enrollments and tuition dollars to maintain financial viability but also, in a sense, to protect the curriculum they offer in a particular subject from being undercut by what they might view as a poor alternative. In some places, there are few or no "market regulations" to prevent poorly designed and supervised or ill-taught CE courses, since various states are at different stages in their efforts to set up standards and to regulate CE programs so that educational abuses do not occur. The National Alliance of Concurrent Enrollment Partnerships (NACEP) is spearheading a nationwide effort to establish accreditation standards that will ensure uniformly high quality in CE courses. But there are still years to go before that milestone is reached.

The growth of these new avenues for acquiring college writing credit before matriculation at a college and the increasing numbers of students choosing these alternative paths are signs that the academic discipline of English—usually the home of college writing programs—needs good answers to several overarching questions: Is the "outsourcing" of instruction in college writing to noncollege "providers" of educational services something to be resisted or embraced? If it is embraced, what are the possible benefits and the possible detriments to students, their parents, their teachers, the educational institutions at both secondary and postsecondary levels, and the public at large? And if these pathways are to proliferate, what are the standards that should be met with respect to student readiness, teacher preparation, curricular content, pedagogical strategies, and learning outcomes? What advice and cautions ought to be given with respect to any of these? Can general "college-level writing ability" be defined adequately? Or would it always have to be defined with reference to expectations at a particular postsecondary institution? Should the education of prospective secondary English teachers change, since many of them will become de facto college teachers as part of the college curriculum migrates into the high schools? What is the evidence for and against the utility and success of these new policies, practices, and providers that are being touted as a cure for the shortcomings of the American secondary education system? What is the risk that the bottom-line economics of selling courses, tests, and credits to students may overpower considerations of readiness, teacher quality, and soundness of curriculum? Will pressures for market expansion, for example, compromise educational quality? Or is competition a plus, something that will spur each provider to work harder to attract more "customers"?

The contributors to this volume shed light on many of these questions, but their answers are not always in agreement with each other. The purpose of the volume, however, is not to find a univocal answer to questions like the above; rather, it is to explore the complexity of the issues, to describe best practices, to point out pitfalls, to establish benchmarks for measuring success, and to lay out possible futures in this brave new educational world. For if things change in the ways envisioned by the authors of *Minding the Gap* and the organizations they represent, the future of college writing programs—and perhaps the general education curriculum that makes up a great part of the first two years of college—will have to change as well.

In the first chapter Kristine Hansen sketches broadly the

"composition marketplace," describing the generic brand of first-year writing offered on most postsecondary campuses and comparing it to the brands offered by IB, AP, and CE. While critical of the AP brand—particularly the AP Literature and Composition test—Hansen acknowledges that the IB brand may actually be giving students the same well-rounded instruction in writing across the curriculum that is sought in university WAC programs. However, she views CE programs as likely the best venue for institutional cooperation in working with students ready to make the transition from secondary to postsecondary schooling, particularly if those programs meet certification standards set up by NACEP. She calls for K–16 teachers to cooperate in creating a writing curriculum that is continuous from grade to grade, integrated with other curricula, and developmentally appropriate for students. She urges resistance to the idea that writing is a bounded and discrete set of skills or a bundle of knowledge that students "acquire" in one simple transaction. A cooperative effort across institutional boundaries to revamp the K–16 writing curriculum, she argues, would support the larger public good of producing the right kinds of human capital for our economic system and knowledgeable citizens for our political system.

By exploring the 1950s roots of the AP program, Joseph Jones points out that the concern of private foundations with high school and college curricula is not a recent phenomenon. However, the aim of those foundations over half a century ago was not to more carefully align secondary and postsecondary education, but rather to offer gifted students college credit while they were still enrolled in elite high schools. Jones shows how a report funded by the Ford Foundation in 1953 reduced composition to a set of basic skills, while privileging the mastery of literature. By describing this history, he speaks also to the contemporary question of whether the ends of the AP program some fifty-five years after its founding mesh with the ends of college writing programs as they are articulated today. Now that AP is not just for gifted students preparing to enter select colleges but is targeted at an ever broader population, he asks whether the AP curricula and tests make sense any longer. Jones concludes they have not kept pace with the changes in the field of rhetoric and composition nor with the ability of individual postsecondary institutions to offer a writing curriculum best designed for local populations and needs.

Kathleen Puhr, on the other hand, argues that recent developments in the AP English Language and Composition course and its corresponding test have brought both into better alignment with most college composition courses. Although she acknowledges that the evolution of the English Language course is not yet complete, Puhr argues that it can be a valid substitute for a first-year writing course on a college campus when the AP course is taught as envisioned by well-prepared teachers. She also describes the College Board's efforts to audit high school AP syllabi, begun in 2007, in an attempt to control the quality of AP courses and to prevent courses that are advanced "in name only." Speaking from her twenty years of experience teaching high school AP courses at Clayton High School in St. Louis, her fifteen-plus years of leading summer workshops for AP teachers, and her five years of service on the committee that develops the AP English Language and Composition Exam, Puhr believes that AP offers some students a legitimate pathway to completing college-level work in writing before they go to college.

One response to Puhr's claim can be found in Colleen Whitley and Deirdre Paulsen's report of results from research they conducted of an honors first-year writing course taken annually by about 700 students who could have skipped the course because of their AP English test scores. Whitley and Paulsen surveyed 176 students, from all over the nation, who compared their high school AP courses and their college honors writing course in terms of the perceived emphasis each gave to various elements of rhetoric, the writing process, and genres of writing. The results show the college honors course added unique value to students' AP education in writing not only by giving students experiences with genres they hadn't learned in AP—such as documented, research-based arguments—but also by enriching the students' conceptions of what writing is and what writers do. Particularly, Paulsen and Whitley show how the AP courses the students had taken focused heavily on the genre of the impromptu timed essay, perhaps to the detriment of their learning research writing skills.

Steve Thalheimer, a high school teacher who now serves as an assistant superintendent of a school district, corroborates Whitley and Paulsen's research by interweaving and analyzing two narratives from his past to make pointed contrasts and derive strong conclusions about the value of both AP and CE programs. First, he compares his own readiness as a student entering college with a 5 on the AP exam with the requirements of the writing he actually had to do in college. He shows how he thought he had "acquired" the ability to write, when what he had really gained was simply passage through the gateway into a new world of college writing. He describes how he was humbled by the expectations of his history professor, whose requirements were not met by the kind of writing that netted Thalheimer his high AP score. Second, as a teacher of CE writing courses in high school for Indiana's Advance College Project for seven years, Thalheimer compares what that course prepared his students for with what students can gain from the AP English course and test, also an option at the small Indiana high school where he taught, albeit an option fewer students took. His experience and comparisons show that high school students can achieve the same outcomes as students taking on-campus college courses. However, he argues students' later success at college depends most on the nature and quality of their high school preparation, particularly on the language used to refer to college credit and the attitude students acquire about their ongoing development as writers.

Barbara Schneider reflects upon the fact that writing courses are increasingly expected to prepare students for jobs in an economy that trades in intellectual property. Noting how private foundations such as Carnegie, Ford, Kellogg, and the Bill and Melinda Gates Foundation are attempting to influence how we educate Americans between the ages of fourteen and twenty-four, Schneider questions whether other societal goals and students' personal goals are well served by this influence. Describing what happened when fourteen-year-old students in TECHS, an early college high school sponsored by the Gates Foundation, were integrated into Toledo University's writing program, Schneider focuses on hard questions raised by such initiatives: Are the students physically, intellectually, and socially mature enough to be in classes with students perhaps eight years older? Are they ready for the adult subject matter often discussed in those classes? Can they perform the writing tasks at the same level as older students? Can the typical teachers of first-year writing meet the demands of working with such young students? Concluding that the jury is still out—though some early signs are positive—Schneider nevertheless is concerned about the nonmaterial goals of literacy education when corporations and foundations take it upon themselves to sponsor such education and try to speed it up.

Likewise, Joanna Castner Post, Vicki Beard Simmons, and Stephanie Vanderslice acknowledge the problems that can arise when state legislatures mandate the meshing of college and high school. Although they are optimistic about the eventual success of CE at their institution, they describe the difficulties they faced in a fast-track transition to offering the University of Central Arkansas writing course in surrounding high schools when the Arkansas state government decided to make CE courses an integral part of secondary education. Their university president asked the faculty in the spring of 2006 to have programs in place by fall of that same year. The authors describe what they learned from that tumultuous time, not least that, according to NACEP survey data, high school teachers felt they were largely capable of taking on the role of teaching university courses, even on short notice. Post, Simmons, and Vanderslice claim that their experience bodes well for positive partnerships between high schools and universities, but they outline changes that still need to be made as the high schools work to send better prepared students to college, and the university's writing department changes to accommodate and challenge these students.

Describing a program that is more settled, Randall McClure, Kevin Enerson, Jane Kepple Johnson, Pat Lipetzky, and Cynthia Pope show how CE can be a win-win program for both high schools and universities in rural areas. McClure and his coauthors—a university dean, a high school principal, and two high school English teachers—speak from a variety of institutional perspectives to the benefits of CE programs in the wake of government mandates in Minnesota requiring students to take postsecondary course work while still in high school. The authors discuss the demographic, academic, and economic needs for CE courses in rural high schools and universities. They also discuss the benefits, which, along with improved fiscal and resource management, include student readiness for advanced work and smoother transition to college, improved college recruitment, greater curricular rigor, and bilateral teacher development, as the high school teachers not only learn from their university colleagues but also offer them new avenues for development as well. The authors conclude that CE is a boon to both secondary and postsecondary institutions in rural settings; in fact, they argue it is superior to all the alternatives.

Miles McCrimmon, a community college professor of English with more than a decade of experience teaching in and administering concurrent enrollment programs, argues that such programs hold great promise when administered effectively and incorporated fully into the respective missions of the institutions engaged in offering the courses. Using the concept of "territory vs. territoriality," he questions why colleges should be troubled about offering composition in the habitat of the high school, when they are already expanding their offerings, real and virtual, into many other settings in the larger community. He argues that because dual enrollment is already causing the boundaries between educational territories to become more blurred and porous, secondary and postsecondary institutions should consider how to take advantage of the new liminal space created and how to spur the evolution of a new "hybrid species" of teacher to succeed in this environment. Unless postsecondary institutions are willing to improve and refine dual enrollment partnerships, McCrimmon asserts, high school curricula are likely to become even more standardized and reductive than the current national testing mania has already made them. Because both colleges and high schools are mutually "environed" by what the other is and does, they need to collaborate in a way that advances their mutual interests. McCrimmon suggests ways to capitalize on the hybrid qualities of dual enrollment and make writing courses richer experiences for both teachers and students.

Patricia A. Moody and Margaret D. Bonesteel argue that Syracuse University's Project Advance, in existence since 1972, offers a national model of best practices for precollege course offerings and evidence of a win-win solution to the debate about the validity of precollege writing experiences. Syracuse's CE program is now offered to approximately 6,600 students in 140 selected high schools in New York, New Jersey, Maine, Massachusetts, and Michigan. By describing their careful teacher selection, regular professional development, generous supportive resources, and the close relationships between the instructors teaching in the high school and the collegiate academic departments, Moody and Bonesteel demonstrate the efficacy of the program, explaining why it is so successful and a model for other universities to follow.

Chris M. Anson acknowledges that the motives behind some universities' CE programs may be unprincipled, particularly when composition, the easy target for outsourcing, is perceived to be remedial rather than "a base for more complex writing experiences in the disciplines." But since dual-credit composition programs are here to stay, he argues, we need clear, theoretically principled standards to avoid judging them subjectively, leveling unfair criticisms at some, and letting others off the hook. Anson proposes a possible set of standards, modeled on those used in writing program assessment, for evaluating dual-credit composition programs. These criteria address pedagogical and programmatic integrity and student needs, along with faculty development and fairness in labor practices. He discusses each standard, using the University of Minnesota College-in-the-Schools Program as a test case, and he suggests how each standard can be applied systematically, using key indicators and methods of assessment that go beyond those reported in other literature on evaluation.

Finally, Christine R. Farris, Indiana University's writing program administrator and coordinator of the long-standing CE writing course in Indiana's Advance College Project, argues that, especially in the face of government-mandated articulation between high school and college, we need to consider one of the biggest differences between the two sites for the delivery of composition instruction, a difference that lies not so much in course content or syllabi but in the degree of inquiry that ideally results in the production of academic writing. She points out that because secondary and postsecondary teachers work in different cultures, the intellectual moves that college writing teachers teach students to make are often reduced to formulas or essay types when taught in the high schools. In order to bridge the gap between the high school and postsecondary culture, Farris calls for real disciplinary collaboration and professionalization that address differences in approaches to the use of texts and ideas in student writing. Improvement in the articulation between secondary and postsecondary composition will require a reshaping of the role high school teachers play in their relationship to college: a transformation from "broker" to that of participant in and facilitator of disciplinary conversations worth writing about.

Taken together, the essays in this volume show that the contributors—including David Jolliffe, author of the foreword, and Douglas Hesse, author of the afterword—are more than willing to consider the benefits of greater flexibility and greater collaboration in teaching writing to students in the transition zone from adolescence to adulthood. These authors are all educators undertaking in good faith the difficult day-to-day work of developing and teaching courses that stretch their students and themselves in new ways. Many are turning willingly to neighboring institutions to engage in common efforts with colleagues they previously never knew. In the process, they are discovering not only the possibilities but also the limits of what education policymakers have envisioned as better ways to teach writing. The authors of these essays have learned that there are no cheap and easy short-cuts for either students or teachers. Outlining a curriculum is only the beginning of the work; ongoing teacher development and assessment must be planned and carried out as well. Most of all, these authors realize that the business of teaching and learning writing requires full and knowledgeable investment not only from teachers, students, and institutional administrators but also from those who put up the capital to make education possible—the taxpayers, the state governments, and the private entities trying to influence the direction and success of the nation's schools. And so these reflections on the new ways of "taking care of" college composition are meant to be read not only by writing teachers and educational administrators but also by the broadest possible audience—by everyone who agrees that deep and widespread literacy is critical for the success of both commerce and civil society. We offer this volume as a contribution to what we hope will be an enlightened and vigorous debate about the place and nature of writing and writing instruction in our schools and colleges.

Works Cited

Achieve. Home page. Achieve, n.d. Web. 5 June 2008.

American Youth Policy Forum. Home page. American Youth Policy Forum, n.d. Web. 5 June 2008.

College Board. "Advanced Placement." College Board, n.d. Web. 5 June 2008.

———. Home page. College Board, n.d. Web. 5 June 2008.

Crowley, Sharon. *Composition in the University: Historical and Polemical Essays*. Pittsburgh: U of Pittsburgh P, 1998. Print.

Hoffman, Nancy, Joel Vargas, Andrea Venezia, and Marc S. Miller, eds. Introduction. *Minding the Gap: Why Integrating High School with College Makes Sense and How to Do It*. Cambridge: Harvard Education P, 2007.

Institute for Educational Leadership. Home page. Institute for Educational Leadership, n.d. Web. 5 June 2008.

International Baccalaureate. Home page. International Baccalaureate, n.d. Web. 5 June 2008.

Jobs for the Future. Home page. Jobs for the Future, n.d. Web. 5 June 2008.

The National Center for Educational Accountability. Home page. The National Center for Educational Accountability, n.d. Web. 5 June 2008.

The National Center for Public Policy and Higher Education. Home page. The National Center for Public Policy and Higher Education, n.d. Web. 5 June 2008.

Smit, David W. *The End of Composition Studies*. Carbondale: Southern Illinois UP, 2004. Print.

CHAPTER ONE

The Composition Marketplace: Shopping for Credit versus Learning to Write

Kristine Hansen
Brigham Young University

One of the questions this book addresses is whether alternate ways of fulfilling the nearly universal college composition requirement are equally as good as, if not better than, the time-honored and ubiquitous composition course taken on a college campus during a student's first year of college. Is the existence of these competing alternatives a boon or a bane—or something in between? I offer a rather complex answer to that question by analyzing four competing "brands" in what I call the composition marketplace: the International Baccalaureate (IB) program, the Advanced Placement (AP) program, dual-credit or concurrent enrollment (CE) programs, and the "generic" brand of first-year college composition, a course that is likely as varied as the 4,000-plus postsecondary institutions at which it is offered. I frame this analysis in economic terms because I believe doing so helps illuminate reasons why avenues for earning college credit in high school have proliferated over the past thirty years. First, I establish a theoretical perspective for viewing composition as a market commodity. Then, I compare and contrast the brands offered in the composition marketplace, evaluating each in terms of its attributes, marketing, costs, and benefits. Finally, I reflect on my own analysis and the questions it raises, and I suggest changes in the relationship between secondary and higher education as well as in the curriculum of postsecondary English. These changes are needed if our goal is to educate students who are knowledgeable, versatile writers and not merely to produce students who have credit hours in writing.

Composition as a Market Commodity

The alternatives to first-year college composition (FYC) are often marketed to students and their parents as a way to "take care of" the college writing requirement or "get it out of the way" while the students are still in high school and thus save time and tuition once they matriculate at college. These tidy phrases reveal an attitude toward writing that, quite frankly, universities have encouraged for over a century, namely that the ability to write is a set of low-level skills that can and should be fairly quickly mastered early in college, or even before, so that the skills can then be transported easily into new settings and efficiently applied over and over again. These expressions also reveal an attitude toward education in general, implying it is a matter of accumulating credit hours in various categories of instruction. So receiving college credit for an AP test score or an IB or CE course in a given subject means one has completed that part of one's education. These expressions also evidence the belief that the whole purpose of education is "getting ahead"—getting ahead of the usual time frame for completing high school and college, getting ahead of other students, and getting ahead financially by making a relatively small investment now for a bigger payoff later—a quicker trip through college or admission into a prestigious university and a well-paying profession.

The idea that the purpose of education is to get ahead is so pervasive today that few even stop to question it. The U.S. Congress passed the No Child Left Behind law to ensure that all public school students will get ahead. We hear continually about the global economy in which the rising generation will have to compete, and we read statistics showing how American youth generally lag behind youth from other developed nations in science, math, reading, and writing. The fear that their children may not get ahead in such a world is part of the motivation behind market-minded parents' desire for what they call "choice" in education—the right to choose the public schools to which they send their children or even to receive vouchers from public funds to help pay tuition for private schools, where they can send their children to get ahead. AP, IB, and CE programs are aimed squarely at those who want to get ahead because they offer students the promise of starting and therefore finishing college early, distinguishing themselves from the common herd, and enhancing their chances of being admitted to a good university, where they will get even further ahead. But in a land where free market competition is highly valued, is there anything wrong with that?

Education expert David F. Labaree believes there is. When we consider education primarily as a way to get ahead, he says, we view it as a tool for social mobility rather than as a way to achieve democratic equality by preparing good citizens or as a way to promote social efficiency by focusing on the human capital demands of the economy. Labaree offers a pithy summary of these three ways of viewing education: "From the perspective of democratic equality, schools should make republicans; from the perspective of social efficiency, they should make workers; but from the perspective of social mobility, they should make winners" (43). These three goals are in constant tension, each predominating at different times, always interacting in ways that are both contradictory and complementary. Democratic equality was the ideal behind the mid-nineteenth-century establishment of the common schools as places where citizens of the republic could be cultivated. Social efficiency was the motive leading to the early twentieth-century establishment of comprehensive high schools with vocational training, tracking, and ability testing to prepare workers to take their places in the American socioeconomic pyramid. In the 1960s and 1970s the pendulum swung back to education for democratic equality, when the civil rights movement made education more accessible to all, regardless of race, class, gender, and ability. The 1980s and 1990s movement for standards in education was a shift toward the social efficiency goal, growing out of concern that schools should produce the right kind of human capital to maintain U.S. economic competitiveness. In tandem with these pendulum swings, the ideal of education for social mobility grew ever stronger—in fact, this goal was the most potent force driving the expansion of the American educational system. As more people had access to postsecondary education, those in the higher socioeconomic strata clamored for ways to distinguish themselves educationally so that they could get ahead or at least maintain their social position (34–35). Since the mid-1990s, Labaree argues, the ideal of social mobility has dominated, providing "the language we use to talk about schools, the ideas we use to justify their existence, and the practices we mandate in promoting their reform" (19). Of course, democratic equality is still espoused by proponents of liberal education, equal opportunity and access, and compensatory programs to help the disadvantaged. And education for social efficiency is always supported by politicians and employers in business and industry, as well as most taxpayers—at least when they think about the system as a whole rather than their own children's education.

The main difference between education for social mobility and education for democratic equality or social efficiency is that the former views education as a private good, while the latter two see it as a public good—like police protection and public libraries, the benefits of which are extended to all, taxpayer or not. Education can likewise function as a public good. When social efficiency is the goal, schools function as a public good by providing human capital for the economy and increasing productivity. When democratic equality is the goal, schools give students the knowledge, values, and motivation to act wisely as citizens, thus sustaining the nation's political ideals and processes. When education is supported as a public good, even childless adults and families with children in private schools benefit from the ensuing economic prosperity and political stability (Labaree 27).

However, when education is pursued mainly as a private good, as it is when social mobility is the goal, then the values and attitudes of the consumer dominate. In this view, says Labaree, the aim of education is to "accumulate forms of educational property," allowing students "to gain an advantage in the competition for social position" (27). A consumer view of education promotes a stratified structure of opportunities within and between schools so that those who qualify for the higher strata can gain status and reputation distinguishing them from those in the lower strata. Ability grouping, curriculum tracks, honors and advanced courses, special pull-out programs, letter grades (rather than narrative descriptions of student progress), standardized tests, and differentiated diplomas are ways schools respond to the consumer demand for distinction. Socially mobile consumers of education are inclined to seek learning not for its intrinsic use value, but for its exchange value, that is, for what it can be traded to help maintain or improve their socioeconomic status.

But when the value of education is more extrinsic than intrinsic, Labaree warns, credentials—grades, credits, diplomas, and degrees—take on a life of their own and become commodities sought for their own sake rather than for the learning they should represent. The danger is that formal markers of education may displace its substance, resulting in schools that allow students to meet modest performance requirements, not demonstrate mastery (Labaree 32). The "relentless pursuit of educational advantage" by acquiring credentials is best explained, Labaree argues, by economic theories of markets. When education is governed by the logic of the market, schools adapt to meet the demands of the consumers seeking credentials, each becoming "an institutional actor that is trying to establish a place for itself in a complex market environment, even if that place is sometimes socially dysfunctional" (4). Markets invite competition as other entities vie to offer the credentials. Economists tell us it is only rational behavior when some students, given many routes to attaining credentials, try to acquire them with the smallest investment of money, time, and energy.

While Labaree identifies the credentials that schools offer as the commodities students are seeking, Richard Ohmann identifies knowledge itself as undergoing commodification: "Capitalism in its [latest] phase extends the logic of the market to encompass areas of production not previously within its scope, and, in particular, seeks to commodify knowledge wherever possible" ("Accountability" 69). Jean-François Lyotard foresaw the commodification of knowledge over thirty-five years ago, when he predicted that the increasing use of computers would change the very nature of knowledge by translating learning into quantities of information that fit the new channels for circulating knowledge. In fact, any knowledge not susceptible to this kind of translation would be abandoned, he said, because the relationship between the suppliers and the users of knowledge would assume the same form as the relationship of "commodity producers and consumers to the commodities they produce and consume—that is, the form of value." Thus knowledge would be produced only "in order to be sold" and "consumed in order to be valorized in a new production: in both cases, the goal is exchange" (4–5).

It takes little reflection to realize we are now witnessing what Lyotard predicted. Knowledge is packaged in discrete quantities and circulated over long distances to be consumed by learners via TV, CDs, the Internet, and even cell phones. The products of professors' research are marketed by entrepreneurial arms of the university. Computer services, with names like IntelliMetric, are for sale, promising to "read" and consistently score student essays for teachers (Branigan). Some public universities have begun charging higher tuition rates to students majoring in fields such as business and engineering, presumably because these majors cost more to offer and the students in them are likely to get high-paying jobs when they graduate (Glater). But perhaps the most telling example of the commodification of knowledge and credentials is the growth of for-profit universities, such as the thirty-one-year-old University of Phoenix, which in 2008 boasted about 23,000 faculty and more than 250,000 students enrolled online and at almost 231 campuses in 42 U.S. states, the District of Columbia, and 4 foreign countries (*University of Phoenix*). On its twenty-fifth anniversary, Darris Howe, president of five satellite campuses, said the labels "diploma mill" and "McEducation" didn't bother him. "Look at McDonald's," he said: "You've got a consistent, quality product. . . . We too deliver a consistent, quality product." They do so by scripting the curriculum for every course taught by any teacher on any campus (Stewart B1). Instead of acting as professionals who make their own decisions about curriculum and pedagogy, teachers thus become mere deliverers of knowledge commodities to student consumers.

Some people see these phenomena as healthy innovations, unsurprising in a nation that values free market competition, even in education. But in a market environment, individual institutions, teachers, and the educational system as a whole may find it difficult to perform in a way that protects and advances the public's interest in high-quality education. This difficulty arises from the four traits of education markets identified by Labaree. Like other markets, he says, an education market is

> radically individualistic (everyone acts independently), entrepre-
> neurial (you make your own way and reap your own benefits),
> calculating (everyone is working his or her own angle), and
> potentially irrational at the collective level (because everyone
> is at the mercy of the cumulative actions of others). (4)

By examining the competitive actors in the college composition
marketplace, I draw attention to the ways these market characteristics can sometimes frustrate the collective efforts of postsecondary institutions to help students learn to write well during their
undergraduate years.

One factor in this frustration is the credit hour, invented,
according to Robert Shoenberg, in the early twentieth century
to make it easy to calculate the "exchange rate" when students
cross borders between schools. Nevertheless, Shoenberg argues,
"The convenience of the credit hour as common currency has
driven out the better but far less fungible currency of intellectual
purpose and curricular coherence." Because the credit hour is a
medium of exchange, students can receive credit at one institution for learning they completed with another institution, even
though they may have had an experience that doesn't align with
the curriculum and educational mission of the institution to
which they are transferring. In the education market, students,
calculating their own advantage, can exchange for three or more
credit hours from many colleges what might be a mediocre level
of writing performance or knowledge of a very different kind of
writing acquired via an alternative to FYC. They can engage in
what we might call "credit laundering": if they know they won't
get the credit they want from the university they like, they can
simply go first to an institution that does accept their AP score,
their IB experience, or their CE course, then later transfer that
credit to a university that has an articulation agreement with the
first college and successfully bypass FYC. Thus the market permits
what individual institutions might prohibit.

I must emphasize here that I am not claiming that any of the
competitors to FYC deliberately attempt to undermine the quality of student writing. I think their intentions are mainly good:
they aim to enhance education by offering students alternatives
to the traditional high school curriculum, which may not challenge or motivate students or may simply not offer enough to

those who have all the necessary credits for graduation before the end of twelfth grade and are ready to begin college. These problems with secondary education are genuine and need to be addressed (see National Commission on the High School Senior Year). However, the four characteristics of markets Labaree identifies—individualism, entrepreneurialism, calculating one's advantage, and collective irrationality—may operate in ways that are counterproductive. I test this assumption next by examining the curriculum or tests offered by four competitive actors in the composition market: the FYC courses of postsecondary institutions themselves, the IB program, the AP program, and concurrent enrollment (CE) programs.

The Competing Brands

I use the word "brand" intentionally here because it is now common to hear educators use it to identify what they hope the public will think of upon hearing the name of their institution and its programs. As Ohmann puts it, the marketing of education has become "a far more self-conscious activity than it used to be: Universities try to identify their niches, turn their names into brands, develop signatures and slogans" ("Citizenship" 41–42). So it's not far-fetched to regard the competitors to FYC and versions of FYC itself as brands—though not all market their brand with much savvy. Reliable statistics about each brand's share of the composition market are hard to come by and constantly changing. However, a survey of public high schools conducted by the National Center for Education Statistics (NCES)—the only survey of this nature to date—found that in the 2002–3 school year, "71 percent of public high schools offered courses for dual credit, 67 percent offered AP courses, and 2 percent offered IB courses" (Waits, Setzer, and Lewis). These figures tell us nothing about numbers of students who got credit at a postsecondary institution for the brand of composition they chose prior to college, how many passed up the alternative brands to wait for the local brand offered at the college they chose, or how many, in effect, got two brands, say AP in high school and FYC at college. What do we know about these brands? What sort of product or service does each offer? Are they, like brands of sugar, pretty much the same and easily interchanged? Are brand loyalties due to discernible and measurable differences or mainly to clever marketing?

The Generic Brand: FYC Courses

To describe FYC courses taught under the auspices of postsec-ondary institutions by employees of those institutions, I use the phrase "generic brand"—without implying such courses are inferior. Like generic brands in the supermarket, they tend to be modest in their marketing and packaging, but they usually offer good value to the consumer. They are varied but have enough in common that it's clear they belong to the same genre. Few attempts have been made to gather systematic data that would allow statistically accurate generalizations about the nature of this brand. Richard Larson's 1994 Ford Foundation report on the subject is difficult to find, infrequently cited, and now out of date. Kathleen Yancey's more recent conference presentations of her 2004 national survey research, "Portraits of Composition," have given some helpful glimpses of the national picture, but a definitive compilation of her survey results has yet to be published. Nevertheless, from thirty years of teaching in and administering composition programs, attending national conferences, examin-ing textbooks, and reading professional journals, I hazard some generalizations about generic FYC.

Obviously, not all courses do all of what I describe; there are no doubt some old-fashioned composition programs still in place. The particular shape of an FYC course will depend on the resources available at an institution and, to a large extent, the education and inclinations of the faculty members who con-struct the curriculum and hire and supervise the teachers.[1] With seventy-plus PhD programs in rhetoric and composition now operating in the United States and Canada, it is likely that the writing program administrator (WPA) on any campus will be, if not a graduate of one of those programs, at least conversant with the growing literature in rhetoric and composition. It is also increasingly likely that the FYC course on a given campus will be grounded in contemporary theories of rhetoric and composi-tion that influence pedagogy. One of the most influential of these theories since the 1980s has been that FYC should introduce students to the rhetorical practices of the academy—the intellectual and discursive moves that are common to all disciplines, moves that students need to know how to make if they are to succeed in college. Yancey's survey indicates that 57 percent of a convenience sample of 1,861 respondents taught a curriculum focused on academic discourse ("Coming" 267).

The most important point to be made about generic FYC is that it is a course about writing, one in which the main objective is to have students produce frequent writing and in which their grade depends mainly on the success of their writing—how well they take and state a tenable position about an issue, address a specified audience effectively, invent and offer evidence that would satisfy that audience, organize the writing according to expected genre conventions, incorporate and cite sources as necessary, and follow conventions of style, grammar, usage, and punctuation. The writing in an FYC course is not merely incidental to other goals, such as demonstrating an understanding of literature, history, or biology. However, reading and discussing ideas and issues normally play a large role in FYC, as teachers stimulate thinking about topics the students will write about. Many FYC courses are organized around a theme, and some are paired with other first-year courses in the curriculum, but the goal of teaching students to write successfully remains paramount to the goal of learning something else.

Another fairly safe generalization about FYC is that students will be taught using "process pedagogy"; that is, they will learn to plan, revise, and edit by writing two or more drafts of papers. With their classmates, they give and receive peer reviews of drafts before revising. They may be required to meet their teacher for draft conferences or visit the campus writing center for advice from a tutor as they revise. Popular FYC textbooks in recent years teach them processes for writing for different purposes and in different genres, producing personal reflections, narratives, analyses, reports of observations, explanations, evaluations, arguments, and position papers. An important goal of virtually all FYC courses is to teach students to use the scholarly resources of a college library and the Internet to locate and evaluate information. Students are taught how to borrow from and cite sources so that they avoid plagiarism in writing research papers. They are often exposed to more than one documentation style, since a goal of FYC is preparing students to write research papers in different disciplines during their college years.

Some FYC courses are beginning to pay attention to such matters as writing collaboratively, creating and incorporating visuals in texts, and designing documents effectively for dissemination in print or via the Web. Students may even be required to make oral presentations with computer-generated visuals to outline and illustrate their speech. It is now commonly assumed in FYC that students will have access to computers and be able to use various software applications. Some courses are conducted largely or exclusively in computer environments, with teachers and students emailing each other, sharing drafts online, posting readings and audio and video clips, conducting discussions via class networks, and conducting much class business in virtual space and time.

In light of the increasing importance of computers in composition, the Council of Writing Program Administrators has added a fifth "plank" to the "WPA Outcomes Statement for First-Year Composition," a statement that perhaps best encapsulates what the generic FYC brand aspires to be. Briefly, the Outcomes Statement outlines four areas in which students should be able to demonstrate specific competencies by the end of first-year composition: rhetorical knowledge; critical thinking, reading, and writing; processes; and knowledge of conventions. The fifth plank of the statement asserts that students should also know how to

> use electronic environments for drafting, revising, reviewing, editing and sharing texts; locate, evaluate, organize and use research material collected from electronic sources, including scholarly library databases; other official databases (e.g., federal government databases) and informal networks, and internet sources; [and] understand and exploit the differences in the rhetorical strategies and in the affordances available for both print and electronic composing processes and texts. (Council of Writing Program Administrators)

Adding this plank only underscores what is already a common practice in FYC courses.

A final safe conclusion about FYC is that, on most campuses, it continues to evolve in response to administrative and faculty desires, curricular pressures, new technologies, staffing changes, and ongoing research and discussions in the field of rhetoric and composition. For example, emulating Debra Frank Dew's example, Douglas Downs and Elizabeth Wardle claim that FYC should reject the typical goal of preparing students to write academic discourse and become instead an introduction to writing studies, a course in which first-year students would be exposed to the scholarly theoretical discourse about rhetoric, language, and literacy in order to understand the field as a genuine discipline like any other. Although Downs and Wardle have successfully taught such courses, they acknowledge the likelihood of their proposal being adopted on a wide scale is presently remote because of the practice of staffing most FYC classes with relative newcomers to the field. Nevertheless, they join Yancey ("Made") and others in urging that FYC stop functioning in a gatekeeping role and become instead a gateway course to an entire array of new courses about rhetoric and writing. These proposals illustrate the flexibility and dynamism of the first-year writing course.

Finally, I note that some writing programs across the nation have risen above generic status and have established a unique brand. Among programs advertising their writing courses as particularly valuable educational experiences that student consumers must have are those at Harvard, Duke, Rutgers, Washington State, the University of Denver, and George Mason University. In most cases, these institutions have been able to establish a name brand through a combination of generous endowments for the writing program and strong support from central administrators. Such support allows innovative WPAs to articulate and enact a unique vision by hiring a highly qualified staff of teachers, creating excellent teaching support systems, and conducting wide-scale assessments to establish the merits of the program. Ironically, even though generic FYC may not be as distinguished as these name brands, it still has market dominance and therefore is the standard to which the competing brands, which I discuss next, are usually compared when questions of equivalency, exemption, and credit for high school learning are raised.

The International Baccalaureate Program

I examine next the smallest and probably least understood brand, offered by the International Baccalaureate, a nonprofit educational foundation established in Geneva, Switzerland, in 1968 (unless otherwise noted, all information that follows is drawn from the IB website). IB did not arise to compete with FYC or any other college course; instead, its purpose was to facilitate the international mobility of secondary students preparing for higher education by providing secondary schools with a curriculum and a diploma that would be recognized by universities around the world. It now seeks to make an IB education available to students of all ages and currently serves more than 706,000 students in 2,595 schools in 134 countries offering three educational programs: a primary program, a middle-years program, and a Diploma Programme (DP) for students aged 16–19. In 2008, the DP was in place in 1,932 schools worldwide. IB has grown at an average annual rate of 17 percent per year since 1971 (*2007 Annual Review* 3).

The DP is a full-time, two-year course of study with six integrated elements: first language (A1), acquired language (A2), individuals and societies, experimental science, mathematics and computer science, and the arts. Students may choose not to study the arts curriculum, replacing it instead with a second course of study in one of the other five areas. Normally, three of the subjects are studied at "standard level," or 150 teaching hours, and three (but not more than four) are studied at "higher level," or 240 teaching hours. At the center of the curriculum is a three-part experience that each student completes: an interdisciplinary "theory of knowledge" course that explores the nature of knowledge across disciplines and encourages respect for other cultural perspectives; a "creativity, action, and service" experience to engage students in artistic pursuits, sports, and community service work outside the school; and an "extended essay," a 4,000-word (fifteen-page) composition on a subject of each student's choosing that demonstrates his or her ability to conduct research and use "writing skills expected at the university."

In order to offer the DP, schools must first complete a strenuous authorization process taking two or more years and consisting of two phases: a feasibility study by the applicant school and a site visit from an IB-appointed delegation that reports on the school's capacity to deliver the curriculum. If approved, the school begins the program, which is evaluated by the IB every five years after authorization. Teachers at the high school offer internal assessments of students' homework, projects, notebooks, and labs; these typically count for 20 percent of students' grades. However, some 5,000 external examiners, hired and trained by the IB in order to ensure "international parity," score the exams of students in each subject and award a score of 1 to 7, with 7 being "excellent." These examiners also evaluate the theory of knowledge essay and the extended essay; their judgments count for about 80 percent of students' grades. The external grading is a criterion-based, not norm-referenced, assessment; it aims to be objective, valid, and reliable, not varying by time or place. Students who meet satisfactory levels of performance (scores of at least 4) in all elements of the curriculum and achieve a minimum of 24 points (out of a possible 45) are awarded the IB diploma. Students who fail to earn the diploma may receive IB certificates for each subject area in which they were examined.

An ambitious program like this requires funding. In its first eight years, the IB was funded by UNESCO, the 20th Century Fund, and the Ford Foundation. In 1977, participating schools began to pay the IB an annual registration fee. In countries where state schools offer the DP, governments pay some of the fees; the 2007 *Annual Review* states that 56.5 percent of IB programs are now offered in state-funded schools (12). These fees allow the organization to offer training workshops, conferences, and teaching materials to IB teachers and to assist schools in implementing and reviewing the DP; the fees also support the external examinations for IB diploma candidates. However, students also pay both a registration fee ($123 for 2007–8) to take one or more exams during a particular examination session and an exam fee of $84 per subject, thus paying as much as $600 in a given year. Students working for the IB diploma pay less, however, than those who are taking individual IB courses. Students who qualify for financial assistance may receive federal and state grants to defray costs. There is no fee for assessing the theory of knowledge essay or the extended essay. In 2007, some 40,386 IB diploma candidates took 299,213 exams with an 80 percent pass rate (*Annual*

Review 2007 19). In 2006, total income was $64.1 million from fees with $1 million from fundraising (22).

In the early 1980s, regional offices were established around the world to promote the IB diploma to universities and governments, especially to help governments understand that the DP is a complement to, not a replacement for, public education, since the IB curriculum meshes with state-mandated curricula and learning outcomes. Increasing market share appears to be an important objective, as the IB website presents statistics in a series of annual reports showing steady growth of the various programs. IB now boasts that its diplomas are accepted at the most prestigious universities in Australia, New Zealand, the UK, and the United States, and it offers an online searchable directory of the IB recognition policies at 2,221 universities in 73 countries. In turn, university admissions officers can search the IB's database to view syllabi and recent examinations.

The IB diploma is generally viewed as a plus for admission to many respected universities. Harvard, for example, offers advanced standing to students who earn the "full International Baccalaureate diploma" and achieve "three higher-level subject scores of 7," a designation that enables students to complete a bachelor's degree in three years (*Harvard College Admissions*). Scott J. Cech reports that Oregon State University offers "automatic admission" and a year of college credit "worth about $6,000 for in-state students and about $18,000 for students from out of state" to any student with an IB final exam score of 30 or higher; it also gives such students a "minimum of $2,000 in scholarship money, renewable annually so long as the student maintains a 3.0 grade point average" ("World"). Other universities and colleges, both selective and less selective, have similar policies that grant college credit for high DP scores or allow students to bypass selected first-year college courses.

Viewed as a product and service in the education marketplace, the IB Diploma Programme operates like a high-end global franchise: The franchisor, IB, licenses its trademark name and proven methods of establishing a curriculum and assessing learning to franchisees, the schools, for recurring fees and periodic audits. The audits ensure the franchisor's quality standards are upheld so that its brand will continue to be respected and sought after by consumers. It is hard to find fault with the IB diploma because it requires considerable school and teacher investment to implement the curriculum and higher than usual student effort to complete it. It also succeeds in giving 80 percent of the students who enroll an integrated package of courses and learning experiences, not just individual ones that can be chosen from a menu. However, for this reason it is also difficult to identify just one part of the DP that might be thought of as the competitor to generic FYC, though the likely choice would be the first language, or A1, course. According to the *Guide to the IB Diploma Programme for Universities and Colleges*, the A1 course is "a pre-university literature course in the student's native or best language." Along with promoting appreciation for literature and culture, it emphasizes oral and written expression "in a variety of styles and situations." At the higher level, the course requires two oral activities internally assessed by the teacher and externally moderated by the IB assessors as well as two formal papers of 1,000 to 1,500 words each (four to six pages) and two written exams, all of which are assessed externally. At the standard level, one less paper is required. Both standard and higher-level courses require a great deal of writing in addition to the externally assessed papers and exams. The European origins of IB are evident here: writing is not viewed as a subject matter in itself but as a vehicle for demonstrating knowledge about other subjects, in this case, literature and culture. In this respect, the similarity of IB to the AP Literature and Composition course comes to mind.

The A1 course on its own may not seem comparable to a contemporary FYC course, but according to Sandra Wade-Pauley, IB university and government liaison for North America, pedagogical practices for teaching writing in IB follow those typically used in FYC: drafting, getting feedback, revising, and editing are emphasized. Presumably, instruction about rhetoric and usage is provided incidentally as students work on papers. Students are also encouraged to think of writing for real audiences, as they can submit an extended essay about a historical topic for publication in the *Concord Review*, a national student journal established in 1988. Throughout the entire DP curriculum there is much writing in many genres, in addition to the externally evaluated course papers and essay exams. Teachers of every subject are supposed to teach writing, something for which university Writing Across the Curriculum (WAC) and Writing in the Disciplines (WID) programs also aim. In addition, the theory of knowledge essay and extended essay are challenging writing tasks, comparable in their length and demands to significant research writing in the university. Thus, provided scores are high, the entire package an IB student presents could be considered strong evidence the student has worked diligently to develop the same kinds of writing abilities aimed for in FYC. Because of the extensive and varied experiences with writing that DP students have, it's not surprising that many universities grant credit for FYC to IB diploma holders, despite the A1 course's lack of congruence with generic FYC courses. However, more information about writing pedagogy and IB students' success with writing in college would be welcome in order to more fully compare the two brands.

The Advanced Placement Program

The Advanced Placement program, offered by the nonprofit College Board, began in the early 1950s. Its originators intended to provide a way for academically advanced students at prestigious prep schools to begin working on introductory college course work in high school and avoid repetition once they matriculated at one of the partnering universities. Because Joseph Jones (this volume) explores the history of AP English in some depth, I note only that the first AP tests were given in 1954, with Educational Testing Services administering the first exam in English literature. In 1955, the College Board became proprietor of the AP program, but it still hires ETS to develop and administer the exams. Over the last fifty-three years the College Board has expanded its market to the point that more than 16,000 schools in North America now offer one or more of 35 AP courses in 20 subject areas (unless otherwise noted, all factual references about AP are drawn from the College Board website). At first the AP program was decidedly elitist, aimed at the top students at prestigious prep schools, but now the College Board is aggressively attempting to democratize the program, announcing ambitious goals such as "offering AP in every school in the nation, with 10 courses in each school by 2010" (College Board, *Access* 3). The program is certainly growing. In 2008, the College Board sold a total of 2,736,445 AP exams worldwide to 1,580,821 students for $84 each, thus taking in nearly $230 million in 2008 just from AP tests. From a financial standpoint, AP tests are clearly a successful product in the education market, since the cost of the tests is within the reach of many students. In fact, in some states, the costs are paid from public funds as legislators look for ways to move students into and through college cost-effectively. However, as AP has expanded its market share by recruiting teachers and students in inner-city and rural schools that formerly did not participate, the number of students receiving the low scores of 1 and 2 on the tests (explained below) has also increased (see Epstein), raising the question of whether it makes sense to invite students to participate in a program for which they are ill-prepared and to spend personal or public funds for tests they will likely fail.

Currently, the AP English program consists of two exams, each of which corresponds to a high school course: English Literature and Composition, established in 1953, and English Language and Composition, established in 1980. However, students may take AP tests without taking the corresponding courses; conversely, they may take one or more courses without taking any AP tests. Though they were originally very similar, the two AP English products have become quite different from each other since 2002. The English course description booklet for May 2007/2008, which describes both courses, explicitly positions the newer Language and Composition course as the equivalent of a college composition course with a focus on rhetoric. (Kathleen Puhr's essay, this volume, explains how the course has evolved in this way.) Noting that the college composition course is "one of the most varied in the curriculum," the booklet asserts that most college composition courses nevertheless focus on "expository, analytical, and argumentative writing" because these are foundational in academic and professional communication and thus are the kinds of writing students should do in the AP Language and Composition course (6). The booklet also stresses the importance of the writing process in college composition courses, with students taking time to "explore ideas, reconsider strategies, and revise their work." Noting that extensive revision "cannot be part of the AP exam," the document nevertheless encourages teachers to have students write essays in stages and drafts as doing so "may help their performance on the exam itself" (7). The booklet particularly recommends that students write "researched argument papers" that evaluate, synthesize, and cite sources, using the sources to take and develop a position in an ongoing scholarly conversation, rather than simply quote and summarize what others have said as a way of demonstrating the ability to use and cite sources (8). Finally, the booklet stresses "intense concentration on language use" in the AP Language course to enhance "students' ability to use grammatical conventions appropriately and to develop stylistic maturity in their prose" (8). As Puhr shows in her essay (this volume) the AP Language and Composition course also has a new statement of desired outcomes that parallels in many respects the "WPA Outcomes Statement for First-Year Writing." Those familiar with FYC as taught at most colleges would recognize the ways in which the AP Language and Composition course—at least, on paper—attempts to model itself after current objectives and practices at many universities.

The same could not be said of the AP Literature and Composition course, as it is described in the same course description booklet. Not mentioning college composition at all—or any other course to which it is supposed to be equivalent—the booklet celebrates AP Literature and Composition as a course that "engages students in the careful reading and critical analysis of imaginative literature." And not just any literature, but Arnoldian works of "recognized literary merit" that "invite and reward rereading and do not, like ephemeral works in such popular genres as detective or romance fiction, yield all (or nearly all) of their pleasures of thought and feeling the first time through" (45). Students read this literature for three purposes: to experience and appreciate it, to interpret it, and to evaluate it. Three kinds of writing correspond to these purposes: first, annotation, freewriting, reading journals, and response and reaction papers; second, "focused analyses on aspects of language and structure" because meaning is held to be "embodied in literary form," and interpretation is defined as "the analysis of literary works through close reading to arrive at an understanding of their multiple meanings"; and, third, writing that judges the artistry of a work and explores "its underlying social and cultural values through analysis, interpretation, and judgment" (45–46). This description of the Literature and Composition course evokes FYC as it was in the 1950s, when AP began.

Although the booklet acknowledges that "critical analysis makes up the bulk of student writing for the [AP Literature] course," it suggests that teachers also consider "well-constructed creative writing assignments" to "help students see from the inside how literature is written" (46). The goals of writing instruction are as formalist as the literary reading goals. The stated emphasis is on helping students develop "stylistic maturity," defined as having "a wide-ranging vocabulary"; using "a variety of sentence structures, including appropriate use of subordinate and coordinate constructions"; organizing logically by using "specific techniques of coherence such as repetition, transitions, and emphasis"; balancing "generalization with specific illustrative detail"; and displaying an "effective use of rhetoric, including controlling tone, maintaining a consistent voice, and achieving emphasis through parallelism and antithesis" (47). This focus on formal features of writing and the narrow definition of rhetoric suggest a stunning lack of awareness of (or a lack of interest in) how the field of rhetoric and composition has developed and shaped FYC over the last thirty years. Granted, the designers of this course may not aspire to have it compared to generic FYC courses today. Granted also, some students take the course for the cultural capital it gives them, a knowledge of canonical literature and a boost in the college admissions process. Nevertheless, it is still thought by many—including students, parents, and high school and college administrators—to be similar to FYC, despite the divergence of its aims and content. And many universities still give credit for FYC to students who pass the AP Literature and Composition test with a score of 5, 4, or often 3.

These overall scores are calculated from each student's performance on the various parts that make up the AP tests. Each of the exams for the two AP English programs is divided into two main sections: a series of multiple-choice questions and a set of "free-response" questions that require students to write timed, impromptu essays. Students have 60 minutes to complete the multiple-choice section, which is scored by computer and accounts for 45 percent of the total grade, and 120 minutes to handwrite the three impromptu essays, which are scored by human readers and account for 55 percent of the total grade. Students' scores on the multiple-choice sections and free response sections are converted by ETS statisticians into a single overall score using a 1–5 scale. The College Board advertises that a score of 5 means a student is "extremely well qualified" for advanced college work; 4 means a student is "well-qualified"; 3, "qualified"; 2, "possibly qualified"; and 1, "no recommendation" (see critiques of these descriptors in Hansen et al., "Argument" and Hansen et al., "Advanced").

Just as the descriptions of the two AP English courses do, the two exams now diverge significantly. In fact, since 2005 different committees have developed the two exams. Inspection of the 2007 Language and Composition exam evidences the committee's determination to actually assess whether students have experienced the conception of the AP Language course described in the 2007–8 course description booklet. The multiple-choice questions about various nonliterary readings ask about each author's rhetorical strategies and use of syntax, style, and even footnotes. The prompts for the three free response essays in 2007 required students to demonstrate the ability to synthesize, analyze, and argue. Since these essays are explained in Puhr's essay (this volume), I note only that the three prompts present students with intellectually challenging writing tasks that would require the best efforts of any writer—but especially adolescents attempting to do justice to each by planning and writing three papers, by hand, in just two hours! The multiple-choice questions for the Literature and Composition exam are rather similar to those in the Language and Composition exam, focusing on such things as genre, point of view, the narrator's attitude, word choice, tone, figurative language, and grammatical and syntactic elements in selections from poetry and fiction. Noticeably different, however, are the three free response prompts, with their terse and very general directions. In 2007, the first prompt simply directed students to "write an essay" in which they compared and contrasted two poems, "analyzing how each poet uses literary devices to make his point." The second asked students to read a selection from Dalton Trumbo's *Johnny Got His Gun* and "write a well-organized essay" analyzing how Trumbo used "such techniques as point of view, selection of detail, and syntax to characterize the relationship between the young man and his father." The third prompt presented students with a list of thirty-nine novels and plays ranging from *Absalom, Absalom* to *Wuthering Heights* and asked the students to choose a listed work or "another novel or play of similar literary merit" and then "write an essay" about how a character in the work "must contend with some aspect of the past, either personal or societal," and "show how the character's relationship to the past contributes to the meaning of the work as a whole" (College Board, *AP English Literature and Composition*). As open as they are, these are challenging tasks, especially for two hours of intense handwriting. But they are not tasks likely to be assigned in most current FYC courses.

Despite its focus on matters not currently central to the objectives of most FYC courses, in 2008 the AP English Literature and Composition exam was taken by 320,358 students, of whom 60.4 percent received a 3, 4, or 5 and were thus judged to be "qualified" or better for college credit. The AP English Language and Composition exam was taken by 306,479 students, of whom 58.2 percent were judged "qualified" or better. Some light is shed on the slight disparity by Puhr's explanation (this volume) that many high schools don't have a separate AP Language and Composition course, but instead use the eleventh-grade survey of American literature as a de facto preparation for the Language and Composition exam, which students are encouraged to take at the end of their junior year (this practice was also mentioned by Olson and Metzger in 1989). It's not clear how widespread the practice is, but it appears that high school teachers of American literature either find a way to shoehorn in some preparation for the AP test or they retool to teach their subject from a rhetorical rather than belletristic perspective. The fact that they are working with younger students and perhaps a divided focus may help explain why the pass rate of students who took the exam in 2008 was somewhat lower.

Similar to IB, AP is attempting to operate like a franchise— though in an interesting twist, the parent corporation, College Board, pays each franchisee high school a rebate for every AP test taken by its students. Compared to IB, the College Board's methods of licensing the AP name and ensuring brand quality are not as rigorous, relying a great deal more on trust and voluntary cooperation of teachers. Unlike the curriculum of the IB Diploma Programme, the curriculum of high school AP courses has never been and is not now standardized. There is no two-year implementation period with site visits, such as IB has, to guarantee a school is qualified and ready to offer the AP curriculum. The College Board offers online materials and summer workshops to help teachers plan a curriculum, but there is no requirement for teachers to avail themselves of this help. As a quality control measure, in 2007 the College Board began for the first time to audit the curricula of AP courses by requiring every school offering any course it called "advanced placement" to submit a course syllabus so that it could be vetted by college instructors to determine its similarity to college courses in the same subject. The *New York Times* described this new audit procedure as "an effort to protect the College Board brand" (Lewin), since some high schools had begun to offer courses labeled AP, even though they weren't in subject areas the College Board had defined as AP. Since syllabi are not common in high school courses and are difficult to follow when tried, the audit brought some skepticism. A teacher who submitted a syllabus complained the audit amounted to an "exercise in producing a syllabus, with no way of knowing that what's on paper is what's being taught in the classroom" (Lewin 2). The audit was also criticized by Barmak Nassirian, associate executive director of the American Association of Collegiate Registrars and Admissions Officers, as "highly susceptible to gaming" because teachers had two or more chances to submit their syllabi and were sometimes coached in person or by phone on how to write them. William Lichten, a noted critic of AP, granted that the audit is a way to "begin to restore quality to the program." But he added, "It doesn't take very much time to write a syllabus" and preparing to implement it well is more difficult (both Nassirian and Lichten qtd. in Cech, "Number").

Where the IB has 5,000 trained examiners who evaluate student papers and exams to ensure that international standards are upheld, the College Board recruits armies of temp workers, mostly high school teachers, who are trained on the job to make holistic judgments of AP exams for eight days every summer. Where IB examiners' judgments are combined with teachers' evaluations to determine student grades, for AP students hoping to score high enough to garner college credit, only the AP exam readers' judgment counts. Everything comes down to the work the student produces for the test. Are these tests sufficient evidence that the AP course has produced the same knowledge and abilities that an FYC course would? Should exemptions from or credit for FYC be granted for an AP score of 5, 4, 3, or possibly even 2, as the AP website recommends? Using data collected from students who took both AP in high school and FYC at college, Colleen Whitley and Deirdre Paulsen (this volume) produce some strong evidence that the answer to both questions is no. Even though the AP Language and Composition course, as it is described on paper, has many similarities to FYC, teachers are only encouraged, not required, to have students learn to draft and revise papers or to produce researched, documented argument papers. Learning to use computers to do research and writing is not even mentioned. The AP Literature course, as described above, is a 1950s version of FYC; it thus lacks face validity as an equivalent to FYC, though it is often accepted as a substitute. As Whitley and Paulsen's data show, the fact that the AP English exams require handwritten, timed, impromptu essays militates strongly in favor of teachers rehearsing students in that exercise alone to the exclusion or detriment of other kinds of writing and learning that are part of a typical FYC course. The very nature of the AP test goes far to undermine all the encouragement that could be given teachers via workshops and audit procedures to place due emphasis on rhetoric, writing processes, research writing, and conventions of writing in their AP courses.

David Jolliffe, former chief reader of the AP Language exam,[2] and Bernard Phelan, veteran AP teacher in Chicago, do not view AP English courses as "an alternative method of delivering traditional, introductory college writing instruction." Instead, they argue, AP's function is to challenge high schools "to develop and teach demanding courses in which students learn to read and analyze the rhetorical effectiveness of texts of all genres—not solely fiction, poetry, and drama—and to write strong, cogent, and persuasive arguments" (89). Noting that AP stands for advanced *placement*, not *exemption*, they assert that AP courses should help students make the transition from high school to college literacy instruction, not replace it. Their position means, however, that colleges must have a sequence of courses in writing and reading, not just one monolithic FYC course, so that there is an appropriately rigorous course for successful AP students to place into. Jolliffe and Phelan specifically criticize the College Board for marketing its AP English products as alternative methods for taking FYC so that students can avoid the course once they matriculate at college (95–96). They also criticize administrators at secondary and postsecondary institutions for encouraging the public in this belief (102). If Jolliffe and Phelan, two teachers long and intimately connected with the AP English program, are not buying the AP products as substitutes for an appropriately challenging FYC course, shouldn't other buyers beware?

Concurrent Enrollment Programs

The newest and perhaps the fastest growing brand in the composition marketplace is the concurrent enrollment (CE) course, in which high school students can earn both high school and postsecondary credits for the same course. Originating in the 1970s, these courses are, like IB and AP, meant to challenge high school students who would be bored with the regular high school curriculum and are ready to begin college work. According to the NCES, during the 2002–3 school year there were about 1.2 million enrollments in CE courses from students in 11,700 public high schools. Of these enrollments, 74 percent were taught at high schools, 23 percent on campuses of postsecondary institutions, and 4 percent via distance education. There are no national data on English composition in particular, though it is reputedly one of the most frequently offered CE courses. Several of the chapters in this volume (e.g., McClure et al.; Moody and Bonesteel; Post, Simmons, and Vanderslice; Thalheimer; Farris) give insights into common practices in designing CE programs for college composition. For example, the most common model is for CE programs to train high school teachers to deliver the college course at the high school, with the colleges offering liaisons who make site visits to consult with teachers and supervise delivery of the curriculum. The CE program described by Miles McCrimmon (this volume) is somewhat unusual in that it may involve college teachers going to the high school. The early college high school described by Barbara Schneider (this volume) is also considered a type of CE program, but it is comparatively rare.

CE courses are becoming increasingly popular with state education policymakers, who view them as a way "to address worries about a lack of rigor and innovation at many high schools" and as "part of a broader strategy to help more students become college-ready" (Klein), particularly those students who might not consider themselves the right consumers for the IB or AP brand, which may seem more for the academically gifted. One reason for state interest in CE courses is that there is some evidence that earning nine or more "accelerated credits" in high school increases the likelihood that students will persist in college to graduation and will cut their average time to graduation by almost half a year (Adelman). However, in a 2004 study, the U.S. Department of Education also noted that states have to perform delicate balancing acts with respect to CE: they must uphold high academic standards while promoting access to postsecondary education for a broad range of students; and they must also prevent the program from becoming a drain on state resources while attempting to provide some financial inducement to prompt schools and individuals to participate (Karp et al., *State*).

It is difficult to generalize about CE because there isn't one national brand, just a lot of local and regional brands. The best and most recent national snapshot of CE comes from Karp et al.'s 2005 study. This update found that eighteen states had policies mandating that high schools inform students of CE opportunities and accept credit; nine had policies making high school and college participation in CE voluntary; eleven had policies that did not specify whether participation was mandatory or voluntary; two had what was described as a "mixed" policy, that is, "high schools have the option of whether to offer dual enrollment, but colleges cannot refuse to participate"; and ten had no state policy. Twelve states allowed only high school juniors and seniors to participate in CE, while five permitted students in grades 9 and 10 to participate, and one had different admission requirements depending on students' ages. Of thirty states having academic requirements for participation, nine required a certain GPA or test scores indicating a student was "advanced"; two required lower GPAs and test scores that indicated a student was "proficient"; six made academic requirements dependent on the course of study; four permitted the secondary institution to determine admission requirements, eight permitted the postsecondary institution to do so, and one state made it a joint decision (Karp et al., *Update*).

The source of funding for CE courses also varies. The 2005 *Update* reports that in ten states the student pays tuition costs, and in six the state does. In ten states either the college or the high school is responsible for the tuition costs, and in seven the two institutions decide who is responsible (these results are somewhat confusing since, if institutions are state supported, the state indirectly pays the cost, one way or another). There is apparently uncertainty about whether the primary responsibility for the students resides at the secondary or the postsecondary level because in two states, the high school loses average daily attendance funding for CE students; in four states, both the high school and the college lose some but not all of their funding for CE students. In ten states, however, neither institution loses funds for CE enrollments; both are fully funded.

Another important issue is standards for teachers and content of CE courses. The *Update* found only twelve states specify requirements for teachers: some require high school teachers to hold the same credentials as college faculty, and some require only that high school teachers participate in professional development or receive approval from colleges. The survey also found only thirteen states have a policy regarding course content: some states limit the types of CE courses that may be offered, while others require approval of the CE course syllabus, textbook, or exams to be given by the partner college or the state education agency. Because of the variability in or absence of state policies, the National Alliance of Concurrent Enrollment Partnerships (NACEP) was organized in 1999 to work toward accrediting CE courses across the nation. NACEP aims to foster excellence by "providing standards of excellence, research, communication, and advocacy." It views CE as a "mechanism for delivering ongoing professional development to America's most talented teachers," restricting its definition of CE to college courses taught during the normal school day in high schools by high school teachers selected and prepared by partnering colleges. It excludes courses in which college teachers go to the high school to teach, courses that high school students take at a nearby college, and AP and IB courses (NACEP).

NACEP's fifteen accreditation standards, approved in 2002, fall into five areas: curriculum, faculty, students, assessment, and program evaluation. All of the standards emphasize that CE students are to be taught and treated the same as fully matriculated postsecondary students. The standards are so rigorous they cannot be met quickly, so a CE program must be in place for five years to gather assessment data before it even seeks accreditation. According to officials who spoke at the national NACEP Conference in 2007, only twenty-six institutions have received accreditation using these standards since 2004, and another eight are in the process of being accredited. Klein notes that thirty-seven additional colleges will likely go through the accreditation process by 2012 and that the first schools to seek reaccreditation will apply in 2011. Clearly, these figures represent only a small fraction of all colleges now involved in offering CE courses. But the totals are likely to begin growing more rapidly because, as Klein reports, Arkansas, Idaho, Indiana, and Minnesota have called for their state CE programs to adopt the NACEP standards. As of 2007, NACEP was also seeking federal recognition as an accrediting body so that these standards can become more powerful and pervasive.

If the NACEP standards were met by all CE courses, I think they would rapidly become the best market alternative to taking FYC on a college campus because students would be assured they were receiving the same kind and level of instruction they would if they had gone to the campus of the college offering the course. If program evaluation is conducted as envisioned by NACEP, there would be solid data to determine whether the teachers, the students, and the high school location of the CE course are in fact producing results similar to those produced on the college campus. As the college changed curricula, textbooks, pedagogical methods, or evaluation procedures on its campus, it would also change them in the CE courses it offers. There would not be the same worries about teacher preparation, equivalence of assignments, depth and breadth of student knowledge, or relevance and currency of pedagogical and evaluation methods that can arise with the IB and AP brands. Of course, this ideal would not be achieved without hard work, as indicated by Christine Farris's description of the effort required to help high school teachers make curriculum changes successfully. However, her account also shows how rewarding it can be to invite high school teachers to campus to act as genuine colleagues who collaborate with their college counterparts to "invent the university" ("The Space Between," 110–12).

Perhaps because of the difficulty of coordinating students, teachers, pedagogies, and curriculum on a large scale in different venues, many are still skeptical of CE programs. They point out that the cultures of high school and college differ, and that, even if students take a strong college course in a high school, the context and culture are simply different. For example, high school classes—even ones being taught for college credit—may be interrupted or even canceled for activities such as sporting events and assemblies. High school teachers are often required to allow makeup work, whereas college teachers usually are not. Unlike college students, failing high school students usually can't drop a course. Because of the age and minor status of high school students, parents have more say in what happens to their children, and they are allowed to see their educational records. However, the Family Educational Rights and Privacy Act (FERPA) allows students who are either eighteen or enrolled in a postsecondary institution to restrict access to their educational records. This law creates a gray area for CE programs: Are seventeen-year-old CE students in high school or in college? Can parents and the high school view their CE course records? Different states and institutions interpret the law differently.

If the concerns about differences between secondary and postsecondary students and culture could be overcome, there would still be other criticisms. Many critics of CE focus on problems related to student selection, teacher credentials, curriculum, teaching materials, and supervision. Klein reports that Tad Perry, executive director of the South Dakota Board of Regents, audited CE courses in his state and found students taking a course for CE credit were mixed in the same classroom with students taking the course for high school credit only, and both groups were using high school textbooks, materials, and assessments. These observations obviously raise questions about the rigor of the curriculum.

Klein notes that other critics worry that students are encouraged to enroll in CE courses too early or without sufficient support to succeed. Klein also quotes Gerald Edmonds, director of Syracuse University's Project Advance, who observed CE programs "certifying a course as college-level without visiting or looking at the syllabus or the credentials of the instructors." He added, "It's like they were selling credits." Edmonds's fear is perhaps the biggest criticism that CE programs need to overcome, namely that they are "cash cows"—vehicles for entrepreneurially minded colleges to increase enrollments and therefore tuition income without necessarily offering a truly college-level course to the students.

In an education market that is still quite unregulated, the potential for CE programs to cut corners is fairly high. In the worst-case scenario, some postsecondary institutions may be too loosely franchising their name to high school courses simply to increase tuition dollars, and such courses may be drawing high numbers of students looking for the easiest way to complete the required FYC course before they arrive on a college campus. In this scenario, the common currency of the market, the credit hour, is seriously devalued as such institutions grant credit to students for courses that do not meet rigorous standards. In the best-case scenario, however, the relationship between the postsecondary and secondary institutions is less that of a loosely operated franchise and more like a cooperative, in which both partners view courses as jointly owned, and both have a stake in turning out students who write well. In this scenario, the currency of the credit hour is solidly backed by the "better but far less fungible currency of intellectual purpose and curricular coherence" (Shoenberg). Where partners in CE programs take a cooperative approach built on high standards, I think they create the corner of the market where postsecondary institutions have the greatest chance of influencing the quality of an alternative to generic FYC. Then institutions can exercise quality control directly through offering their own programs, or they can exert pressure on state education systems to ensure that CE-sponsoring institutions in their state or articulation network are meeting high standards. Because IB and AP brands are privately owned and have their own agendas focused mainly on their relationship with secondary schools, they are less susceptible to this kind of influence from universities.

Shopping for Credit versus Learning to Write

At the beginning of this essay, I promised to reflect on my analysis of the composition marketplace and to raise questions about it. While there is merit in using the perspective and vocabulary of economics to study the competition between brands of composition, I must admit I have set up a false dichotomy in my final heading—shopping for credit vs. learning to write. A student who goes shopping for writing credit cannot get it merely by paying money, except from an unscrupulous and unaccredited supplier. Although education usually involves the exchange of money, it is not a transaction like buying a car, in which the value of the product is dependent almost entirely on the producer. In education, the value of the "product" relies heavily upon student input; even excellent teachers using the best materials cannot produce valuable outcomes without significant student effort. Thus, even though students may be acting partly like consumers as they compare and choose from among IB, AP, CE, and generic FYC options, most likely will understand that the real value they carry away from a course will depend heavily on their own efforts to actually learn to write. A few may even realize that, regardless of the curricular path they choose, their education in writing will have to continue long after the course is complete. Still, I am concerned that students may be encouraged to employ consumerist thinking by the way the various brands promise savings, efficiency, and equivalence of products. Do students really have enough information to understand that exchange value may not correlate with use value? Are they too strongly conditioned to believe that credit is credit and the object is to get it, then forget it?

I have also oversimplified matters by writing as if there were a single educational market, when in fact there are many overlapping markets defined by the complex interplay of geography, institutional mission, faculty quality, tuition costs, public or private institutional status, student ambition and ability, family income and social class, availability of financial aid, course offerings, and many other factors that influence the choices a student can make about how and where to seek education. This variation in markets means that it is impossible to have a consensus definition of phrases like "college-level" or "college-ready," as both Terrel Rhodes and several contributors to *What Is College-Level Writing?* point out (see, for example, Blau; Gunner; and White). Yet when the competitive actors in the composition marketplace act as if there were only one market and when the common currency of the credit hour tends to support that assumption, we begin to get what Labaree fears: a situation in which independent entrepreneurs, each angling for their own advantage, create incoherence at the collective level. We have student consumers presenting IB, AP, or CE grades and scores that might be suitable to exchange for credit in one market but not another. We have perplexed students (and sometimes angry parents) who have confused exchange value with use value, who have mistaken credentials for ability, and who can't understand why they didn't get credit at a particular institution, or why their old strategies and familiar formulas for writing aren't working in college, or why they are getting low grades. We even have teachers and administrators who have lost sight of the use value that education in writing should produce.

Here I must re-emphasize that I believe most educational administrators and teachers, especially those in nonprofit institutions, do not primarily see themselves as engaged in building market share, earning profits, turning out products, or otherwise participating in a business. They see themselves, rather, as developing human potential and transmitting knowledge that, yes, helps make commerce possible but that, more importantly, sustains civil society and nourishes human desires the market can't satisfy. True educators work diligently in whatever program they are employed to bring about student learning, not merely to award credit. I am not belittling the efforts of those who have devoted their lives to educating the young, whatever schools or programs with which they may be associated. But I am asking whether it is possible that all of us are so busy in our individual enterprises that we don't stop to think about the goals we have in common. Do our locations blind us from seeing all around us? Are we contributing to the collective irrationality of the market by thinking in individualistic and entrepreneurial ways? Do we advertise our work in ways that make students, parents, and school administrators think learning to write is something to "take care of," to "get out of the way"?

I hope this analysis calls attention to the fact that making education a market enterprise can become pernicious, especially if techniques of branding and advertising lure students to confuse the trappings of education with the thing itself or to mistake completion of one course or one test in writing as evidence they have learned to write, once and for all. Unfortunately, the first-year writing course is particularly susceptible to this confusion because it is just that: one or two semesters of instruction that are widely thought to impart skill in writing sufficient to see a student through a college career, if not, indeed, through life. A skill-based ideology of writing instruction has kept writing in a tenuous and marginal position at the university for over a century. This ideology has bred the desire to quickly and efficiently "take care of" the function of making students literate enough to succeed in college. It has also bred the desire to have someone else do it, if possible, to "get it out of the way." Ironically, the cause of a pernicious competition is that literacy—which can never be contained—is packaged and sold as if it could be, both in FYC and by its competitors. In Gunner's terms, capitalist culture has reified writing as a commodity, so that it has become "disembodied and asocial"; but when "writing [is] separated from the writing subject" (112), it becomes a mere "credential that can be impersonally produced," and its "teaching becomes a matter of boxing, bundling, and otherwise delivering learning packages through a process that standardizes all products" (113). FYC, IB, AP, and CE are all various ways of "containing" writing. But in this, the Information Age, the needs of students, of teachers, of employers, and of nations for ever-greater literacy will always exceed the parameters of this packaging. This fact urges us, presses us, to acknowledge that literacy is at the heart of all education, in all fields of education, and that students can never be literate enough. We must stop thinking of writing as something that students "take care of" or "get out of the way" and that universities can conveniently "outsource."

Those who work at universities and those who work at high schools and even middle schools and elementary schools need to come to an understanding of what we jointly hope to accomplish in the literacy development of the same students we all teach at different points in their lives. If those who work at high schools and universities can partner with each other to build stronger curricula, by all means let us cooperate in doing so. Let's develop stronger CE courses that energize the high school senior year and smooth the transition from secondary to postsecondary education. Let's call on the College Board to get rid of its narrow, outdated AP exams and instead require portfolios of students' writing that demonstrate their abilities in many genres, including documented, research-based arguments. If high school teachers can prepare some students for more challenging instruction once they reach college, by all means let universities build new sequences and networks of writing courses so that well-prepared students can find rich and meaningful ways of expanding their literacy when they arrive at college. Let's heed the warnings sounded by Joseph Petraglia, David Russell, and Lee Ann Carroll, among others, who question simplistic notions about transfer of "general writing skills." Let's undertake joint longitudinal studies of how literacy abilities develop as students mature cognitively and socially; then let's plan courses and write instructional materials that are appropriate to different developmental levels. Let's strengthen Writing Across the Curriculum programs in high schools and Writing in the Disciplines programs in colleges so that students experience the deeper, more meaningful, and more lasting learning that comes when they must verbalize what they are studying. Let's make sure we don't cheat students out of the opportunities to mature and to develop their writing and reading abilities fully by pushing them through high school and college too fast. Doing so will shortchange not only the students but their future employers and our political system, both of which depend on fully grown and fully literate citizens. Instead of competing in a marketplace, let's explore how we can cooperate in a coherent and rational K–16 educational system to help students develop their writing abilities in a broad repertoire of real genres for a wide range of real audiences. Let's not sell writing or our students short.

Notes

1. The majority of teachers who staff the generic brand courses at large baccalaureate and research institutions are part-time faculty and graduate

students because composition teaching is a labor-intensive job, requiring many small sections to enroll all students in what is usually a required course. Most universities find it financially impossible to staff all these sections with full-time teachers. Yancey's preliminary data indicate that of 1,861 respondents from all types of postsecondary institutions, only 27 percent had an educational background in composition and rhetoric; 33 percent reported a background in literature (McLeod 98). These results reflect the dominance of literary studies in undergraduate and graduate English curricula. The practical implication is that writing program administrators of generic FYC must give on-the-job training in rhetoric and composition to a constantly overturning staff of teachers. This fact has obvious implications for my argument about brands of composition instruction, but I opted not to try to compare teachers in the four competing brands, since I have no good empirical basis for doing so. I think the teachers of any other brand may be just as likely to be strong or weak depending on local circumstances. However, the issue of teacher quality remains a salient one and ought to be addressed in further research.

2. Jolliffe deserves much of the credit for transforming the description of the AP Language and Composition course into one that parallels generic FYC and for transforming the related test, insofar as it has been transformed. As I have implied, however, timed, impromptu handwritten essays indicate the need for further evolution.

Works Cited

Adelman, Clifford. *Principal Indicators of Student Academic Histories in Postsecondary Education, 1972–2000.* Washington: U.S. Department of Education, Institute of Education Sciences, 2004. *Ed.gov.* Web. 3 Dec. 2007.

Blau, Sheridan. "College Writing, Academic Literacy, and the Intellectual Community: California Dreams and Cultural Oppositions." Sullivan and Tinberg 358–77.

Branigan, Cara. "Pennsylvania Tests Essay-Grading Software." *ESchool News.* ESchool Media Inc., 1 Jan. 2001. Web. 1 June 2008.

Carroll, Lee Ann. *Rehearsing New Roles: How College Students Develop as Writers.* Carbondale: Southern Illinois UP, 2002. Print.

Cech, Scott J. "Number of Schools Offering AP Falls after First Audit of Courses." *Education Week.* Editorial Projects in Education, 9 Nov. 2007. Web. 1 June 2008.

———. "With World Growing Smaller, IB Gets Big." *Education Week*. Editorial Projects in Education, 30 Oct. 2007. Web. 1 June 2008.

College Board. *Access to Excellence: A Report of the Commission on the Future of the Advanced Placement Program*. Princeton: College Board, 2001. Print.

———. "Advanced Placement." College Board, n.d. Web. 13 Apr. 2009.

———. *AP English Course Description: English Language and Composition, English Literature and Composition, May 2007, May 2008*. College Board, 2006. Web. 1 Mar. 2008.

———. *AP English Literature and Composition 2007 Free Response Questions*. College Board, 2007. Web. 1 Mar. 2008.

Council of Writing Program Administrators. "WPA Outcomes Statement for First-Year Composition." WPA, Apr. 2000. Web. 11 Apr. 2009.

Dew, Debra Frank. "Language Matters: Rhetoric and Writing I as Content Course." *Changing the First-Year Curriculum*. Ed. Christine Farris. *WPA: Writing Program Administration* 26.3 (2003): 88–104. Print.

Downs, Douglas, and Elizabeth Wardle. "Teaching about Writing, Righting Misconceptions: (Re)Envisioning 'First-Year Composition' as 'Introduction to Writing Studies.'" *College Composition and Communication* 58.4 (2007): 552–84. Print.

Epstein, David. "Tons of Test Takers." *Inside Higher Education* 8 Feb. 2006. Web. 3 Dec. 2007.

Farris, Christine. "The Space Between: Dual-Credit Programs as Brokering, Community Building, and Professionalization." Yancey, *Delivering College Composition* 104–14.

Glater, Jonathan D. "Certain Degrees Now Cost More at Public Universities." *New York Times*. 29 July 2007. Web. 3 Dec. 2007.

Gunner, Jeanne. "The Boxing Effect (An Anti-Essay)." Sullivan and Tinberg 110–20.

Hansen, Kristine, Suzanne Reeve, Jennifer Gonzalez, Richard R. Sudweeks, Gary L. Hatch, Patricia Esplin, and William S. Bradshaw. "Are Advanced Placement English and First-Year College Composition Equivalent? A Comparison of Outcomes in the Writing of Three Groups of Sophomore College Students." *Research in the Teaching of English* 40.4 (2006): 461–501. Print.

Hansen, Kristine, Suzanne Reeve, Richard Sudweeks, Gary L. Hatch, Jennifer Gonzalez, Patricia Esplin, and William S. Bradshaw. "An Argument for Changing Institutional Policy on Granting AP Credit in English: An Empirical Study of College Sophomores' Writing." *WPA: Writing Program Administration* 28.1–2 (2004): 29–54. Print.

Harvard College Admissions. Harvard University, n.d. Web. 3 Dec. 2007.

International Baccalaureate. A Guide to the International Baccalaureate (IB) Diploma Programme for Universities and Colleges. International Baccalaureate, n.d. Web. 3 Dec. 2007.

———. *2007 Annual Review.* International Baccalaureate, n.d. Web. 11 Apr. 2009.

———. Home page. International Baccalaureate, n.d. Web. 11 Apr. 2009.

Jolliffe, David A., and Bernard Phelan. "Advanced Placement, Not Advanced Exemption: Challenges for High Schools, Colleges, and Universities." Yancey, *Delivering College Composition* 89–103.

Karp, Melinda Mechur, Thomas R. Bailey, Katherine L. Hughes, and Baranda J. Fermin. *State Dual Enrollment Policies: Addressing Access and Quality.* Washington: U.S. Department of Education, Office of Vocational and Adult Education, 2004. *Ed.gov.* Web. 3 Dec. 2007.

Karp, Melinda Mechur, Thomas R. Bailey, Katherine L. Hughes, and Baranda J. Fermin. *Update to State Dual Enrollment Policies: Addressing Access and Quality.* Washington: U.S. Department of Education, Office of Vocational and Adult Education, 2005. *Ed.gov.* Web. 3 Dec. 2007.

Klein, Alyson. "Acceleration under Review." *Education Week.* Editorial Projects in Education, 31 July 2007. Web. 29 Nov. 2007.

Labaree, David F. *How to Succeed in School without Really Learning: The Credentials Race in American Education.* New Haven: Yale UP, 1997. Print.

Larson, Richard. *Curricula in College Writing Programs: Much Diversity, Little Assessment.* A Report to the Ford Foundation on the Project on College Curricula in Composition, n.p. July 1994. Web. 3 Dec. 2007.

Lewin, Tamar. "College Board Tries to Police Use of 'Advanced Placement' Label." *New York Times.* 18 July 2007. Web. 3 Dec. 2007.

Lyotard, Jean-François. *The Postmodern Condition: A Report on Knowledge*. Trans. Geoff Bennington and Brian Massumi. Minneapolis: U of Minnesota P, 1984. Print.

McLeod, Susan H. *Writing Program Administration*. West Lafayette: Parlor, 2007. Print.

National Alliance of Concurrent Enrollment Partnerships (NACEP). Home Page. NACEP, n.d. Web. 27 Nov. 2007.

National Commission on the High School Senior Year. *The Lost Opportunity of Senior Year: Finding a Better Way*. 2001. Web. 3 Dec. 2007.

———. *Raising Our Sights: No High School Senior Left Behind*. 2001. Web. 3 Dec. 2007.

Ohmann, Richard. "Accountability and the Conditions for Curricular Change." *Beyond English Inc.: Curricular Reform in a Global Economy*. Ed. David B. Downing, Claude Mark Hurlbert, and Paula Mathieu. Portsmouth: Boynton/Cook, 2002. 62–73. Print.

———. "Citizenship and Literacy Work: Thoughts without a Conclusion." *Tenured Bosses and Disposable Teachers: Writing Instruction in the Managed University*. Ed. Marc Bousquet, Tony Scott, and Leo Parascondola. Carbondale: Southern Illinois UP, 2004. 36–45. Print.

Olson, Gary, and Elizabeth Metzger. "The Language and Composition Course." *Advanced Placement English: Theory, Politics, and Pedagogy*. Ed. Gary A. Olson, Elizabeth Metzger, and Evelyn Ashton-Jones. Portsmouth: Boynton/Cook, 1989. 116–29. Print.

Petraglia, Joseph, ed. *Reconceiving Writing, Rethinking Writing Instruction*. Mahwah: Erlbaum, 1995. Print.

———. "Writing as an Unnatural Act." Petraglia 79–100.

Rhodes, Terrel. "Accelerated Learning for What?" *Peer Review* 9.1 (2007): 9–12. Print.

Russell, David. "Activity Theory and Its Implications for Writing Instruction." Petraglia 51–77.

Shoenberg, Robert. "'Why Do I Have to Take This Course?' or Credit Hours, Transfer, and Curricular Coherence." *General Education in an Age of Student Mobility: An Invitation to Discuss Systemic Curricular Planning*. Washington: Association of American Colleges and Universities, 2001. 1–9. Web. 27 Nov. 2007.

Stewart, Kristen. "Learn While You Earn: Nation's Largest Private University Is Flourishing in Utah." *Salt Lake Tribune* 27 Aug. 2001: B1–B2. Print.

Sullivan, Patrick, and Howard Tinberg, eds. *What Is "College-Level" Writing?* Urbana: NCTE, 2006. Print.

University of Phoenix. University of Phoenix, n.d. Web. 27 Nov. 2007.

Wade-Pauley, Sandra. Personal interview. 6 Nov. 2007.

Waits, T., J. C. Setzer, and L. Lewis. *Dual Credit and Exam-Based Courses in U.S. Public High Schools: 2002–03.* NCES 2005–009. Washington: U.S. Department of Education, National Center for Education Statistics, 2005. *NCES.* Web. 3 Dec. 2007.

White, Edward M. "Defining by Assessing." Sullivan and Tinberg 243–66.

Yancey, Kathleen Blake, ed. *Delivering College Composition: The Fifth Canon.* Portsmouth: Boynton/Cook, 2006. Print.

———. "Made Not Only in Words: Composition in a New Key." *College Composition and Communication* 56.2 (2004): 297–328. Print.

Yancey, Kathleen Blake, with Brian M. Morrison. "Coming to Terms: Vocabulary as a Means of Defining First-Year Composition." Sullivan and Tinberg 267–80.

ADVANCED PLACEMENT: ISSUES AND ANSWERS

CHAPTER TWO

The Beginnings of AP and the Ends of First-Year College Writing

JOSEPH JONES
Memphis State University

In the early 1950s, objections about the direction of American schools and, more specifically, the ways gifted and talented students were being underserved reached a sort of critical mass. The concern was not so much that no child be left behind: the concern was that the "best" students were not being challenged and advanced as quickly as they should be. For many of the critics of public education, the schools' inattention to the needs of such students was symptomatic of a host of ills often conveniently lumped together under the term "progressivism." The schools' wrongheaded—or, at least, misguided—efforts to focus on the average student and his or her interests meant squandering the opportunities to engage the exceptional pupil in challenging, academically centered curricula that mirrored the best—and most traditional—college curricula.

The Advanced Placement (AP) program arose from this milieu, and identifying and analyzing the contexts from which AP arose provides a fuller sense of why AP English is as it is, for its substance hasn't changed much in the last fifty years. The size of AP, however, has changed. Five hundred hand-picked students took a first version of the exams; more than a half-million students now take one of the two AP English exams each May. Those currently involved in designing AP English curricula have grown more self-conscious about the shortcomings for which AP is most often faulted, and aspects of the program and the exams have been modified over the years. Most recently, the College Board has begun requiring and reviewing syllabi of those courses seeking the AP imprimatur, and the AP English Language and Composition exam was altered to include a timed essay requiring students to synthesize a variety of secondary sources. Yet the traditions of English teaching that informed AP English at its inception remain tenacious insofar as the courses and exams are concerned, particularly the isolation of textual features for literary analysis and the reduction of composition to basic skills constrained by timed writing. It is the values of those traditions and their implications that this essay seeks to make clearer as a means to more fully understand the implications of AP English for college English.

Rescuing the "Academically Talented"

The counterpoise of tradition and reform in high school English described by Arthur N. Applebee in *Tradition and Reform in the Teaching of English* provides a useful means of framing the beginnings of AP. If one follows the narrative Applebee composes regarding the teaching of English in American secondary schools, it is possible to locate the origins of the Advanced Placement program within a period of contention and transition in American high schools. Of course, public education seems always in periods of contention and transition; it is the particular tensions and trends that rise and subside. Criticisms of progressivism in public education made possible the conditions from which the Advanced Placement program arose during the 1950s. Critics charged that progressivism's concern for the whole child meant neglecting the intellectual training the most able students deserved and, as Cold War fears intensified, that society needed for its brightest students.

The first formal gestures toward establishing AP are generally identified in College Board materials as occurring in 1951. Education historians cite the launch of Sputnik in 1957 as among the most pivotal occurrences in American education, for it "became a symbol of the failure of the schools and a milestone marking the end of one era and the beginning of another" (Applebee 188). Yet Sputnik is only a symbol, a convenient marker at which to locate the significant shift in emphasis that occurred in the public schools away from progressivism and its efforts at "life adjustment" toward more traditional academic standards. In fact, the "reemphasis of academic achievement was already well underway" before 1957 (189–90). The College Board's William H. Cornog writes in "The Advanced Placement Program: Reflections on Its Origins" that AP "grew out of some pre-Sputnik tree-shaking and hollering in the groves of academe" (14). The tree-shaking and hollering led to a revival of interest in special programs for "academically talented" students and a rejection of the trend toward non-subject-specific high school coursework. Progressive educators had argued since the 1930s against dividing the high school curriculum into discrete subject matters to mirror college curricula and argued instead for a more unified, broadly conceived general education for secondary school students that developed skills for effective social living beyond school. That said, James Fraser's *The School in the United States: A Documentary History* offers an important reminder: "Progressive education had as many definitions as it had proponents—or, later, critics" (181). In fact, he argues—as do most other education historians (see, for example, Kliebard)—that because progressive education was associated with educational reform on so many fronts, ascribing a delimited meaning to the term is nearly impossible. Fraser identifies several groups involved in public education who identified themselves as progressive: "administrative progressives, who sought consolidated management" for schools and school systems; "militant teachers, who sought a greater role for themselves" that ranged from issues as basic as increasing teacher pay and encouraging an emerging sense of professionalism to desires for greater curricular autonomy; "child centered curriculum reformers," who traced their lineage to John Dewey; and even "advocates of testing and measurement," who "saw themselves as scientists above the squabbles of the other groups" with little interest in educational reform as a means of societal reform (182). It was the attitudes of the "child centered curriculum reformers" that drew fire from critics at midcentury, for it was they who most effectively argued that secondary school curricula should offer students fuller educational experiences than only college preparation.

Applebee credits perspectives ascribed to Dewey and appropriated by progressive reformers in the 1930s and 1940s for

forging three attitudes that "contributed directly to the emanci-
pation of the high school from the college program in English"
(48). First, an "intentionally progressive society" uses its schools
as a means of social reform. Second, progressive educators, motivated by the desire to reach all students, rejected the contention that only the "classics" could purvey culture. Third, there
was "Dewey's conviction that democracy demands education in
the problems of living together for *all* in the community; there
could be no provision for a cultural elite" (48). Such progressive
attitudes were not universally adopted, of course. Nor did they
receive approbation from all quarters. The editors of *Public Education under Criticism*, published in 1954 to refute the charges
against progressivism by its detractors, could declare, "Changes
in educational philosophy and practice that have been closely
associated with the term 'Progressive Education' constitute the
most influential and most criticized educational development of
the Twentieth Century" (Scott and Hill 81).

Typical of the criticisms of progressivism were arguments
advanced by Arthur Bestor, professor of history at the University of Illinois and author of the influential critique *Educational
Wastelands*, who faulted schools for greater concern with the
"life adjustment" of students than their "intellectual training."
He recommended relieving "professional educators" from sole
responsibility for devising school curricula and proposed instead
the creation of "a Permanent Scientific and Scholarly Commission
on Secondary Education" composed of "scholars" (presumably
university faculty) because "the learned world can provide responsible leadership to the millions of Americans who believe both in
democracy and in sound education and who are anxious to rescue
the schools from those who act as if democratic education were
synonymous with intellectual mediocrity" ("Anti-Intellectualism"
44). Such criticisms were not new. For example, in an article published in a 1940 issue of the *Saturday Evening Post*, "Lollipops
versus Learning: A High-School Teacher Speaks Out," the author
objects that progressivism "is not a system at all; it is, rather, an
attitude" (Crockett 82). Of course, that "attitude" seemed to be
anything critics found objectionable, but in general terms, what
most antagonized those allegiant to more conservative educational
approaches was what they saw as progressivism's tendency to

privilege pedagogy over subject-matter content. Moreover, they faulted the reluctance in most public high schools to differentiate among student abilities. They argued that by adhering to more traditionally rigorous curricula focused on content rather than teaching methodology, students could be more effectively sorted, classified, and taught. Progressivism was subjected to sustained and compelling enough criticism that in "the 1950s, progressive education, in most of its many guises, had lost its energy" (Fraser 222), and educational interest groups reacting to progressive education began to coalesce in an "academic resurgence which dominated secondary school instruction from the late fifties till the late sixties" (Applebee 185). The Advanced Placement program emerged from this coalescence, and its "model of special attention to intellectually gifted students offered the public schools one relatively direct way to respond to the growing criticism of progressive education" (190).

Educational initiatives for the academically talented gained considerable impetus in 1951 from the Ford Foundation's Fund for the Advancement of Education. Known simply as the Fund, it had $70 million, a termination date set sixteen years in the future, and, according to its historian Paul Woodring, a mandate "to advance and improve formal or institutionalized education in North America"(10): "The Fund for the Advancement of Education was in operation during a time of national affluence, population expansion, international tension, growing social unrest, educational turmoil, rapid social change, and the adventure into space" (3). After World War II, college enrollment increased dramatically, an upward swing that continued for decades. College enrollment (including community colleges) increased from 2.6 million students in 1949–50 to 3.2 million in 1959–60 (Valentine 67). During the 1950s, some forty million American babies were born, and Fund administrators were concerned that "the schools were not prepared for them and the taxpayers were not prepared for the shock of having to pay for their education" (Woodring 4). Some at the Fund were particularly afraid that America's most talented students wasted time in the last two years of high school and first two years of college because of curricular redundancy between the upper high school grades and the lower college years. This sentiment was articulated by Philip H. Coombs, secretary and director of research for the Fund: "There is currently a tremendous upsurge of concern throughout the country over our future supply of what is invariably termed 'high ability manpower,' 'specialized talent,' or 'leadership'"; he concluded that "we are presently wasting a vast amount of potential talent" (v). The talented were threatened by the school system's insistence on age-level, grade-level grouping and advancement: "The most serious victims—the most handicapped under this lock step arrangement—turn out to be our ablest youngsters for whom the pace is too slow and the academic diet too thin" (vii). There was also concern, given the war in Korea that had followed so soon after World War II, that the draft would continue to interrupt the supply of talented young men entering the labor force, so there was interest in exploring ways that especially talented students might get some college under their belts before entering military service.

In 1951 the Ford Foundation's Fund sponsored three projects to study the relationship between the last two years in secondary school and the first two years of college because of the concern that "some of the most able students found themselves marking time during their last years in high school, facing assignments too easy for them, losing interest in learning, and developing poor work habits" (Woodring 153). One Fund project, an early admissions program, was short-lived due to the concerns of high school principals that their schools were losing their ablest students. The second project, the School and College Study of General Education, and the third project, known as the "Kenyon Plan" (discussed next), are the acknowledged progenitors of the AP program.

Formative Attitudes toward Composition

The report that emerged from the School and College Study of General Education, *General Education in School and College: A Committee Report by Members of the Faculties of Andover, Exeter, Lawrenceville, Harvard, Princeton, and Yale*, deserves extensive consideration because its values regarding the production and consumption of texts were instantiated in the first AP English examinations, and the vestiges of those values can be found still. The authors of the committee's report acknowledge that their "thinking has been based, in part, on current practices in our six institutions" (40), which in itself makes the report an interesting artifact for the version of English it discloses. Appended to the committee's study is its recommendation to enable qualified students to enter college with sophomore standing. The committee concludes that a set of achievement tests is needed to determine which students deserve such "advanced placement." The committee's final report makes clear, however, that such a program is not intended for most students: "There is no intent in what follows to call for reform of the whole American educational system for the sake of a relatively small group of students" (2). Of course, such a disclaimer is so laden with elitism that one is less inclined to appreciate its frankness than to take exception to its smugness.

The headmaster at Andover, John M. Kemper, oversaw the project. In a letter to the Ford Fund's Clarence Faust, Kemper wrote: "Boys from the best independent schools often report that their early courses in college are repetitious and dull" (qtd. in *General Education* 2). The final report described a study of 344 alumni from Andover, Exeter, and Lawrenceville who subsequently attended Harvard, Princeton, and Yale, and it concluded that there was much needless duplication between high school courses in English, history, and science. The committee examined the school and college records of the students and collected survey data in ten different subjects from instructors in those programs. Fifty-eight of the young men in the graduating college class of 1952 completed "a twenty-page questionnaire of the essay type . . . designed to explore the students' feelings about what was good and bad in their school and college experience, what stimuli or hindrances to intellectual growth they had encountered, and why" (4–5). The report identifies the cause of student disengagement as "a failure of the school and college to view their jobs as parts of a continuous process, two halves of a common enterprise" (4). The report further identified "certain basic convictions" that motivated the committee's work and guided its analysis: "We believe first of all in individual excellence," and "we are old-fashioned enough to believe that content is just as important as method in education" (10). While those basic convictions deliberately reproach progressive education, the authors self-consciously conceded that they were nevertheless "modern enough to be concerned with the intimate connection of the *mind and emotion*" (10; italics in original) and "tried always to remember the total development of the student in any recommendations on the intellectual side" (11), a nod in the direction of the progressive educator's invocation of commitment to the "whole child."

The *General Education* committee's report includes recommended courses of study in eight curricular areas (English language, literature, foreign languages, mathematics, natural sciences, social studies, the arts, and "values"), consistent with "the problem which is the central subject of the entire report: the construction of a tightened, sharpened curriculum joining the work of school and college"(40). The committee clearly demarcates between the English language—by which it means composition, grammar, and speech (or rhetoric)—and literature; the two are treated as entirely different subjects. The division is made for two reasons, one implicit, the other explicit. The explicit reason cited for the division of composition from literature is seen in the committee's declaration that "training in language is the English teacher's first task because verbal skills are central to the curriculum as a whole," though "there is no area of learning which is more clearly everybody's responsibility" (47).

The implicit reason for the separation of composition and literature can be discerned in assertions reflecting the typical mid-century privileging of literature and diminution of composition:

> The responsibility for training in the use of the English language is a joint and continuing responsibility of the school and of the college. Nevertheless, a sound foundation can and must be given in the schools. Elementary courses in language skills do not belong in the college. Until ways can be found to bring secondary school students to an adequate level of competence in such skills, higher education in America cannot do its proper work. (41)

Considering the colleges involved in preparing *General Education in School and College*, the contention that the teaching of writing is primarily the responsibility of the schools is to be expected, for such an attitude began at Harvard in the 1870s. The first freshman composition course was offered at Harvard in 1885, largely to address the failure of more than half the students on its first entrance examination in written English in 1874. Nevertheless, "the required freshman course was never meant as a permanent English offering but was instead a temporary stopgap until the secondary schools could improve" (Connors 48–49). John Brereton notes in his history of college writing instruction that shortly after Harvard instituted its written composition exam, "it began to prod its preparatory schools about improving their writing instruction, beginning a twenty-year-long acrimonious debate over composition in the schools," a debate that included Harvard publishing "lengthy official reports pinpointing the problem and laying blame on the preparatory schools" (27). These reports were "part of an attempt to get the secondary schools to improve their writing instruction; in effect, though, they diminished the role of first-year composition and expressed the hope of removing it entirely from the college curriculum and placing it in the schools" (26).

The lower status of composition compared to literature is also evident in the *General Education* committee's closing remarks regarding the teaching of English, which identify "one other problem which faces the secondary school teacher of English, responsible for both language and literature": the "multiplicity of aims and responsibilities of his field will prevent his concentrating his efforts effectively" (47). It is essential, according to the report, that high school English teachers recognize that their primary responsibility is in teaching language—that is, the "skills" and structure of language and writing—presumably so that college instructors could be relieved of those onerous tasks and freed to teach literature, which "has traditionally been the central humanistic study of the curriculum"(78), a statement that, among other things, offers a skewed, inaccurate history of the college English curriculum.

The attitude toward composition expressed in the *General Education in School and College* report is the same one that Daniel Mahala and Michael Vivion criticize the AP English programs for perpetuating, "the popular understanding that English [composition] inculcates 'basic skills' preliminary to the intellectual work of the university" (46). That attitude also considers students with poor writing skills a burden upon the colleges that the schools must alleviate; thus, the report concludes, it falls upon the colleges "to encourage and stimulate increased concern for good writing on the part of the schools—student and teacher alike" (*General Education* 43). Toward that end, the *General Education* committee recommends that colleges "support the effort to institute a general composition test as a regular feature of college entrance examinations" (43), a recommendation that would finally be realized some fifty years later in 2005 in the "new" SAT exam.

To address the ostensible problem of talented students languishing in redundant general education courses, the committee proposed an "advanced placement program" based on a series of examinations they hoped would be developed by the College Board. The *General Education* committee's recommendations for formal grammar instruction were typical of the time and no doubt articulate attitudes that persist—and guide—many contemporary teachers of AP English. For example, the report describes the necessity of "giving the student a clear sense of the way in which the elements of a sentence—subject, predicate, object, and predicate noun, in words, phrases, and clauses—work together to express a unit of thought. . . . Without such solid foundation, a student's use of language, however fluent and colorful, remains, in our experience, uncertain and shaky" (43). Imbedded in such a formulation is the basic skills approach to the teaching of writing, one that starts with parts of speech and sentence structure before allowing the student to engage meaning or expression: "On the basis of such foundation of grammar and accompanying it, the student can then be given training, adapted to his increasing awareness and maturity, in the nature of language and what is involved in the concept of meaning—a highly complex affair" (44). Those who teach composition know that there is much useful writing instruction that can occur between teacher and student in considering sentence construction. Yet the assumption that students should be taught to identify the elements of sentences and the parts of speech before being turned loose to write whole compositions reflects an atomistic approach toward writing instruction that views writing not as the making of meaning but as the avoidance of error.

One encounters in the committee's description of language the same terms that subsequently appeared on the AP English exams (and still do). According to the report, the student, at an early stage, should "gradually learn how tone, mood, and attitude affect meaning and how to handle abstractions, symbols, figurative language, irony, satire, and fantasy, all of which, without experience, baffle the literal minded" (44). *Tone, mood, attitude,* and *figurative language* are vital terms in AP English. Indeed, commercial prep materials for AP identify a dozen or so of the most common literary terms, or *devices* (a term once common in AP English materials) or *techniques,* used on the English exams and drill students in their identification and explication. Two of the three analyses on the free-response sections of the AP Literature exam delimit the student's interpretation of texts by asking them to engage such considerations. The recently modified AP Language exam now has at least one such free-response question. One of the 2007 AP English Literature exam essay prompts is typical: "Read carefully the following passage from Dalton Trumbo's novel *Johnny Got His Gun* (1939). Then write a well-organized essay in which you analyze how Trumbo uses such techniques as point of view, selection of detail, and syntax to characterize the relationship between the young man and his father" (College Board, *AP English Literature* 3).

Advancing Literature

Besides separating composition from reading literature, the *General Education* committee advanced a view of literature that is best described as decidedly New Critical. The committee reported from its survey: "In English, where it is normal for boys to study literature in both the 12th and 13th grades, we found a striking similarity between the 12th grade course in all three schools and the standard freshman English course at two of the universities" (13). It's useful to keep in mind the universities in the study: Harvard, Princeton, and Yale. The committee does not claim for the colleges the exclusive privilege of teaching literature, and, in fact, states that "there should be no sharp break between the work of the school and the college; rather a steady, uninterrupted growth in the student's understanding of good books, each step forward based on a solid foundation of knowledge, skills, and appreciation" (78). The committee does, however, describe and divide different approaches to literary texts between school and college. Schools should stress the "direct, immediate experience of good books, a deepened personal response, emotional as well as intellectual, to a writer's vision of life" (80). The committee has less to say about the teaching of literature in college, perhaps because the intended audience of the committee's report is not college literature faculty—most of whom, it might be safely assumed, would have little interest in, and would not be influenced nor inconvenienced by, the committee's recommendations. It is nevertheless noted that a "student's interest in craftsmanship is apt to mature later than his interest in ideas. Also, an interest in style is more a special than a general interest, and detailed analysis of form, unless handled with rare imagination by the teacher, can easily become irrelevant to the main purposes of all but the potential specialist" (81). Such observations suggest doubts about the abilities of secondary school teachers while describing an emphasis on form and style prevalent in mid-twentieth-century literary criticism.

The *General Education* committee's discussion of the teaching of literature is a mixture of the practical and the conventional. The committee suggests, for example, that a few texts, carefully and thoughtfully explored, are preferable to what many of their survey respondents described as "an education which consists disproportionately of passive, and often hurried absorption of the written word in great quantities" (83). The committee also endorses the traditional chronological presentation of literature, though it offers a "new—and flexible—principle of order" by proposing "that schools and colleges work out an experimental plan whereby the schools, in their upper years, would teach a few key works in common from a set list which permitted options" (84–85). Such a list would recognize "the importance of a shared tradition with which to help unify society," for it is the "school's responsibility" to provide "sound training in reading skills" and to "equip students who go on to college with the fundamentals of our literary heritage": "Without familiarity with the Bible, classical mythology, and great epic and legendary material, intelligent reading at the college level is exceedingly difficult; and colleges have a right to count on such knowledge in their entering students" (84–85). The texts mentioned as examples for such a "flexible" plan include many of the usual suspects—*Macbeth, Antigone, Billy Budd*—and others that now seem historical peculiarities, the province and concern only of college literature majors or graduate students: *Babbitt, Quentin Durward, Le Bourgeois Gentilhomme*, Shaw's first Fabian essay, and *Henry Esmond*. The suggestion of a common reading list likely disquieted those who had endured or had heard of the colleges' uniform lists that so bedeviled secondary schools in the first quarter of the century. Moreover, the committee's desire for a "shared tradition" recalls a time when the Eastern colleges and the prep schools that supplied them with students could assume a homogeneous population that shared beliefs and cultural values. From its inception, AP English has valued and reified the more conservative approaches of both college and secondary English. Given the school population it was originally intended to serve and their postsecondary school destinations—at least in the earliest days of AP—that conservatism seems entirely consistent.

Critics of AP English Literature often find fault with the formalist approach to literature the exam embodies, for such an approach operates on the assumption that meaning is located only in the text. Today the multiple-choice portion of both the AP Literature and AP Language exams, which accounts for 45 percent of each test's final value, presents to students excerpts from literary and "rhetorical" texts for analysis. Given the demands of scoring reliability, many of the questions are the sort that requires students to identify the most accurate paraphrase of a given line or a predetermined textual interpretation. Such an approach reduces reading to a set of skills employed in the decoding of texts having a relatively finite set of features (tone, diction, imagery, figurative language, etc.) that can be identified and compartmentalized in ways that offer a tidy, self-contained textual interpretation, innocent of the social and political contexts in which texts are actually produced and read. In his critique of AP English written over thirty years ago, Richard Ohmann declares that such an approach to literature "actually teaches the students *not* to respond to literature, not with . . . feeling"; instead, the student's role is reduced "to that of the neutral instrument, recording and correlating the facts and drawing conclusions" (57). AP's particular version of formalism also discourages students from reading *against* the work; students are taught not to challenge literature so much as to dissect it in ways that fit an examination methodology. Dynamic texts are rendered collections of static textual features, or "literary and rhetorical devices."

Selecting and Testing Students for Selective Colleges

Appended to the committee's 1952 *General Education in School and College* report is "A Proposal for an Experiment in Advanced Placement" in which they propose to place under the direction of the College Board the following "experiment":

1. To see whether it is possible to get sufficient agreement on the content and objectives of certain college freshman courses to make feasible the construction of valid tests for advanced placement.

2. To see whether such tests could be produced, administered, and scored at reasonable cost.

3. To see whether there would be enough able and willing students to make an advanced placement program worthwhile on an extended basis.

4. To see whether college teachers would accept good performance on an advanced placement test as equivalent to passing college courses. (129)

The committee describes the schools' and colleges' responsibilities in such an experiment as threefold: identify students who have "special competence" in any of the given subject areas; provide students, "probably at the 12th grade, with courses that anticipate college work" in that area; and, finally, "permit such students, on the basis of adequate tests, to skip the ordinary freshman courses and move directly into advanced subject matter" (129–30).

The process recommended by the committee's report for selecting students to prepare for advanced placement testing is more extensive—with more gatekeeping functions—than is current practice in most schools. Currently, each high school determines its own policy about its AP classes and who may enroll in them. The committee, however, suggested screening criteria for the advanced placement program that included school recommendation, SAT score, and performance on CEEB Achievement Tests (which have since been transformed into the SAT II exams). Today many high schools do in fact screen students before permitting them into the AP classroom. Some schools require teacher recommendation or approval by faculty committee. Other schools review the "strength" of the student's transcript or SAT scores. Some high schools even require a test for admission into their AP English courses. Many schools place students on an honors or "pre-AP" track early in high school and only permit those students to eventually enroll in AP.

The committee also called for a three-hour test, the content and form of which would be set for each subject by a Committee of Examiners. In English, the test decreed was "English Literature and Composition":

> The principal feature of the advanced placement tests . . . would be their power to measure a student's maturity in those intellectual processes required by each subject. Thus, a substantial section of the test would emphasize ability to reason with known facts and to solve problems. Whenever appropriate to the subject, essay questions would require the student to organize ideas, to write coherently, and to show intelligent critical sense in dealing with the ideas of others. (130–31)

Furthermore, in a description of reciprocity that makes clear the limited participation the committee imagined for an advanced placement program, the committee imagined that the relationship between schools and colleges would be so close that it recommended that "all participating colleges . . . incorporate parts of this preliminary material annually in their regular final examinations. This procedure would not only keep the tests abreast of any changes in the curriculum but would provide the colleges with expertly constructed tests on which to base their final marks" (132). This, obviously, never happened. And it's certain that no one involved in the report imagined that this educational experiment directed toward a select number of students destined for the highly selective colleges of the East would one day involve, according to the College Board's "Program Summary Report 2008," 1,580,821 students taking 2,736,445 exams, chosen from, according to the 2007–8 *Bulletin for AP Students and Parents*, 37 different exams in 22 subject areas (4).

The School and College Study of General Education provided the theoretical foundation and justification for the Advanced Placement program, and the schools involved in that study were the blue-blooded stock of the College Board, which would assume responsibility for the nascent AP program in 1955. There was, as identified earlier, a second, independent committee also funded by the Ford Fund that concurrently addressed concerns and explored options for the academically talented through advanced placement. The School and College Study of Admission with Advanced Standing (SACSASS) actually initiated the testing of students for advanced college placement. In a 1952 article in the *College Board Review*, Frank Ashburn, head of the College Board's Subcommittee on Achievement Tests (formed in 1950, before the Ford Fund and the formation of either the *General Education* committee or SACSASS), describes the subcommittee's efforts to identify the proper purposes for achievement tests in secondary schools. He writes that the subcommittee envisioned two possibilities: a set of tests to identify "broad aptitudes" that colleges might use for admission decisions, and a set of subject-matter tests given at the end of the school year that would be "of value to the schools in rating their students on a completed segment of learning, and to the colleges for purposes of placement, credit, and guidance" (315). When the subcommittee learned of the recommendations in *General Education in School and College*, they enthusiastically endorsed them, Ashburn writes, as "a carefully worked out practicable plan, closely related to ours. Where we were vague, this was specific; where we were far-flung, this was workable" (315). When the subcommittee later learned of the SACSAAS study, they unanimously decided to shelve their testing recommendations for those articulated in the *General Education* report.

Gordon Chalmers, president of Kenyon College, conceived the School and College Study of Admission with Advanced Standing, organizing presidents or deans from Bowdoin, Brown, Carleton, Haverford, M.I.T., Middlebury, Oberlin, Swarthmore, Wabash, Wesleyan, and Williams. The motivation for what would be known as "the Kenyon Plan" (and then, later, the Advanced Standing Program) was informed by the same antipathy toward progressive education described earlier. In his reflection on the origins of AP, the College Board's William Cornog, who was principal of Philadelphia's Central High School when he accepted appointment as the SACSAAS project director (Valentine 82), described the perspective from which the School and College Study viewed things—and repudiated progressivism—as "radical conservatism." Cornog notes, "Gordon Chalmers was fond of saying that our program was not for those colleges that had 'taken a header into general education'" (15). Furthermore, Chalmers identified two of the "opinions, or prejudices" that informed the SACSASS undertaking: "For the bright student who is well taught, the American system wastes time," and "the best teachers of 17-year-olds are as likely to be found in schools as in universities" (309).

The SACSASS identified eleven subjects for which its dozen participating college members would give full or partial first-year credit and invited select high schools to join its initiative and help develop course outlines that were available to secondary school teachers at the beginning of the 1953 school year. They also involved ETS from the beginning in the preparation of exams based on those course outlines (Valentine 83, 84). In the spring of 1954, 18 secondary schools had 532 students take 929 exams; in 1955, 925 students from 38 schools took 1,552 exams (Keller, "AP" 23). There were two English exams, one for composition and one for literature, and the three-hour exams consisted entirely of essays. Scorers developed the now familiar 1–5 AP score ranking, with test scores of 3 and higher the recommended range for college credit. Initially, it was assumed that the most selective colleges would grant credit only for test scores of 4 or 5, but McGeorge Bundy, then dean of Harvard and manager of a Ford Foundation grant, announced Harvard would consider the score of 3 sufficient for credit (Cornog 17). (When Harvard announced a few years ago that it would accept only AP scores of 5 for credit, it was news enough for the *New York Times* [Lewin].) Cornog notes that SACSAAS feared that too much emphasis would be placed on the exam—rather than the course—and that the exam would be confused with "proficiency" exams. Some of the teachers involved in the Kenyon Plan also feared that if they ceded control of the program to the College Board and ETS—which they did after the second year in an effort to sustain it—that they "would somehow turn the program into one more objective testing enterprise" (Valentine 85). Of course, the committee's fears were not unfounded.

The College Board, spurred as well by the recommendation of the *General Education in School and College* committee report, assumed responsibility for administration of the Advanced Placement program and exams in 1955, though there was reluctance within the College Board to take on the AP program because it seemed to offer little potential for growth. A grant from the Ford Fund actually defrayed costs during the first year of the board's sponsorship (Valentine 86), though College Board President Frank Keller, in his 1956 report about the new program, declared: "It is an inordinately expensive enterprise for the College Board to operate, because there are office and travel expenses, publications, conferences, and predominantly essay-type examinations which have to be prepared, administered, read, analyzed, and reported" ("Piercing" 19). The essay responses were initially to be forwarded to the colleges in which the student examinees had enrolled so that faculty could review incoming student performance (Keller, "AP" 22). (Colleges can still request students' test booklets after the June grading sessions; few do.) The College Board first offered its Advanced Placement exams in the spring of 1956 to 1,224 students from 110 schools who took 2,187 tests and later enrolled in 133 different colleges (23). Former AP director Harlan P. Hanson recalled in 1980 that the twelve hundred students who took AP exams in 1956 represented "several of the founders' notion of its ultimate clientele. In its second year it served 2,068 students from 212 schools, thereby 'exhausting' its apparent 'market' in a manner that was to be as regular as its growth" (9). The 2007 *Advanced Placement Report to the Nation* counts participation by 16,000 high schools and boasts that just under 25 percent of all graduating seniors in 2006 took at least one AP exam while in high school (83). If one considers the $83 fee for each of the 2.5 million exams taken by all high school students in 2007, the $210 million generated by this "inordinately expensive enterprise for the College Board" seems a decent return on its investment in America's "academically talented" high school students.

The Ends of First-Year College English

A common complaint against AP is that the exams—which are, at last, the instantiation of what *really* matters in AP English—test little of what is most emphasized in many contemporary first-year writing programs. Such complaints, perhaps not surprisingly, are not new. College Board historian John Valentine cites a comment from an early survey of college reactions to the AP program from one institution that refused to award credit "'because the courses did not duplicate' their own courses" (87). Despite recent thoughtful considerations by some involved in AP English exam development that the program is about *placement* rather than *exemption* (see Jolliffe and Phelan), it's clear that the original intentions were to develop a test as a means of exempting high school students from the first-year college English course.

David Foster, in "The Theory of AP English: A Critique," asserts that the central question those in college English must ask is "whether what the examinations teach is really what we want students to learn about writing and literature" (20). One answer to that question is offered by Edward M. White:

> But that argument [that AP scores should not be accepted because they are in conflict with curricular ends] makes the common mistake of confusing a curriculum with an assessment; the exam is seeking information about students who do have conscious control of their writing process and can show it on an essay test. Only such students deserve credit by examination; the rest will appropriately enough go through the curriculum. (37)

Such an explanation, however, doesn't address the question that follows of whether the "conscious control" of a timed writing process is, in fact, reason enough to exempt someone from first-year composition. Few first-year college writing programs teach or valorize timed writing; most devote their instructional efforts toward helping students develop the processes of research, revision, and the composition of more fully developed essays. Perhaps even more problematic is the conclusion reached in one study that former AP students were convinced "that they were finished developing as writers—a message that the decisiveness of the AP exam and subsequent waivers from college writing requirements unfortunately reinforce" (Spear and Flesher 47). Among the important discoveries detailed by Kristine Hansen et al. in a comparative study of writing abilities among college sophomores is that those who took AP English in high school and scored a 3 on either of the exams displayed no greater efficacy than students who didn't take AP English—and significantly less efficacy than those who not only scored higher on an AP English exam but also took their college's first-year English course.

One of the ironies associated with AP English is that, as it has become more widespread and egalitarian, there has arisen an implicit mistrust of this program that began as a sort of gentlemen's agreement between elite secondary and postsecondary schools. An increasing number of "highly selective colleges"—that certainly demonstrate a preference for applicants who have taken AP English—have grown stingier in using it as an equivalency exam to exempt students from their required first-year English courses. William Lichten argues that the rapid growth of AP, far from being cause for celebration, has caused its degradation as a valid measure for college credit. That is, as the College Board has concentrated on increasing the number of participants, the quality of student performance has actually declined, despite College Board claims to the contrary. By more carefully considering the credit awarded by the postsecondary institutions in which students actually enroll (the real determiners of success, he states), Lichten demonstrates that those "highly selective" colleges have actually grown less amenable to awarding college credit for AP scores: "English Literature seems to have slipped farther than other subjects. Some colleges, not all highly selective, will not even accept a '5' for AP credit. The shift from a '3' to a '4' in selective colleges occurs more often for English Literature than for other subjects" (2). Furthermore, Lichten attributes the major difference between what the College Board claims as "qualified" and what selective and highly selective colleges accept as "qualified" to "a yawning gap in communication between CEEB and the colleges" (4).

The 2007–08 *Advanced Placement English Course Description* notes: "The goals of an AP Language and Composition course are diverse because the college composition course is one of the most varied in the curriculum" (6). (It's instructive to contrast that statement with a similar one offered in the 2000 course description book: "The college composition course for which the AP Language and Composition course *substitutes* is one of the most varied in the curriculum" [College Entrance Examination Board 7; emphasis added]. Implicit within that observation is the recognition by those at the College Board that there is no common curriculum for first-year college composition. Indeed, first-year English courses vary in emphases and objectives from institution to institution, which is one reason many in college writing programs resist and resent AP. A well-conceived and designed first-year college English course responds to local needs and conditions; it also serves a particular student population. When it comes to first-year composition, one size does not fit all, and that has come to be considered a virtue rather than a shortcoming. The increased reluctance to trust the exam, or the high school course that students took to prepare for the exam, is also a likely result of the disciplinary emergence of rhetoric and composition and recognition by those trained in such graduate programs of the possibilities for, and benefits of, a theoretically sound first-year college course. It would be an overstatement to assert that the first-year college English course has achieved universal approbation in every postsecondary institution that requires it for its incoming students, but it is unlikely that most working in first-year writing programs consider their courses primarily remedial and of little value to students who demonstrated competence in the skills inculcated by the AP courses and exams.

Fifty years ago, the ostensible concerns that led to the creation of AP were for the intellectually gifted student adrift in the curricular backwaters of high school. The remedy was imagined to lie not in a more individualized curriculum of personal challenge or in more innovative secondary school programs but in introductory college classes. And because the model for academic work for the gifted high school student was the college curriculum, "the proposed changes in high school programs followed very closely what went on—or what was thought to go on—in college classrooms" (Applebee 191). Therefore, more significant than the yawning gap between the College Board and the colleges bemoaned by Lichten is the gap between the colleges and the high schools. Generally speaking, first-year college composition classes are profoundly different sites of instruction than they were in 1952. First-year college writing programs endeavor to develop in students the abilities to engage in the recursive processes of composition, and most particularly value revision as well as peer response and collaboration—none of which, of course, is required for the AP English exams. Yet for high school AP English teachers, AP continues to represent "college English." Otherwise, why would colleges award credit for it?

The "WPA Outcomes Statement for First-Year Composition" from the Council of Writing Program Administrators (see Harrington et al.) offers the most significant articulation of purposes for the first-year college English course. A comparison of those outcomes with the goals offered for the AP Language course reveals some parallel language and suggests some shared values. The goals for the older, more popular AP Literature course, however, make no mention of first-year college composition, which suggests a course insulated from the practices of most first-year writing programs. Dispiriting stories describing high school AP English classrooms dominated by multiple-choice and timed essay practices are common. It would be unfair to assume that such approaches are the norm, for the typical high school AP English teacher takes great pride in developing a thoughtful, challenging course for students. However rich such courses may be, though, the AP exam in May tends to trump most other impulses. It isn't that some of the skills acquired in AP English are of no use in college English; it is that many of the skills emphasized by AP are useful primarily for AP test taking. Furthermore, the traditional AP approaches to the production and reception of texts become especially problematic insofar as they come to represent to students—and their teachers—the most important ways meaning is made when encountering and composing texts. The *General Education* report of 1952, based on its survey of students, decried a "lack of contact between school and college curricula, particularly in the duplication of course content" (4). The lack of contact between most schools and colleges endures. The problem is no longer the duplication of course content but the discrepancy between curricula created in the absence of shared enterprise—in the absence of agreement on what the ends of English composition instruction should be. AP English doesn't address that discrepancy so much as perpetuate it.

Works Cited

Applebee, Arthur N. *Tradition and Reform in the Teaching of English: A History*. Urbana: NCTE, 1974. Print.

Ashburn, Frank D. "Recommendations for Achievement Testing." *College Board Review* 18 (1952): 13–15. Print.

Bestor, Arthur E., Jr. "Anti-Intellectualism in the Schools." *New Republic* 128.3 (19 Jan. 1953): 11–13. Rpt. in Scott and Hill 40–44.

Brereton, John C., ed. *The Origins of Composition Studies in the American College, 1875–1925: A Documentary History*. Pittsburgh: U of Pittsburgh P, 1995. Print.

Chalmers, Gordon K. "Advanced Credit for the School Student." *College Board Review* 18 (1952): 309–12. Print.

College Board. *Advanced Placement Report to the Nation: 2007*. College Board, 2007. Web. 23 Jan. 2008.

———. *AP English Course Description: English Language and Composition, English Literature and Composition, May 2007, May 2008*. College Board, 2006. Web. 24 Jan. 2007.

———. *AP English Literature and Composition 2007 Free Response Questions*. College Board, 2007. Web. 23 Jan. 2008.

———. *Bulletin for AP Students and Parents: 2007–08*. College Board, n.d. Web. 23 Jan. 2008.

———. "Program Summary Report." College Board, 2008. Web. 12 Feb. 2009.

College Entrance Examination Board. *Advanced Placement Course Description: English*. New York: Educational Testing Service, 2000. Print.

Connors, Robert J. "The Abolition Debate in Composition: A Short History." *Composition in the Twenty-first Century: Crisis and Change*. Ed. Lynn Z. Bloom, Donald A. Daiker, and Edward M. White. Carbondale: Southern Illinois UP, 1996. 47–63. Print.

Coombs, Philip H. "Talent, Education, and Democracy: A Foreword." *They Went to College Early*. Evaluation report no. 2. New York: Fund for the Advancement of Education, 1957. v–viii. Print.

Cornog, William H. "The Advanced Placement Program: Reflections on Its Origins." *College Board Review* 115 (1980): 14–17. Print.

Crockett, Ann L. "Lollipops versus Learning: A High-School Teacher Speaks Out." *Saturday Evening Post* 16 Mar. 1940: 29+. Rpt. in Scott and Hill 81–86.

Foster, David. "The Theory of AP English: A Critique." Olson, Metzger, and Ashton-Jones 3–24.

Fraser, James W. *The School in the United States: A Documentary History*. Boston: McGraw-Hill, 2001. Print.

General Education in School and College: A Committee Report by Members of the Faculties of Andover, Exeter, Lawrenceville, Harvard, Princeton, and Yale. Cambridge: Harvard UP, 1952. Print.

Hansen, Kristine, Suzanne Reeve, Jennifer Gonzalez, Richard R. Sudweeks, Gary L. Hatch, Patricia Esplin, and William S. Bradshaw. "Are Advanced Placement English and First-Year College Composition Equivalent? A Comparison of Outcomes in the Writing of Three Groups of Sophomore College Students." *Research in the Teaching of English* 40.4 (2006): 461–501. Print.

Hanson, Harlan P. "Twenty-five Years of the Advanced Placement Program: Encouraging Able Students." *College Board Review* 115 (1980): 8–12. Print.

Harrington, Susanmarie, Keith Rhodes, Ruther Overman Fischer, and Rita Malenczyk. *The Outcomes Book: Debate and Consensus after the WPA Outcomes Statement*. Logan: Utah State UP, 2005. Print.

Jolliffe, David A., and Bernard Phelan. "Advanced Placement, Not Advanced Exemption: Challenges for High Schools, Colleges, and Universities." *Delivering College Composition: The Fifth Canon*.

Ed. Kathleen Blake Yancey. Portsmouth: Boynton/Cook, 2006. 89–103. Print.

Keller, Charles R. "AP: Reflections of the First Director." *College Board Review* 116 (1980): 22–23. Print.

———. "Piercing the 'Sheepskin Curtain.'" *College Board Review* 30 (1956): 19–23. Print.

Kliebard, Herbert M. *The Struggle for the American Curriculum: 1893–1958*. 3rd ed. New York: RoutledgeFalmer, 2004. Print.

Lewin, Tamar. "Harvard to Require Top Score to Earn Advanced Placement." *New York Times*. New York Times, 22 Feb. 2002. Web. 25 Feb. 2009.

Lichten, William. "Whither Advanced Placement?" *Education Policy Analysis Archives* 8.29 (2000). Web. 23 Jan. 2008.

Mahala, Daniel, and Michael Vivion. "The Role of AP and the Composition Program." *WPA: Writing Program Administration* 17.1–2 (1993): 43–56. Print.

Ohmann, Richard. *English in America: A Radical View of the Profession*. 1976. With a new introduction. Hanover: Wesleyan UP, 1996. Print.

Olson, Gary A., Elizabeth Metzger, and Evelyn Ashton-Jones, eds. *Advanced Placement English: Theory, Politics, and Pedagogy*. Portsmouth: Boynton/Cook, 1989. Print.

Scott, C. Winfield, and Clyde M. Hill. *Public Education under Criticism*. New York: Prentice-Hall, 1954. Print.

Spear, Karen, and Gretchen Flesher. "Continuities in Cognitive Development: AP Students and College Writing." Olson, Metzger, and Ashton-Jones 25–51.

Valentine, John A. *The College Board and the School Curriculum: A History of the College Board's Influence on the Substance and Standards of American Education, 1900–1980*. New York: College Entrance Examination Board, 1987. Print.

White, Edward M. "An Apologia for the Timed Impromptu Essay Test." *College Composition and Communication* 46.1 (1995): 30–45. Print.

Woodring, Paul. *Investment in Innovation: An Historical Appraisal of the Fund for the Advancement of Education*. Boston: Little, Brown, 1970. Print.

CHAPTER THREE

The Evolution of AP English Language and Composition

KATHLEEN M. PUHR

Clayton High School, Missouri

When Charles Darwin wrote about the process of natural selection—about the need for species to adapt to changing environments—he wasn't giving a prescient description of AP English courses and exams. But he could have been. Over the past half-century, the discipline of English has changed, and with it AP English courses. Where once existed only an AP English Literature course and exam, a second species of AP English now thrives: AP English Language. And whereas for some years that new species of AP English struggled to define itself, it has now taken on a distinct identity, differentiating itself ever more clearly from AP English Literature. Although AP English Literature remains a course concerned with literary comprehension and interpretation, AP English Language is becoming a rhetoric course, designed to provide high school students with a curriculum closely aligned with a college composition course. A debatable issue is whether AP English Language is, in fact, the equivalent of a college composition course; another is the role that an AP English Language course plays vis-à-vis a college composition requirement. Let me suggest that although the AP English Language course is becoming more like rhetoric-based college composition courses, further evolution is required. So let me suggest further that the two courses should function complementarily, with the shared goal of improving students' thinking and writing.

As a former college composition teacher myself, I can argue the merits of college writing courses and of requiring that all undergraduates enroll in them. A college composition course, often intimate in size, is invaluable: it provides a means for easing students' transition from high school to college, for acquainting them with college culture, and for orienting them to the college library and its online resources. Best of all, through such activities as peer response, class discussion of student work, and writing conferences, college composition courses level the playing field: students with often wide-ranging backgrounds acquire an understanding of what college writing entails. I'm sure that most, if not all, teachers have encountered the first-year student who, after earning a C or B on the first essay, laments, "But I always got A's on my papers in high school," and we have had to explain that, big surprise, college is not high school.

Recently, when I tutored a first-year student enrolled in Writing 1 at Washington University in St. Louis, I saw firsthand how challenging the course work was: demanding readings, such as Foucault's "Panopticon," and the onerous but imaginative writing assignments. These assignments called for analysis of visual images and of a campus locale, rhetorical analysis of a student-selected passage from one of the readings, and a researched essay supplemented with both an abstract and a metacommentary on the essay. Although the student had attended an outstanding high school, he likely had not encountered such sophisticated nonfiction readings or essay assignments in his English classes. His college composition course stimulated his growth as a reader and writer, building on the more rudimentary skills he had learned as a high school student.

In other cases, however, AP students in high school experience a level of rigor and kind of instruction similar to that offered in many college composition courses, especially if the course is taught by an experienced, well-trained teacher and if it is truly a rhetoric class and not just a literature class. As a twenty-five-year veteran of high school teaching, as a designer and teacher of honors and AP English courses, as a former member of the AP English Test Development Committee, and as an AP English Language teacher consultant, I can assert that well-designed AP courses, aimed at high school juniors and seniors, can often be as challenging as introductory college courses. By explaining how the aims and structure of the AP English Language course and test have evolved since 2002 and by describing my own evolution as an AP English teacher since 1986, I argue that well-taught AP courses can fulfill much the same function that many college composition courses do, thus making room for colleges to develop advanced courses that can add significant value to the knowledge and skills strong AP students bring to college.

Although there are two AP English courses available to students, AP English Literature and AP English Language, the latter is the course now designed to be the equivalent of a college composition course. The newer of the two AP English courses, AP English Language has undergone a number of changes since its inception in 1980 as an alternative to the AP English Literature course. The English Language course was created due to changes in the college composition course, primarily the movement away from writing about literature. And it was also designed for high school students who wanted an AP English course but did not want to study and write about literary works. In fact, in the 1980s the English Language and English Literature AP exams were scheduled at the same time, requiring students to choose between them. AP English Language was not intended to be the junior year AP English course, which it has largely become, but rather an alternative and equivalent course to AP Literature.

AP English Language, like the AP English Literature course, still emphasizes the study of works from a variety of periods and genres and provides a spectrum of writing experiences. Both courses culminate in exams consisting of two sections: a multiple-choice section (55 to 60 questions, 60 minutes total) and a free response or essay section (3 essays, 120 minutes). Students' raw scores are converted into exam scores of 5 through 1, with a score of 3 or higher usually required for most colleges to grant credit for first-year writing. The exams, however, are optional. Some high schools require AP students to take the exams; some do not. Because the AP English exams are now distinct and are available each year on different testing dates, students can take either or both of them.

However, until recently, the AP English Test Development Committee designed both English exams and consequently influenced high school curricula profoundly. This committee consisted of "Literature" teachers and "Language" teachers, who were responsible for creating both exams. The AP English Literature exam has, from its inception in the early 1950s, emphasized analysis of poetry and prose fiction. AP English Literature, being the older course and exam, sometimes overshadowed AP English Language, rendering its identity somewhat uncertain. In fact, in their first years, the two exams shared a common "literary analysis" question. So for quite some time, AP English Language was "sort of" about literature, "sort of" about nonfiction. To illustrate, the 1994 AP English Language exam asked students to compare two passages—one from Austen, the other from Dickens. Both were marriage proposals and encouraged an analysis of strategies of persuasion, but the exercise was still literary in focus. For about the first twenty years, the AP English Language exam included many passages from other belletristic writers as well.

Even when the exam questions included nonfiction passages, students were often asked for stylistic analysis and were directed to consider such traditional "literary" elements as diction, syntax, figurative language, and tone. Thus, an exam ostensibly about rhetoric abridged what true rhetorical analysis entails, namely consideration of all five canons of rhetoric. Analysis of poetry was the only type of exam question that did not appear on the Language exam. The exam did, however, include an argument question—an essential element of rhetoric—so early on, the exam showed signs of evolving away from its parent, the AP Literature exam. Since 2002, this evolution has begun to speed up, and AP English Language has been working to clarify the skills central to it and also to align them with the skills taught in college composition.

The development of my AP courses mirrors in many ways the changes that have taken place in the AP Language and Composition course and exam. First, I should note that I was fortunate to teach in an exemplary school district and specifically at a high school—Clayton High School in suburban St. Louis—that boasted an unusual, and expensive, writing program, the Conferenced English Program (see Puhr and Workman). Since 1962, all students in Clayton High School's English classes have had the opportunity to participate in one-on-one writing conferences with their English teachers. English teachers teach three classes during an eight-period day. The rest of the time they offer individualized writing instruction to the students in those three classes. At least five times each semester, each student sits down with his or her teacher for half-period writing sessions (twenty to twenty-five minutes) at which the student and the teacher discuss the specific draft that the student has produced and ways to revise it. Obviously, Clayton's conference program offers the ideal way to teach writing, but it is costly: for a school of about 900 students the district employs about 20 English teachers. Given this student-teacher ratio, Clayton teachers have the luxury of pushing their students to become better writers by individualizing instruction and offering challenging assignments. Students, even in nonhonors and non-AP courses, write in a variety of genres on a variety of topics. Most of the formal assignments require analysis and argument; some require synthesis; others offer students the chance to write personal experience essays.

In 1986, I first began preparing students for the AP English Language exam within the context of the eleventh-grade honors American literature course that I was teaching. (Clayton High School began offering a separate AP English Language course only during the 2006–7 school year.) The emphasis in the AP Language course and exam then was mainly on literary analysis, with only a nod to rhetoric—and that nod was mainly to the canon of style. One of the assignments was a close-reading essay, with a student-selected passage from either *The Great Gatsby* or *The Grapes of Wrath*, analyzed primarily in terms of style. Students also wrote a précis of a critical essay about one of the authors that we studied in the course: an assignment requiring students to synthesize key ideas from the source. So my own course was slowly moving in the direction that AP English Language has now taken, but I still had far to go in teaching students about the full range of rhetorical analysis and about argumentation and synthesis.

When I moved to the twelfth-grade AP English course in 1993—a course designed to prepare students for either the AP English Literature or AP English Language exams—I incorporated some nonfiction, requiring students to do a close reading analysis of a passage from an essay by Dillard, Didion, or Orwell rather than a passage from a work of fiction. Students also wrote arguments and practiced synthesis within the context of a research paper and presentation. We talked about texts in terms of rhetorical choices and applied them to the choices students were making, or could make, in their own writing.

In addition to participating in writing conferences during which we discussed those choices, my students also engaged in peer review that led to revised and polished essays, not just timed writing. One particularly successful approach involved students bringing a draft to class, stapling a blank piece of paper to the back, and then routing their papers around the classroom to at least five other students. After students read classmates' drafts, they wrote positive comments about them as well as suggestions for revision, and signed their names. During the last five minutes of the class, we gathered a list of effective features and then urged students to incorporate one or more of them into their next draft. Because of all of these experiences with writing—including many in-class, impromptu, fifteen-minute writing assignments—students performed well on both the AP Literature and Language exams. Even if they were required to take college composition, they were well prepared for the course.

Just as I was able to evolve in my teaching of AP Language, I believe that other high school teachers could successfully remake their AP Language courses by taking greater advantage of various programs the College Board offers to ensure that teachers have the training to create courses that are aligned with introductory college courses, and that incorporate the best resources and strategies possible. Those remain the AP program's twin goals. The College Board has supported the evolution of the AP Language course and exam, and it stands ready to help teachers make a parallel evolution in their own teaching. Interestingly, the major climate change that precipitated the recent, rapid evolution of the AP English Language course occurred in 2002, when representatives from the AP English Test Development Committee along with an experienced AP teacher met with writing program administrators at the WPA conference in July. This conference of college composition directors provided fertile ground for frank, productive conversations between the AP representatives and those responsible for the shape and direction of college composition. AP English Language folks have attended the WPA conference every year since. Significant adaptations in the AP Language exam, and thus in the courses designed to prepare students for it, resulted from the 2002 meeting, adaptations that have helped to make AP English Language a rhetoric class focused primarily on the study of nonfiction.

The closer relationship between the AP English Test Development Committee and the WPA has yielded a number of changes in the AP English Language world. Led by the outgoing (in both senses) AP Language chief reader, David Jolliffe of the University of Arkansas, and by the incoming chief reader, Gary Hatch of Brigham Young University, members of the AP English Test Development Committee, who were interested in changing the English Language exam, held several meetings to talk about the types of questions that should appear on the exam. (I served on that committee during 2002–6.) Three overarching skills emerged from the conversations and became the focus for curriculum and assessment: analysis, synthesis, and argument. They have become the new holy trinity for AP Language teachers and students because they are fundamental to reading and writing in any discipline and are the focus of most college first-year writing courses. Although argument had been tested on the AP Language exam from its inception, analysis and synthesis are new or at least spruced up. Analysis far too often had concerned only the third canon of rhetoric—style—and had not invited students to consider the broader rhetorical landscape. Now, the recommended course and exam encourage rhetorical analysis—the meaning, purpose, and effect of various types of rhetoric, including print and visual texts from many disciplines, as well as the nature and operations of the appeals used in them.

The third skill, synthesis, is a genuine innovation, but obviously central to college courses. It's a vital skill in a world of information overload, multimedia input, and clashing moral and ethical systems. The newly added essay question testing this skill gives students a prompt that requires them to develop a contention about a topic, drawing on at least three of the six or seven sources provided. Students have 15 minutes at the beginning of the free response section to read and annotate the sources. Because analyzing visual texts has become increasingly important in a post-print world, students are given a visual text as one of the sources for the synthesis question, such as a chart, graph, map, photograph, painting, cartoon. The synthesis question made its debut on the 2007 AP English Language exam (administered to about 285,000 students nationally) with a question about the effects of advertising on American culture. (Form B of the exam, given to approximately 2,000 American students overseas, asked a question about factors for museum acquisitions directors to consider in choosing a new museum piece.)

In 2005, the AP English Language Test Development Committee became a separate entity from the committee that develops the literature exam and, as a consequence of the inevitable but benign evolutionary process, recommended one other change that has occurred to the multiple-choice section of the exam. That section now includes at least one passage containing footnotes or endnotes, with a few other questions about the citations themselves, in addition to the usual questions about the rhetorical features of the passage. Like other changes, this one was an attempt to align curriculum and assessment more closely with that in college composition courses, which usually include study of the purposes and forms of documentation. However, the nature of the test permits asking students only about their recognition of documentation conventions and precludes asking students to produce documented writing.

To help prepare students, and teachers, for the changes in the exam and especially for the new synthesis question, the Language Test Development Committee members and the College Board organized a series of events designed to spread the word. An online presentation, via AP Central, the official AP website, took place in the spring of 2006. In addition, at the end of the AP Language Reading in June 2006, high school teachers learned more about the synthesis question in a day-long workshop that was mandatory for AP consultants—those who offer regional workshops to AP teachers. The workshop presenters explained the item and suggested ways that teachers could teach synthesis (and citation) in their courses. Those AP teachers who had received the training then conducted workshops for other teachers at which they explained the new item type as well as the course's and exam's more concentrated focus on nonfiction. Adding the synthesis question has in many ways been a boon to AP Language teachers, further enabling them to promote their course as decidedly different from AP Literature and more in line with the kinds of skills asked of college composition students.

Along with articulating the skills of analysis, synthesis, and argument, as central to the AP Language course, meetings with the WPA have also helped the Test Development Committee, and consequently AP teachers, to learn about and implement the "WPA Outcomes Statement for First-Year Composition" (adopted in April 2000). These outcomes fall into four categories: Rhetorical Knowledge (appreciation of rhetorical situation and choosing appropriate strategies for that context); Critical Thinking, Reading, and Writing (evaluating and synthesizing sources); Processes (the writing process, collaboration, using a variety of technologies); and Knowledge of Conventions (genre conventions, citations, usage and grammar). The AP English Course Outcomes, presented in the Course Description Booklet for AP English Language (College Board), closely parallel those WPA Outcomes, as Table 3.1 illustrates.

Obviously, the skills that AP English Language students should have practiced, and ideally even mastered, by the end of the course are largely the same as those envisioned for students who have completed a college composition course. If an AP English Language student is also fortunate enough to have experienced a high school–wide effort to promote writing in all content areas, the result is a student who appreciates the importance of writing as a tool for learning and who has begun to recognize the disciplinary differences in conventions, genres, and contexts for writing.

The outcomes listed in Table 3.1 can be achieved in exemplary AP English Language courses that are, first and foremost, taught by experienced teachers (more about teacher training later). The curriculum in such exemplary courses emphasizes nonfiction, and when it includes works of fiction, it either positions them within the landscape of rhetorical analysis or links them thematically with works of nonfiction. Everything written, after all, is a negotiated text involving audience, writer, context, and purpose, and such considerations involve omissions as well as inclusions of which students should repeatedly be reminded. One way that many successful teachers drive home this idea is

TABLE **3.1.** A Comparison of the WPA Outcomes Statement for First-Year Composition and the AP English Language Course Outcomes

Main Points of the WPA Outcomes Statement	AP English Language Course Outcomes
By the end of first-year composition, students should be able to:	Upon completing the AP English Language and Composition course students should be able to:
• Focus on a purpose • Respond to the needs of different audiences • Respond appropriately to different kinds of rhetorical situations • Use conventions of format and structure appropriate to the rhetorical situation • Adopt appropriate voice, tone, and level of formality • Understand how genres shape reading and writing • Write in several genres • Use writing and reading for inquiry, learning, thinking, and communicating • Understand a writing assignment as a series of tasks, including finding, evaluating, analyzing, and synthesizing appropriate primary and secondary sources • Integrate their own ideas with those of others • Understand the relationships among language, knowledge, and power • Be aware that it takes multiple drafts to create and complete a successful text • Develop flexible strategies for generating, revising, editing, and proofreading • Understand writing as an open process that permits writers to use later invention and rethinking to revise their work • Understand the collaborative and social aspects of writing processes • Learn to critique their own and others' works • Learn to balance the advantages of relying on others with the responsibility of doing their part • Use a variety of technologies to address a range of audiences • Learn common formats for different kinds of texts • Develop knowledge of genre conventions ranging from structure and paragraphing to tone and mechanics • Practice appropriate means of documenting their work • Control such surface features as syntax, grammar, punctuation, and spelling.	• Analyze and interpret samples of good writing, identifying and explaining an author's use of rhetorical strategies and techniques • Apply effective strategies and techniques in their own writing • Create and sustain arguments based on readings, research, and/or personal experience • Write for a variety of purposes • Produce expository, analytical, and argumentative compositions that introduce a complex central idea and develop it with appropriate evidence drawn from primary and/or secondary sources, cogent explanations, and clear transitions • Demonstrate understanding and mastery of standard written English as well as stylistic maturity in their own writings • Demonstrate understanding of the conventions of citing primary and secondary sources • Move effectively through the stages of the writing process, with careful attention to inquiry and research, drafting, revising, editing, and review • Write thoughtfully about their own process of composition • Revise a work to make it suitable for a different audience • Analyze image as text • Evaluate and incorporate reference documents into researched papers.

by teaching the mnemonic device SOAPStone as a lens through which to approach texts. Using this device, students identify the subject of the piece, the occasion (the medium in which the piece was first presented and any subsequent media), the audience (both primary and secondary), the purpose, and the speaker (notably the speaker's persona or role). Finally, students identify the tone of the piece and any places in which the tone shifts. This device offers an effective starting point for rhetorical analysis. In teaching argument, AP teachers invite students to approach an issue using an Aristotelian model, presenting counterarguments and refutations (a procatalepsis paragraph) near the end of the essay. Some teachers also have students practice Rogerian argument, and others the Toulmin model. Regardless of approach, students learn to acknowledge counter-arguments to their claims. Recent AP Language exams have required that students present both sides of an issue before aligning with one of them. To teach synthesis, teachers ask students to generate a list of topics, find sources offering different perspectives, and develop essays or presentations in which the students incorporate those sources in support of their own arguments. Students are learning to analyze and synthesize visual texts as well—everything from graphs and charts to cartoons and illustrations for op-ed pieces.

In teaching these skills, AP English Language courses invite students to consider an array of texts from a variety of eras; these texts encompass many genres and are sometimes grouped around one theme, addressed in different times and places. AP English Language courses also invite classical rhetoric's fourth and fifth canons, memory and delivery, into the conversation. For memory, students consider the cultural context out of which the text emerged and the cultural values subsumed within it. The fifth canon, delivery, urges students to evaluate the medium through which the text is delivered and the limits that the medium imposes. AP English courses encourage students to question texts, to doubt their claims, evidence, and warrants. Above all, these courses call on students to be engaged in their world and become alert citizens, not just passive consumers, who examine issues in terms both of current commentary and historical context. They are students of the media who become more attuned to rhetorical appeals and to logical fallacies by analyzing them in class exercises and in homework assignments. They learn about satire, irony, and parody. They learn to read visual texts as well as the printed page. From the ideal AP English Language class should emerge not only our best students but also informed and thoughtful citizens.

The growth of AP English Language, at least as evidenced by the numbers of students taking the exam, suggests many students are enrolled in AP Language courses around the country. Admittedly, they cannot all be taking the type of course described in the previous two paragraphs. In truth, the evolution of the course is proceeding unevenly. All AP English Language courses are supposed to be created equal, but some are more equal than others—in other words, not all the courses produce the outcomes that they should. This fact results from three major issues: (1) the piggybacking of the AP English Language curriculum onto the traditional junior year American Literature survey; (2) unprepared students enrolling in the course; (3) untrained or underqualified teachers.

Although not originally designed to be a junior year AP English course, more often than not AP English Language has become the eleventh-grade course, with AP English Literature the senior year course. And, since many schools require juniors to take an American Literature survey course, AP English Language has, in effect, involved a study of American literature. Certainly American literature can be taught quite successfully from a rhetorical perspective. The problem occurs if the course focuses on literary analysis rather than rhetorical analysis. Part of the evolutionary process for AP English Language has involved helping teachers to teach American literature primarily through rhetorical analysis. Teaching teachers about this emphasis on rhetoric takes time, and in some cases students might still be taking a course that is essentially a literature course that emphasizes literary analysis exclusively, offering little opportunity for rhetorical analysis or argument. Or they might be taking a course that is focused on the old AP Language exam questions—ones emphasizing stylistic analysis rather than rhetorical analysis, and not even addressing synthesis, citation, and analysis of visual texts. Based on some of the essays readers saw at the 2007 AP English Language Reading, some students are still thinking that rhetorical analysis equals an analysis of style. For example, they approached the passage from Scott Russell Sanders's book *Staying Put: Making a Home in a Restless World*, a rebuttal of Salmon Rushdie's piece about moving, as a chance to identify examples of diction, syntax, and tone. And they applied a similar approach to the sources for the synthesis question. It's sad that some students weren't better instructed, sadder still that some AP English Language teachers weren't better informed. Still, we remain optimistic that the news will spread and that teachers will learn to reshape their curriculum so that students can apply skills of rhetorical analysis to the texts they study and can understand why analysis, argument, and synthesis are fundamental to all textual study, in any discipline.

The second problem, that of unprepared and underprepared students enrolling in AP courses, results from the College Board's commitment to "access and equity," that is, its desire to spread the benefits of AP curricula to as many students as possible. However, a one-semester course, even a one-year course, can't make up for years of less-than-challenging instruction. Students who earn C's and D's in an AP course and a score of 1 or 2 on the AP exam definitely need to take a college composition class or two. Merely having taken an AP course does not mean that this kind of student is ready for college-level writing, so all AP courses should not be judged entirely from the kinds of students who may have enrolled in some of them. I suspect that when these less successful AP students appear in college composition courses, instructors may assume that they are "typical" AP students when, in fact, they are far from it. Depending on the college's placement policy, the more typical AP student may have already earned advanced placement through success on the Language or Literature exam and thus not be enrolled in the introductory college composition course.

With more students signing up for AP courses, it follows that more AP teachers are needed, but an enrollment boom can lead to assigning teachers who are not yet ready for prime time. This is the third reason that the evolution of AP Language courses has not been equally successful in all schools. Although the best AP teachers usually have taught for several years, sometimes teachers with only a year or two of experience are asked to teach the AP Language course, resulting in a raw deal for both the teacher and the students. Assigning untrained, inexperienced teachers to these AP courses is an unfortunate consequence of the rapid growth of AP English Language. Students emerging from such courses would benefit from the training in rhetoric that a college composition course offers. Moreover, before they are asked to teach AP English Language, teachers would benefit from having time to attend workshops and summer institutes and to rethink their curriculum in light of what the AP English Language course is supposed to do and what the test will require.

One might think of this AP English Language program as an incompletely evolved, sprawling organism covering millions of acres but sustained and nurtured by one "remote brain," if you will. That brain is the College Board, which, through its national and regional offices, is trying to hasten the evolution of AP English Language into a course equivalent to college composition. Obviously, teacher training is the essential nutrient in this process. One element of teacher training is workshops. One- and two-day sessions are offered in both the fall and spring at various sites around the country. At these workshops, which are led by trained AP consultants, new and experienced AP teachers exchange teaching ideas, recommend texts and other materials, and learn more about the recent exam and how students performed on it. In the summer teachers can participate in week-long institutes, during which they are given opportunities to develop complete teaching units for their students.

At both workshops and institutes, teachers who often have had little formal training in rhetoric learn more about what it means and how to move from literary analysis to the more challenging rhetorical analysis. Consultants provide examples of passages and student essays from recent AP English Language exams, helping teachers to understand what effective rhetorical analysis looks like. They suggest strategies and activities for teaching this skill as well as the skills of argument and synthesis. Consultants remind teachers of the kinds of materials that work well in an AP English Language course and encourage them to avail themselves of the College Board's website, AP Central. Of course, participating teachers share strategies, texts, and assignments with one another. One synthesis assignment making the rounds is a final course activity that has students devise their own synthesis question and compile five or six relevant sources.

Students then exchange their synthesis questions and write an essay answering the one they've chosen or been given.

Teachers in rural areas who may not have the opportunity to participate in person at a workshop or institute may do so online through discussion groups and online "live" events. In the spring of 2006, for example, one of these online events, lasting over two hours, dealt with the new synthesis essay question. Along with the more formal presentations from two experienced teachers were the ongoing question-and-answer components and the chance for teachers from around the country to exchange ideas with one another. The AP website, AP Central, is a rich repository of articles, previous exam questions, annotated bibliographies, and reading lists. A number of publications pertinent to specific courses are available through this website. Teachers are free to contact publishers to receive examination copies of rhetoric texts, readers, grammar and usage handbooks, and other resources.

Even more of an issue for some teachers teaching an AP English Language course is that they themselves have never taken a rhetoric class. The irony is that English majors frequently "test out" of introductory composition classes and may even earn their degree without taking a writing class other than, perhaps, creative writing. For these teachers in particular, taking a rhetoric class—especially a graduate-level rhetoric class—would make them more familiar with rhetorical theory and its classical and contemporary figures. Short of that, teachers should read a book about rhetorical theory or browse some of the texts used in college composition in order to have a better sense of today's college composition courses. If high school teachers are to prepare students for the analytical and argumentative moves they will have to make in all their college courses—moves that good college composition courses teach students to make—high school teachers need to understand what those courses and those rhetorical moves are about. All of the above are my suggestions, from one AP teacher to all the others, for getting our own house in order.

One other housekeeping chore for AP teachers remains to be discussed. Because of the tremendous growth of the AP program, the College Board in 2007 created a "course audit" for all AP courses. (AP English Language is one of the fastest-growing programs and is second or third among all AP courses in the number of exams scored each year; only AP U.S. History and, possibly, AP English Literature are larger.) Admittedly an attempt to make AP courses more uniform by requiring them to meet certain standards, the audit required all AP teachers to submit a course syllabus for any AP course they teach. Each syllabus is reviewed by two different college professors. The two AP English courses must meet different criteria for the audit, and in this way, too, the courses are becoming more distinct. For AP English Language, syllabus approval is contingent upon each syllabus meeting the standards, mentioned earlier, in the AP English Language Course Description booklet—essentially the same standards that the WPA approved for college composition courses. To be approved, the syllabus must require students to read works from a variety of historical periods, draft and revise a number of pieces, write in a variety of genres and for a variety of audiences and purposes, learn research skills, including citing sources, and attend to vocabulary development, syntactical variety, organizational skills, and control of tone and voice. It must specifically address the skills of analysis—including analysis of visual texts—as well as synthesis and argument. (For a complete listing of all the syllabus criteria, interested readers may see the AP English Language home page.) If the syllabus fails to address these requirements, the course is not allowed to be called an AP course. Obviously, mere approval of the syllabus does not guarantee that the course will actually deliver what the syllabus promises—not unless the College Board sends spies into every AP classroom—but it does show that the teacher whose syllabus has been approved has at least become familiar with the criteria that constitute a college-equivalent course.

The audit sends an important message: that the content of the course is at least as important as the score that a student earns on the exam. In addition to ensuring that each AP course compares favorably to a similar college-level course, the goal of the audit is to make AP courses roughly comparable to one another while still giving teachers the freedom to use their own methods. Because it is a skills-based rather than content-based course, AP English Language (as well as AP English Literature) affords teachers the opportunity to be innovative and flexible while still addressing the required elements for the audit. (I should point out, however, that students are allowed to sit for any AP exam, regardless of whether they have taken the course to prepare them for it.)

Regardless of how they score on the AP exam, students who take AP courses think differently than they did before about the subject and about scholarship in general. True, some students take AP courses primarily to pad their transcript rather than because they have a genuine passion for the subject. True as well: some students take AP courses to "get out of" introductory college courses. As Jolliffe and Phelan remind us, though, "the name of the program is Advanced *Placement*, not Advanced *Exemption*" (89). As for AP English Language specifically and its alignment with college composition, if colleges require all students to take a composition course, students are not going to be irrevocably harmed. Even students who have earned A's in their AP English Language course and a 5 on the exam can always work at becoming better writers. However, students who have taken an AP English Language course that is closely aligned with college composition may find themselves thinking, if they're required to take Comp. 1, "This is *déjà vu* all over again." So college composition courses need to evolve, too, in order to accommodate the students who have honed their skills in a rhetoric-based AP English Language course. Colleges will need to offer more options—honors or advanced composition courses, for example—so that well-prepared students continue to be challenged and continue to develop as writers. The changes in the AP English Language course and exam resulted from the College Board and high school teachers taking their lead from college writing program administrators and teachers. College composition teachers and administrators should now take their lead from AP English Language teachers and instigate changes in college writing programs that will lead to the further evolution of college writing programs.

Works Cited

College Board. *AP English Course Description: English Language and Composition, English Literature and Composition, May 2007, May 2008.* College Board, 2006. Web. 26 Nov. 2007.

Council of Writing Program Administrators. "WPA Outcomes Statement for First-Year Composition." *WPA: Writing Program Administration* 23.1–2 (1999): 59–63. Print.

Jolliffe, David A., and Bernard Phelan. "Advanced Placement, Not Advanced Exemption: Challenges for High Schools, Colleges, and Universities." *Delivering College Composition: The Fifth Canon.* Ed. Kathleen Blake Yancey. Portsmouth: Boynton/Cook, 2006. 89–103. Print.

Puhr, Kathleen, and Gail Workman. "Monitoring Student Progress through a Conferenced Writing Program." *English Journal* 81.2 (1992): 49–50. Print.

Sanders, Scott Russell. *Staying Put: Making a Home in a Restless World.* Boston: Beacon, 1993. Print.

CHAPTER FOUR

What Do the Students Think? An Assessment of AP English Preparation for College Writing

COLLEEN WHITLEY AND DEIRDRE PAULSEN

Brigham Young University

A common avenue to college credit for work completed in high school is earning a score of 3, 4, or 5 on the Advanced Placement (AP) tests. At many universities these scores on the AP English Literature and Composition exam or the AP English Language and Composition exam will exempt students from first-year composition (FYC) classes. In most cases, students who pass one or both of the AP exams in English composition have also taken a corresponding high school course; thus, any college credit they earn suggests that the institution granting the credit views the high school course as equivalent to or at least an adequate substitute for FYC. In some cases, however, students have not had either AP course but have simply taken an AP test and scored well enough on it to earn an exemption at college. For this research we questioned whether it is justified to assume equivalence or satisfactory similarity between AP courses and tests and college FYC courses. We report here evidence from students who have taken both courses that the widespread assumption of equivalence is largely mistaken. The main reason for their lack of equivalence, we found, is that AP courses focus so heavily on preparing students to write timed, impromptu essays for the AP test that they have little time to focus on other genres of writing—particularly research-based writing—usually emphasized in FYC.

Some studies questioning the practice of granting credit for high school work have focused on the history of AP; for example, Joseph Jones (this volume) and David Foster both point out that originally AP programs were designed for students at elite schools and were not considered a path to be taken by as many high school students as possible. Other critics, such as Gary A. Olson and Elizabeth Metzger, have emphasized the disparities between the curriculum of FYC courses and that of the AP English Literature and Composition exam; the latter, they claim, should not be considered equivalent to FYC at all. While Olson and Metzger believe that the AP Language and Composition course can and should be taught to produce the same knowledge and skills as a typical FYC course, they note that it is sometimes actually a survey of American literature, a fact they call "a perversion of the intent and nature of the AP English curriculum" (117).

Only a handful of studies have examined how AP students perform once they are in college. Karen Spear and Gretchen Flesher's interview research with twenty students suggests that AP students who bypass FYC tend to think they are better prepared as writers than they actually are. Such students "manifest a sense of closure toward writing—that what is to be known about writing is limited to mastery of skills, and they have mastered them" (40). Spear and Flesher found that, compared to AP students who took FYC at college, students who skipped FYC "lacked the intellectual gusto of the others"; they speculated those students would make the same intellectual gains as the others "only by overcoming much of what they have learned, at least about writing, in AP" (47). But Spear and Flesher's findings are hard to generalize because of their small sample.

A 2006 study by Hansen et al. ("Advanced") examined a much larger sample of students to answer empirically the question of whether AP English and first-year college writing courses prepare students equally well for college writing. According to survey data they collected from 497 students, there were significant gaps in students' experience with high school writing compared to what the FYC course taught. These students reported that the most heavily assigned types of writing in high school were the five-paragraph essay, book reports, comparison-and-contrast papers, and answers to questions about reading assignments. In comparison, the FYC course used a text-based rhetoric approach that focused on helping students write in the various genres required by their college courses, including documented research writing that taught students to use the university's library and online sources. More importantly, through an empirical study of 182 sophomore students' writing, Hansen et al. found that in two writing assignments for a history of civilization course "those students who had taken an AP English course and a suitable FYC course performed significantly better than those who had only AP English or only FYC" ("Advanced" 461). The authors speculate that more writing instruction in college solidifies high school learning and fills in gaps.

In a 2004 article, Hansen et al. question the basis for granting college credit for FYC in exchange for AP scores, a practice that uses grade studies rather than curriculum comparisons or empirical studies of student writing ability. The College Board regularly studies whether AP students who received credit for FYC earn grades in subsequent English courses that are just as high as or higher than grades of those who didn't have AP credit. If the grades are the same, the presumption is that bypassing FYC caused no harm to the AP students, since they performed just as well as other students. Hansen et al. argue that grades "constitute a very blunt instrument" to use in making such a determination ("Argument" 40). They are not opposed to students taking AP courses in high school; however, given results of their empirical study of sophomore writing, they caution that AP courses are not an adequate substitute for a strong FYC course, especially for students who score only a 3 on the AP exam.

Likewise, David A. Jolliffe and Bernard Phelan point out many reasons why AP English courses are valuable for high school students, but the authors argue that AP scores should lead to advanced *placement* rather than the all-too-common current practice of *exempting* students from taking any introductory college composition course at all. They argue that high school courses simply cannot substitute for college writing courses, and they encourage postsecondary institutions to have in place challenging writing courses for AP students to take once they matriculate at college. They are concerned that *both* high school and college courses be as rigorous as possible to challenge students and foster high levels of achievement.

Evidence that students need rigorous high school course work to be prepared for college comes from the 2005–06 ACT

National Curriculum Survey. Asked about their perception of whether high school courses prepared students for college, the majority of more than 10,000 high school teachers and nearly 13,000 college professors did not believe that "today's students are better prepared than their predecessors, despite explicit attempts toward this end" (*Aligning* 4). ACT states that one of the implications of this survey is that "states should seek empirical evidence that their standards and assessments are actually fostering, preparing and measuring student readiness for postsecondary work as validated by actual student success data in college" (8). Because ACT is a testing organization with a vested interest in recommending more assessment, this conclusion must be taken with some skepticism. Still, the call for actual data on student success in college suggests a need for something more substantial than grade studies—perhaps longitudinal studies and multiple measures that probe student performance in both high school and college to validate the quality of instruction.

To date, however, much assessment of student achievement in high school and readiness for college has relied on one-time snapshots of student abilities as revealed in easily evaluated assessments, such as multiple-choice tests and timed essays. Because the nature of assessments nearly always drives the focus and shape of instruction, when assessments superficially measure discrete bits of knowledge, instruction tends to focus on drilling students to perform well on the assessment. In 2005 the National Council of Teachers of English issued a scathing report about the timed writing test of the new SAT, proclaiming that "the test is unlikely to improve writing instruction in the nation's schools in ways that are consistent with the principles articulated in NCTE's *Beliefs about the Teaching of Writing*." The report also noted that the "potential detrimental impact of the test on writing instruction in secondary schools is cause for genuine concern" (1). NCTE supports this judgment by noting that "the kind of writing required for success on the timed essay component of the SAT is likely to encourage writing instruction that emphasizes formulaic writing with specific but limited textual features" (5). NCTE states that the writing tasks on the timed SAT writing tests are "generally decontextualized and artificial with no reference to the crucial rhetorical matters of audience and purpose," stating that the biggest travesty is the following:

> Careful, in-depth inquiry into a topic, attention to stylistic or structural features that may be suitable for specific audiences or rhetorical situations, creativity and innovation—all these important components of effective writing are likely to be implicitly or explicitly discouraged by teachers who will understandably be concerned about helping students manage the required writing tasks in the short allotted time. (5)

We think NCTE's criticisms of the SAT essay could also be leveled against the AP exams, particularly the timed, impromptu essay exams. However, those who support AP's claim to offer students the equivalent of college courses might respond to this criticism that the AP tests measure only a small part of what students are capable of. In the AP courses, they would argue, students are getting the same instruction in rhetoric, writing processes, and using research sources to write documented argument papers typical of in FYC. But does this actually happen? We designed the following study to answer this question.

No study we are aware of has investigated what students themselves think about the comparability of their AP course and their FYC course. Such a study would be hard to conduct because many AP students do not take FYC, being exempted from it, so they would have no basis for comparison. However, at Brigham Young University (BYU) we have a large group of students who are required to take FYC, despite their AP success. They are the first-year students who commit to graduating with university honors and then enroll in Honors 150 (H150). They constitute a convenient population to survey because they are sizable in number, come from all over the nation, and have significant experiences to help us answer the question of whether the AP course is substantially similar to or different from FYC. In what follows, we report and analyze the results of two surveys we administered in the 2006–07 school year. We first describe the H150 course, its reason for being, and the teachers who staff it. Next we describe the population and the survey instrument we sent to 717 students who had just completed H150, asking them to compare the writing instruction received in their high school English AP courses and H150 courses. We also surveyed the Honors 150 teachers to learn their perceptions of what the students brought with them to the course as well as what they gained from it, and we use some of these findings to complement the student data. We present our quantitative results in two tables and eleven graphs, focusing our discussion mainly on the areas where the AP students reported they were best and least prepared for college writing. In several cases, the results are clear and unexpectedly dramatic in indicating important gaps in the writing knowledge and experience of AP students. Then we discuss the qualitative results in detail, quoting students' own words. The students in our survey repeatedly said that while their high school AP courses had prepared them to enter H150, the AP courses were not replacements for it. Finally, we draw conclusions we believe should influence university policies about awarding college credit for high school writing.

Honors 150, the Course of No Exemptions

From its inception in 1960, the directors and faculty associated with the BYU Honors Program have regarded writing as a crucial component of students' education. For the first sixteen years of the program, the need was filled by honors sections of the regular FYC course offered by the English department. However, James Kearl, a former director of the honors program, related that as "high schools pushed more and more students into AP, we . . . were concerned about what was happening to the 'best' students we admitted, particularly as high schools pushed AP English to the junior and even sophomore years of high school—which meant that an 18-year-old freshman had last taken an English class as a 15- or 16-year-old." Consequently, the honors program created its own class, "Intensive Writing," for which AP credit could not be substituted (renamed "Honors University Writing" in 2005). Because the program directors realize some students may already be at the level required to pass H150, there is an option for students to challenge the requirement by submitting samples of their writing. Fewer than three apply annually, and course directors can recall only one student in the past fifteen years who earned an exemption (Laing; Jorgensen).

What is this FYC course that allows virtually no exemptions? H150 focuses primarily on teaching students how to think and read critically and to write academic discourse to prepare them for writing assignments they will encounter in later courses. The teachers are all currently part-time instructors, although some have previously taught full-time. All hold at least a master's degree or MFA, and several have PhDs or JDs. All are experienced teachers and writers: several have published books; some serve on editorial boards for magazines or journals; several have won writing awards. Some edit and have even founded journals; others serve as faculty mentors for student publications and foster contact between student writers and publishers. Many are actively involved in the national profession of writing teachers and have presented at national conferences. All view themselves as mentors to students who want to excel as writers. All in all, they are a stable, highly qualified group of teachers, and several have taught the course for ten to fifteen years. Teachers new to the program are carefully mentored by experienced teachers. In addition to hiring and supporting a well-qualified staff, the honors program has developed a challenging curriculum for H150. Assignments include the following:

- Working with the library personnel, instructors train students in how to locate, read, and evaluate the reliability of source material and how to successfully incorporate borrowed evidence as support for their writing. These skills are used in a traditional research paper, a multigenre research project, and in other major papers.

- One or more argumentative or persuasive papers, following instruction in critical reading and reasoning where students learn to reason logically, identify premises and unstated assumptions, draw sound inferences from evidence, avoid fallacies, project a credible ethos, use emotional appeals justifiably, and so on.

- A critical analysis or interpretation of a work from the Honors Great Works list, a catalog of influential works of art, architecture, literature, drama, film, music, dance, and science from ancient to modern times, with which all honors students must become acquainted.

- A personal narrative/essay focusing on developing voice, style, audience awareness, use of concrete detail and dialogue, and so forth.

- ◆ Other informal papers such as "postings," journal entries, letters, reflection essays, evaluations, proposals, abstracts, and so on.

- ◆ Collaborative learning opportunities and/or a service learning project in many sections.

The focus of the H150 curriculum is on critical reading and writing, not on literature. Readings—usually short expository, argumentative, or personal essays—are used to develop critical acumen and support the teaching of writing. Students typically produce between thirty and forty pages of polished final-draft writing, and every paper goes through at least two drafts. Peer review of drafts and draft conferences with teachers are also standard pedagogical practice.

Research Methods

Participants

BYU is a private university with an enrollment of 30,000; it draws students from every state in the nation and 130 foreign countries. Admission requirements are high. According to the registrar's office, in fall 2006 the average ACT score of entering students was 27, and the average SAT score was 1230. Their average high school GPA was a 3.7, and the average GPA for any college work done prior to admission at BYU was 3.6. The majority of entering students come from a public school background. Like many universities across the country, BYU grants an exemption from FYC for an AP score of 3 or higher on either or both of the AP English exams. This policy has been in place for more than forty years. In fact, BYU was one of the first major universities to accept AP credit and is currently one of the top ten universities for numbers of students entering with AP credit. However, as noted above, those students who plan to graduate from BYU with university honors are not exempt from FYC. Typically some 700 AP students each year choose to start down the path to honors graduation. These students are thus required to take H150 regardless of their grades on the AP exams. (A few take Philosophy 150 or an honors section of English 150 instead.)

All students enrolled in H150 during fall semester 2006 and winter semester 2007, a total of 717, were asked to complete our survey, administered between April 2007 and July 2007. Of the total, 292 (40.7%) responded. Of those, 253 (86.6%) had attended public schools. Eleven students (3.8%) came from private schools; 10 (3.4%) were home-schooled; 4 (1.2%) attended international schools; 9 (3.1%) were in International Baccalaureate programs; 4 (1.2%) listed "other" without any defining explanation.[1] The total group included students from thirty-three states, from all regions of the country—New England, East Coast, South, Midwest, Southwest, Rocky Mountain, Pacific Coast, and both Alaska and Hawaii. Ten students came from foreign countries.[2] All but twenty-two of the respondents were eighteen to nineteen years old; eighteen were twenty to twenty-two years old; and four were twenty-three or older. Seventy-five percent were female, and 25 percent male. All but twenty-seven graduated from high school in 2006; five each graduated in 2004 and 2005; the rest graduated prior to 2004.[3]

Of the students who responded to the survey, 176, or 60.3 percent of the total, had taken AP classes and tests. These students represented 69.6 percent of the public school graduates in our population. We were somewhat surprised that only about 60 percent of students in this survey had taken AP courses since so many college-bound students are now taking AP courses in hopes of gaining some college credits. Those respondents who did not take AP classes gave a range of reasons: they came from outside the United States, or they were in private, correspondence, or home schools and did not have access to AP classes. Among public school students, by far the most common response was that they simply chose to take another kind of writing class or workshop altogether. Some who had not taken AP classes said that they felt they were actually better prepared for college writing than some of their classmates in H150 who had taken AP classes. For example, IB students observed they had a different focus; since the IB program requires research and documented paper(s), creative writing, and service projects that are not ordinarily a part of the AP program, they felt they were much more prepared to take a college-level writing class than some of their classmates who had taken AP.

Instruments

To obtain the students' views on their AP experience as compared to their Honors 150 experience, we constructed a survey that students could answer anonymously. The survey first asked a series of questions regarding demographic information. Students were then asked to rank on a scale of 1 through 5 the emphasis they perceived their teachers gave to specific elements of writing in both their high school writing classes and their H150 course. These elements included steps in the writing process (prewrite, draft, review, revise, edit) and the six traits designated by the Northwest Regional Educational Laboratory in Portland, Oregon: idea development, organization, voice, word choice, sentence fluency, and conventions. The survey also asked students how often they experienced such approaches to writing instruction as peer review, workshopping, and teacher or student critiques. They were asked how much their teachers emphasized matters such as documentation, plagiarism, argument, thesis and topic sentences, and library research as well as the extent to which they taught about audience, purpose, format, and voice. Finally, there were six open-ended questions that allowed students to express opinions and offer comments of a qualitative nature. In addition to the student survey, we designed a similar instrument to ask H150 teachers about student attitudes and preparation as they entered the course and about student attitudes and achievement as they exited it. We do not report extensively on the findings of the teacher survey, but the instructors did offer insights that helped us in interpreting the student survey data.

Procedures

Some sections in fall 2006 were given paper copies of the survey that students filled out anonymously and returned. All other sections in fall semester 2006 and winter 2007 received an email with a request to respond on a website that guaranteed their anonymity. Results from the online survey were totaled automatically; then a careful count, repeated three times, from the hard copies was added to the online results to determine the final numbers.

Quantitative Results

As already noted, not all respondents to this survey had taken an AP course in high school. In the following presentation and discussion of results, only the responses of the 176 students who had enrolled in AP courses are considered; they represent 60.3 percent of the 292 total respondents. (Where the number of respondents differs from 176, on Tables 4.1 and 4.2, readers will see a note.)

Table 4.1 presents aggregated results of the student answers generated by items 9 and 12 of the survey. The data in Table 4.1 are presented in four categories—rhetoric, process, structure, and library research. As the reader will note, students perceived H150 to give more emphasis, on the whole, to each of the four elements of writing or pedagogical activities identified than did their high school AP courses.

Figures 4.1 through 4.9 take individual items of data from Table 4.1 and graphically show the differences between AP and H150 emphases. Each of the figures is discussed in turn. Figure 4.1 shows students' perception of the differing emphases given to all of the elements or activities of writing in all four areas—rhetoric, structure, process, and library research—in both AP and H150 classes. The sharp upward slope of the H150 line indicates that a higher percentage of students perceive their H150 course to have given more than moderate or very strong emphasis to these concerns. In contrast the flatter slope of the line for AP courses indicates they perceived their AP teachers to have given less overall emphasis to these concerns.

In Figure 4.2, the fact that the two lines are relatively similar reveals that students perceived both their AP and their H150 class to give similar emphasis to the concept of writing with a thesis. Likewise, Figure 4.3 indicates a great deal of similarity in the emphasis both courses placed on editing for content, grammar, punctuation, and spelling, though the AP line peaks at "more than moderate" emphasis, while the H150 line continues to rise. Student responses to the open-ended questions indicate that the slightly higher emphasis on editing they perceived in H150 may have come from the emphasis given to revision and precision in writing as well as from learning—in many cases for the first time—how to organize and cite materials in research papers. One

TABLE **4.1.** Comparison of Emphases in High School AP and Honors 150

Shaded areas contain student responses to the question, "Please indicate the extent to which your **high school AP teacher** emphasized each of the following elements or steps of writing." White areas contain responses to the question, "Please indicate the extent to which your **Honors 150 teacher** emphasized each of the following elements or steps of writing." Students were asked on both questions to put only one check in the appropriate box for each row.

Amount of Emphasis	*Little or none*	*Little or none*	*Some*	*Some*	*Moderate*	*Moderate*	*More than moderate*	*More than moderate*	*Very strong*	*Very strong*
	High School	H150	High School	H150	High School	H150	High School	H150	High School	H150
•*Rhetoric*• Writing for a specified audience	5.9	0.0	13.5	5.8	33.5	16.8	21.2	36.9	25.8	40.5
Purpose	1.2	0.0	7.1	1.7	20.1	13.4	30.8	40.7	40.8	44.2
Voice	6.4	1.2	6.4	4.7	23.8	16.3	24.4	27.3	38.9	
•*Process*• Prewriting	6.5	1.2	21.9	9.4	28.4	19.9	27.2	31.6	15.9	38.0
Drafting	10.0	1.2	20.6	4.0	27.1	14.5	27.6	31.2	14.7	49.1
Revising	6.5	1.2	11.2	1.2	21.3	8.7	38.5	28.5	22.5	60.5
Peer review, critique, workshopping	6.5	1.2	10.0	1.7	24.7	7.5	28.8	23.7	30.0	65.9
•*Structure*• Organizational strategies for papers	4.7	0.6	9.9	4.7	24.4	19.1	32.6	37.6	28.5	38.2
Format	14.5	4.0	16.3	9.2	32.6	29.5	21.5	25.4	15.1	31.8
Topic sentences	4.7	2.3	8.9	6.9	21.3	27.9	32.5	31.9	32.5	30.8
Thesis sentences	0.06	0.5	5.8	1.7	8.7	19.7	30.2	23.1	54.7	54.9
Transition sentences	4.1	1.2	9.3	9.8	31.4	20.8	24.4	32.4	30.8	35.8
Editing for content, grammar, punctuation, spelling	4.1	1.7	8.8	7.5	23.5	22.5	40.0	31.2	23.5	36.9
•*Library*• Library research	20.9	0.0	23.8	2.3	23.3	10.4	20.9	31.2	11.0	56.1
Documenting library sources	18.7	0.0	18.1	3.5	25.6	11.6	21.1	27.2	17.5	57.8
Avoiding plagiarism	7.1	1.2	11.8	3.5	15.3	11.0	27.1	26.7	38.8	57.6

Note: Not all 176 students answered every question; 4 answered no questions on high school at all. Percentages are calculated for each question based on the exact number who did respond, varying on this table from 169 to 171. Responses are shown as percentages for each specific question rounded to the nearest tenth.

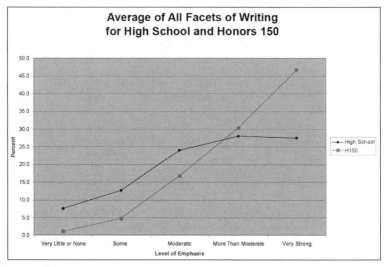

FIGURE 4.1

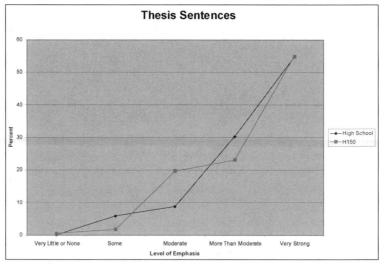

FIGURE 4.2

student said the difference between high school and H150 was "the post-writing process—revising and editing. In high school, we were told to do it, but never really told what things to look out for when evaluating our own writing. Honors 150 explained how

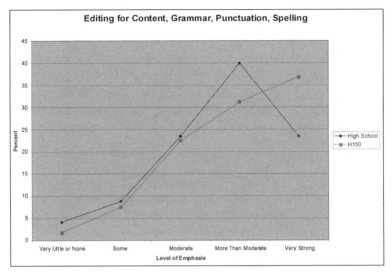

FIGURE 4.3

to evaluate your own and others' work much better." Another observed that "the things I learned in Honors 150 will be useful for writing research and understanding how to format the paper appropriately," while another "appreciated the step-by-step walk through of writing research papers."

Elements of the writing process, including prewriting and drafting, were emphasized much more strongly in H150 than in AP, as shown in Figures 4.4 and 4.5. In some cases, students were experiencing these for the first time. When asked the difference between AP classes and H150, one student said, "I barely ever did pre-writes in my high school class—I did one draft and turned it in. In my Honors 150 class, I did a lot of drafting and revision." Another observed that in H150 "we really revised and improved the writing."

Revision, particularly peer reviewing and workshopping each other's writing, was a new experience for some students, as shown in Figures 4.6 and 4.7. One student observed, "In my high school class we never focused on the format or peer reviewing." One teacher reported that when her H150 class broke into small groups to examine and critique each other's work, one student asked, "Isn't this cheating?" Further discussion revealed that the

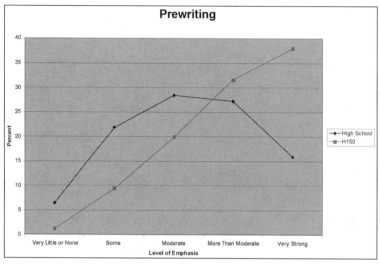

FIGURE 4.4

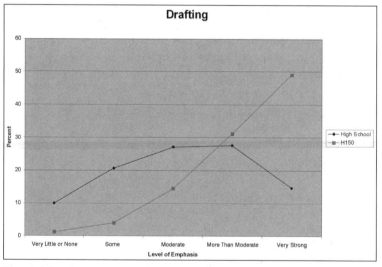

FIGURE 4.5

whole concept of collaborative work had never been presented to this student in his AP class. That student is not alone, judging by the 10 percent who said the concept had received less than moderate emphasis in their AP course, and the 6.5 percent who reported it had received very little to no emphasis at all.

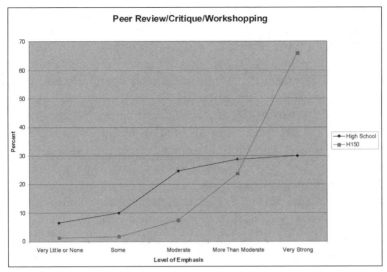

FIGURE 4.6

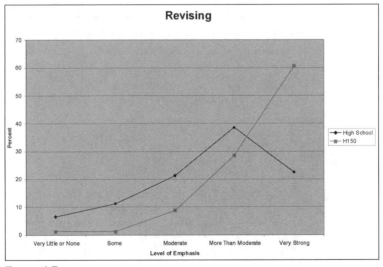

FIGURE 4.7

One of the most revealing sets of responses concerns library research. Only 11 percent of the respondents said their AP course gave a very strongly emphasized to library research, while an additional 20.9 percent said their AP training included more than moderate emphasis. But 20.9 percent also said they had little to no library work, 23.8 percent said the emphasis they received was less than moderate, and 23.3 percent indicated a moderate emphasis. In contrast, 31.2 percent of the respondents said their H150 class gave more than moderate emphasis to library research, and 56.1 percent said the emphasis was very strong. Figure 4.8 reveals the dramatic difference students perceived between their AP and H150 experiences in this area of instruction. Likewise, Figure 4.9 shows a striking difference between the two courses in the amount of emphasis given to the related skills of how to document library sources.

In survey items 10 and 11, students were also asked to rank the amount of emphasis they saw given to the following specific genres in both their AP and their H150 classes: timed, single-draft essays; analysis of reading, narrative, personal essays, descriptions, argumentative or persuasive writing; and research papers. Results are given in Table 4.2. The most striking differences between students' experience in AP and in H150 are related to the amount of emphasis given to timed, single-draft responses to a question—much more emphasis in AP than in H150—and the amount of instruction and experience students received in

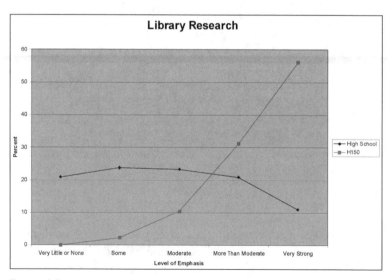

FIGURE 4.8

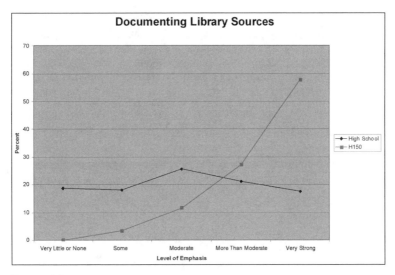

FIGURE **4.9**

writing library research papers—much more emphasis in H150 than in AP.

Figure 4.10, based on the data in Table 4.2, shows dramatically how research papers received much higher emphasis in H150 than they did in students' AP classes. Even when the "more than moderate" and "very strong" emphasis categories are combined for AP focus on research papers, the percentage equals only 41.6 percent, while the total for "very strong" emphasis in H150 is 65.7 percent, with another 27.9 percent saying the emphasis was "more than moderate."

In their answers to open-ended questions at the end of the survey, several students commented on encountering a research paper, or even library research, for the first time in college. One admitted, "I had never done actual research until Honors 150." Another responded, "I had not really written any research papers before that class, so writing a research paper for it was a good learning experience." Yet another pointed out the difficulty of encountering such a major element of learning for the first time in college: "I had never written [a research paper] before college, and it was really hard and time consuming." The disparity between AP and FYC is particularly important in this area because

TABLE 4.2. Comparisons of Emphases on Genres in AP and H150 Courses

Shaded areas contain responses to the question, "Please indicate the extent to which your **high school AP teacher** emphasized each of the following elements or steps of writing." White areas contain responses to the question, "Please indicate the extent to which your **Honors 150 teacher** emphasized each of the following elements or steps of writing." Students were asked on both questions to put only one check in the appropriate box for each row.

Emphasis given	Little or none	Little or none	Some	Some	Moderate	Moderate	More than moderate	More than moderate	Very strong	Very strong
	High School	H150	High School	H150	High School	H150	High School	H150	High School	H150
Timed, one-draft essay of about five paragraphs	5.8	55.8	4.6	24.4	9.8	9.3	26.0	4.7	53.7	5.8
Analysis of reading	0.6	0.6	4.0	12.8	10.9	27.9	21.4	26.2	63.5	27.3
Narratives	12.8	1.8	12.2	4.7	31.9	15.2	27.7	37.4	16.3	40.9
Personal essays	13.9	0.6	15.0	4.7	32.4	12.2	21.4	33.7	17.3	48.8
Descriptions	7.6	1.2	13.9	8.7	29.1	26.7	30.8	30.8	18.6	32.6
Argumentative or persuasive writing	6.4	0.6	10.4	2.3	17.9	12.2	34.1	36.6	31.2	48.3
Research paper	21.4	0.6	15.0	0	21.9	5.8	26.0	27.9	15.6	65.7

Note: Not all 176 students answered every question; percentages are calculated for each question based on the exact number who did respond, varying on this table from 171 to 173. Responses are shown as percentages for each specific question rounded to the nearest tenth.

research in libraries, in labs, and on the Web is the basis for much undergraduate work, as students are required to learn about the evolving conversation in a particular field. Students need to know how to read sources critically and then to summarize, quote, paraphrase, and cite the facts and ideas they find there. In many cases, they also need to know how to add their own voice to this conversation by producing a paper that synthesizes existing views and offers new ones. These difficult and time-consuming competencies cannot be quickly taught or easily gauged by a simple test, especially a multiple-choice or timed test. One student's comment

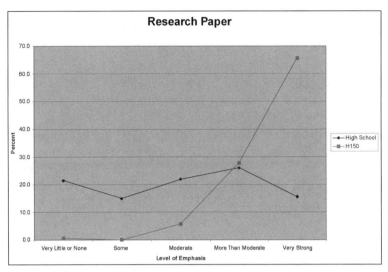

Research Paper

FIGURE **4.10**

is typical: "I definitely think [the H150 research paper] helped me with research papers in other classes."

The library research portion of H150 is particularly strong because, in addition to the teachers' instruction, university librarians provide a self-guided audio tour of the facilities and conduct two classes for students on research, demonstrating how to locate both print and online resources. Open labs and mini-courses geared to various subject areas are available to students who need additional help. Students learn how to locate a variety of materials presenting different viewpoints, including everything from newspapers to academic journals, and how to tell the difference between reliable and biased sources. Students recognized the value of their library training. "I learned a ton about the library and writing center resources. I know what's available and who to go to for help," one said. Another commented, "Honors 150 is a very necessary class for anyone and everyone, if for nothing else but the emphasis on research writing. Becoming familiar with the library and its resources, for example, is completely invaluable for the rest of one's college career." Still another admitted, "I don't know that I ever would have understood the library, especially, as well as I do now."

Another marked difference between AP and H150 courses is quickly apparent from Table 4.2: the amount of emphasis placed on timed writing in AP courses as compared to H150. The difference is graphically represented in Figure 4.11, where the two lines practically mirror each other, providing strong evidence that high school AP teachers put far more emphasis on timed, one-draft essays than do H150 teachers.

The reason for the differences in the two lines in Figure 4.11 is obvious. Frequently, students' comments were like this one: "My [high school] teacher focused almost entirely on preparing for the [AP] test (i.e. timed essays or practice tests)." One student observed that "we wrote a timed essay every Monday, which became very annoying." The ability to write a well-focused and clearly organized essay under time constraints is no doubt useful in college, particularly for essay exams; however, practicing this skill at the expense of learning how to read academic discourse and work with the ideas of others in their own documented writing seems counterproductive. It mainly serves to help students pass the AP tests. And if an AP test score allows them to bypass the FYC course where they would learn how to read and synthesize academic discourse in documented research writing, students are ill-served.

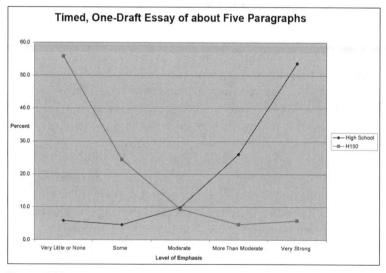

Figure 4.11

Qualitative Results: Students in Their Own Words

While numbers from the survey clearly demonstrate the students' overwhelming belief that their high school AP experience was not comparable to H150, their responses to the open-ended questions offer insights the numbers do not reveal. Question 14 for students was, "What were your initial feelings when the honors program required you to take a writing class despite your AP test score?" Teachers were asked a corresponding question: "At the beginning of the semester, did any of your students express their feelings about the honors program requirement that they take a writing class despite their AP test scores? If so, please specify." Samples of responses to questions 14–19 have already appeared in the above discussion of answers to the quantitative questions. Summaries of all responses to the open-ended questions now follow. While only a few answers are directly quoted, they are, in fact, typical of the bulk of the students' comments for each question.

Question 14. "What were your initial feelings when the honors program required you to take a writing class despite your AP test score?"

Not surprisingly, many of the students surveyed were unhappy to learn that their AP scores would not be accepted for graduation with university honors. The most common expressions of regret included the words "upset," "frustrated," "annoyed," or "miffed." One said, "I was a little frustrated that I would have to 'waste' credits and time." Another was "surprised" because "I felt that I had tested out of it because I performed so well on the AP tests." Many students assumed that their AP scores indicated high proficiency. One was "resentful and thought I knew all I needed." Another said, "[I thought] the writing class would be superfluous because of my prior education." And, "I did not think that it was fair because my AP class was very difficult because I had to write over 40 papers over the course of the class, and I thought that that would be sufficient."

Surprisingly, however, many students did not mind being required to take the course. They agreed with two who said, "A little extra writing never hurt anyone," and "I needed the extra experience, so I was in favor of the requirement. I planned on taking a higher-level writing class anyway. Even though I did well in AP, I knew that I was far from being an excellent writer." Another commented, "I was okay with it because I knew that taking a class that focused on writing would help me with other classes." One respondent's comment suggests another group that should, perhaps, be surveyed with regard to expectations about AP credit: "I didn't care that much. I took it as an opportunity to learn more about writing at a university level. My parents were very upset though." That statement was the only one in the entire survey that expressed any information about parental attitudes, but it is revealing since the AP test is marketed as something that will help students get through school faster so they will have to pay for fewer credits, a prospect attractive to parents.

Teachers observed much the same attitudes. One said "occasionally students grumble a bit"; and another said, "Sometimes they imply that they don't need the class because they know everything from their AP class." Yet another teacher reported she "had two [students] with sincere chips on their shoulders" because they were not exempted from FYC.

Question 15. "What are your feelings about having to take Honors 150 now that you have completed the class?"

If the AP course really does substitute for FYC, students who had completed the H150 course should have found the class redundant. But, on the whole, they did not. Only 11 students (4%) of the total 292 responders said they did not feel that taking H150 was worth their time, with 4 of those saying it was a waste of time. Two of the eleven had attended private schools, one had been in an IB program, and one listed "other" without specifying the kind of school. The seven who had attended public schools had all taken the AP exam. Of those, only 4, or 2.3 percent of those who had taken AP classes, declared H150 to be a complete repetition of their high school experience. One of those was a student who already had seventy-five university credits, obviously someone who had decided long after the first year to graduate with university honors. Two others observed that while they knew most of what was included in H150, the introduction to the library and the library paper were "very valuable." Another noted H150 had lost its value only because she or he had decided not to graduate with honors.

Another 8 students, 4.5 percent of the total respondents, had slightly negative responses, or perhaps more accurately, passive half-positive responses, such as this: "Still unhappy, but it wasn't as bad as expected." Three did not like their specific teachers but thought the class itself was good. Another thought the class was all right, but she or he had decided not to graduate with honors and felt annoyed at having taken the course. And though three students liked the course, they felt they really should have been able to use their AP scores to skip the class.

The rest of the students, 93.5 percent of the total and 89.2 percent of those who had received AP credit, raised no objections whatsoever. In fact, they emphatically stated that they were glad they had taken H150, feeling far better prepared for college-level work than they had been before. The specific words "loved," "glad," "grateful," or "awesome" appeared in 35 percent of the answers. Two randomly selected quotations: "I learned more about writing in one semester than in all of high school combined!" and "I was so happy I was forced into it!"

Both students and teachers recognized that AP, focused largely on a test, can leave students with an artificial, inaccurate sense of what good writing is. One said, "[H150] will last my life. Being able to write a ten-minute essay loses all value the minute AP testing is over." Another said, "My high school writing classes were so focused on teaching to standardized tests, like the state writing test or the SAT or ACT writing sections, that we didn't learn about writing itself, we just learned how to write for a test. It was much better in Honors 150." Teachers' perceptions of the value of the course aligned with those of the students. One teacher commented, "By the end of the semester they seem to have forgotten any complaints they may have had initially." Another quoted a student's feedback form: "Highly recommended even if one already has the first-year writing requirement fulfilled by AP credit!" That teacher also added, "That is always (yes . . . always) the sentiment."

Question 16. "How well did your high school writing class prepare you for Honors 150?"

In answer to this question, students tended to mention particular items that were different from one class to the other, most frequently library use, research paper, and the writing process, including peer review and revision. However, 229 students, or 78.4 percent of all students, opened their statements with brief, specific phrases that allow at least a rough set of classifications. Twenty-three students, or 10 percent, thought their preparation was excellent; other responses included in this group were "great," "extremely well," and "splendid." Another 52 students, 22.7 percent, said they were well prepared. And 120 students, 52.4 percent, said they were prepared ("sufficient," "some," "adequate," "fairly well," and "OK"). Only 17 students, or 7.4 percent, said they were not well prepared, and an identical number said they were badly prepared or not at all prepared.

Virtually all of the students in this survey, with the few exceptions discussed already in the responses to question 15, echoed one student's observation that the high school class "prepared me. . . . I had an adequate basis of understanding to build on." They agreed, however, that while their high school experience had prepared them to take a first-year college writing class, it definitely did not equal what they had experienced in H150 in every area. One said, somewhat uncharitably, "Eh, I guess it [my AP class] built the foundation but that's all." Historically, however, that foundation has been what was expected of high schools, and they have provided it very well. Even those students who praised their high school classes said some fundamental elements of writing had not been adequately stressed. One summarized a commonly repeated theme: "Some of what I did in my AP classes in high school prepared me for my H150 class, but I felt under prepared in some areas. Most of the work I did was meant to prepare me for the test and not for real life, so I learned how to write short essays very quickly with very little revision, but I didn't have much experience writing well-planned, longer essays. I had a hard time learning to revise and strategize for better thought-out essays."

Virtually every teacher observed that H150 had given their students a sense of freedom in writing. One said, "They are usually excited to learn they are not restricted to the 5-paragraph essay." Another said that the students were "almost relieved that writing doesn't have to always be confined to these forms."

Question 17. "What has been the greatest difference between your high school writing class and Honors 150?"

Overwhelmingly, the students said that the fundamental difference between their AP and H150 classes was the focus. Students from the AP literature classes said, "In my high school writing class, we focused on reading and analyzing literature, whereas Honors 150 actually focused on OUR writing." That focus on literature doubtless reflects the fact that the majority of students in this survey, 79 percent, took AP Literature and Composition in high school, preparing for a test in which they would analyze a literary work. The AP Language and Composition class was taken by 51 percent, and 30 percent of the students took both classes and both tests.

Nonetheless, concern about focus was echoed again and again: "My high school writing class focused mostly on analysis of literature. Honors 150 was more about actual writing—research paper, analysis, great works papers, etc. I think the college class was more broad." Another student observed, "Honors 150 taught me how to write in many different styles and that each different type of writing required a different mindset, voice, and set up. My AP class taught me mostly about the works of other authors, how to holistically understand them, and how to effectively describe and/or argue my point about texts." One student recognized the synthesis that occurs in learning: "My high school writing classes taught me how to write clearly and eloquently; Honors 150 taught me to write intelligently. I was given the trimmings before the foundations, which helped me once I finally figured everything out halfway through the semester." But another student saw the relationship the other way around: "High school writing teaches basic principles and teaches how to score well on the AP exam, whereas Honors 150 teaches more practical kinds of writing that apply to writing research papers or argument papers."

Teachers were asked, "What to you were the most noticeable differences in the abilities of your Honors 150 students as they began the semester and as they ended it?" Several teachers noted the students' shift from preoccupation with rules to a greater ability to express their own ideas. One said, "By the end they've usually become much more sensitive to accuracy and conciseness in choosing words and constructing sentences and paragraphs." One teacher replied, "They are ready to jump through the usual hoops at first, but by the middle of the semester, they couldn't see uniform hoops (or even discernible ones)." The phrase, "jumping through hoops" in high school occurred again and again through both student and teacher responses.

Question 18. "How well do you feel Honors 150 has prepared you for the rest of your college career?"

As with the question about how well high school prepared them for H150, many students responded with discussion of things they had learned, now often relating H150 specifically to their own majors. Specific phrases used by 145 respondents permit a rough classification. Seventeen students, 11.7 percent, said they were extremely well prepared ("excellent," "wonderfully," "fabulously," "righteous," and "10+"). Eighty-four students, 57.9 percent, said they were very well prepared ("great," "significantly well," "a lot," "very nicely"). Thirty-five students, 24.1 percent, said they were well prepared ("good," "decently"). Eight students, 5.5 percent, said their preparation was all right ("somewhat good," "so-so"). Only two students, 1.3 percent, felt the H150 class had done them no good at all because it did not match the writing needs of their specific majors. In contrast, several other students noted that, "I've already used what I learned in my Honors 150 course in every other class I've taken. I'm really glad I took it."

In marked contrast to those students who said in response to Question 14 that they had already learned all they needed to know in high school, respondents to this question frequently realized they needed to learn still more. One said, "I think I still have a lot to learn. However, I am much more confident about writing in college because of Honors 150." Another said, "I think it has given me an advantage in writing, but I know that there is a lot that I still need help with. I would like to learn more about organizational strategies for research papers and how to use the library more effectively." Another added, "I feel that I still have a great deal to learn but am glad that I enrolled in H150."

While students felt well prepared for college through their studies in H150, some continued to compare it with their high school experience. Said one, "I thought that Honors 150 was well prepared and delivered for a writing class. If it was a more general English class, I think that it should have more novel reading, like my high school class had. However, Honors 150 is a writing class, not a reading class, so I thought it was well done." The issue of focus came up again and again. One called H150 "a good transition from high school to college writing." This, of course, is exactly what FYC is supposed to be.

Question 19. "Is there anything else you would like to say about the differences between your high school and college writing classes?"

Several students left this question blank or simply responded with some kind of "no." But most did reply, some writing at length, discussing both classes in detail and observing several things we had not included (nor even imagined) in any of the earlier questions. Some helped to put their own responses into perspective. One, for example, recognized one of life's great realities: "In college I wasn't a big fish anymore." Conversely, one said that since college writing classes are small (H150 enrollment is capped at twenty), "This class was like a step back to high school—small group, classroom banter, and a professor that knows your name." Students wisely perceived that the culture of the two classes had either helped or hurt their learning. Several appreciated the greater focus and maturity of college students. "The students in my high school class didn't seem to care as much about writing. In Honors 150 I found plenty of people with the same level of passion for thinking, feeling, and writing." Another said, "We had better participation (especially in effective peer review groups) in Hon150 than in high school. Most people in my class were very respectful of others' opinions (something that was uncommon in high school). I enjoyed it more and felt like I accomplished and grew more in Hon150 than in high school." Another said simply, "There's just a lot more maturity expected in your writing in college, and that's coming from someone who was blessed with an amazing English department in high school, so I'd say that the average high schooler would really find a challenge with college writing."

Several respondents also recognized that the abilities of individual teachers can either make or break the class. One simply dismissed his H150 teacher as "a nut case," while another charitably observed, "In high school my AP English teacher was brand new. It was his first time teaching AP English ever. I think that's why I felt the class was disorganized." But another noted that a good teacher can surmount nearly anything, saying his AP class prepared him for college "extremely well," adding that his AP teacher, who was state teacher of the year several times, demanded "what seemed almost unreasonable to most people for high school students. It was a workload meritorious of the title 'Advanced Placement.' Where most AP classes were somewhat of a joke, my AP English class was more demanding and worthwhile than most classes I have taken at BYU. I would say that it was easily the most worthwhile class I took in high school, and it prepared me to easily master my Honors 150 class."

Similarly, several students noted that while the structure and required papers for H150 broadened their repertoire of writing genres and expanded their knowledge and skills, the talents of their individual H150 teachers provided additional merits. "I loved my Honors 150 teacher—he really makes you think outside the box." Fifteen, speaking anonymously, named their teachers and cited specific qualities that helped them learn. One said that taking Honors 150 from a certain teacher was "liberating . . . it was very inspiring to know that it's OK to think outside the box." Another, referring to a teacher who was eight months pregnant at the time, demonstrated that idiom does not necessarily reflect fact: "I loved [my teacher]. She's the man."

Conclusion

Whatever specific differences the students in this survey may have observed among teachers or institutions, nearly all agreed that while the AP classes and tests are touted by the College Board as equivalent to a first-year college writing class, the focus on timed essays in the AP test tends to foster a formulaic, five-paragraph approach. Since the AP test so often determines how the course is taught, students overwhelmingly responded on both the numeric scales and in the open-ended questions that their high school experience, while in many cases excellent, failed to match in depth and variety what they found in H150.

The course description from the 2007–08 College Board AP handbook for AP English Language and Composition states that, upon completing the course, "students should be able to analyze and interpret samples of good writing; . . . write for a variety of purposes, produce expository, analytical, and argumentative compositions; . . . move effectively through the stages of the writing process with careful attention to inquiry and research, drafting, revising, editing, and review; . . . revise a work to make it suitable for a different audience; . . . evaluate and incorporate reference documents into researched papers" (9). However, students in our study consistently said they had little to no experience in learning to achieve any of these goals in writing; their greatest focus in their AP courses was on writing timed essays to practice for the test. The AP English Literature and Composition portion of the same handbook does not state the same aims as the Language and Composition course, yet, judging from what our survey respondents said, the literature AP course also focuses heavily on practicing timed writing.

Excellent though their high school AP classes were, competent though their teachers had been, virtually all students agreed that neither the AP class nor the test does, in fact, take the place of a college-level writing experience that teaches writing processes, rhetorical awareness, research and all its components, and a variety of other genres as well. One student who had passed the AP exam summed up most respondents' feelings very well: "I think all students should be required to take first-year writing, regardless of AP test scores. The level of learning I achieved in my college class far surpassed what I experienced in high school." Several students noted the need for taking English/writing classes on both the secondary and postsecondary levels. One student said, "While the two experiences were very different, and the two classes approached literature and composition from two different ways, I'm glad that I was able to take both courses. One class simply can't teach all that there is to know about writing and the English language, and so I believe that people really do need both courses."

We believe our findings strongly imply that university policymakers should carefully think through the ramifications of using AP scores to exempt students from FYC. Since students on the whole found that H150 added much value to their high school writing experiences, we see a benefit in requiring FYC of AP students. This benefit is particularly pronounced in helping students negotiate a university library and the scholarly resources of the Internet responsibly and skillfully. We firmly believe that FYC ought to be required of those students with at least a score of 3 on the AP exam, since Hansen et al. found that students with scores of 3 who bypassed FYC later demonstrated only limited proficiency in writing. However, they also found that those students who scored 4 or 5 on the AP exam but took FYC anyway tended to write significantly better than others, so even they benefited from further instruction (Hansen et al., "Advanced"). Since writing ability is developed iteratively with practice, and since the ability to write well in college and in the workplace is paramount in today's world, it makes little sense to encourage students to bypass writing courses.

However, if postsecondary institutions are to require more writing of AP students, schools must ensure that students have challenging new courses to take so they do not feel their high school AP success is devalued or that they are just repeating instruction they have already had. We think H150 is a good example of just such a challenging course. Staffed by experienced and dedicated faculty, it offers a rigorous curriculum requiring diverse types of writing—especially research-based writing. If postsecondary institutions can offer students a strong, advanced FYC course such as H150 for AP students to place *into*, rather than just the option of placing *out* of the regular FYC course, then AP students will be well served.[4]

Notes

1. All percentages in this chapter are calculated to the nearest tenth of the total respondents to that specific question. As a result, totals may be slightly more or less than 100 percent.

2. The countries were Australia, France, Hong Kong, Marshall Islands, Mexico, New Zealand, Singapore, South Africa, and the United Kingdom.

3. Both the skewed gender ratio and the presence of older students in the sample are explained, at least in part, by the fact that BYU is sponsored by the Church of Jesus Christ of Latter-day Saints, and many young people, particularly men, spend two years in voluntary missionary service for the church. Men typically serve at age nineteen; women, at twenty-one. Some men may serve before they begin college, so they enter the university at an older age than usual, while many leave at the end of their first year of college. Since the online portion of the survey was administered in June and July, after the school year ended, a number of men may well have been unavailable to reply.

4. The authors gratefully acknowledge the assistance of Susan Jorgensen, coordinator of Brigham Young University's Honors 150 classes, and the following H150 instructors: Lara Candland Asplund, Sue Bergin, Jane Brady, Kris Chandler, Matthew Clarke, Rebecca Clarke, Liz Crowe, Cheri Earl, Kacy Faulconer, Stephen Fullmer, Lisa Harris, Lisa Johnson, Mary Lee, Rachel Ligairi, Dian Monson, Kimberly Parry, Boyd Petersen, Erika Price, Kerry Spencer, Ethan Sproat, Greg Taggart, Donlu Thayer, Kylie Turley, and Scott Walker. We are grateful also for the assistance of John Baxter Oliphant in designing and running the online survey.

Works Cited

ACT. *Aligning Postsecondary Expectations and High School Practice: The Gap Defined. Policy Implications of the ACT National Curriculum Survey Results, 2005–2006.* ACT, 2007. Web. 4 Dec. 2007.

———. *ACT National Curriculum Survey, 2005–2006.* ACT, 2007. Web. 4 Dec. 2007.

College Board. *AP English Course Description: English Language and Composition, English Literature and Composition, May 2007, May 2008.* College Board, 2006. Web. 26 Nov. 2007.

Foster, David. "The Theory of AP English: A Critique." Olson, Metzger, and Ashton-Jones 3–24.

Hansen, Kristine, Suzanne Reeve, Jennifer Gonzalez, Richard R. Sudweeks, Gary L. Hatch, Patricia Esplin, and William S. Bradshaw. "Are Advanced Placement English and First-Year College Composition Equivalent? A Comparison of Outcomes in the Writing of

Three Groups of Sophomore College Students." *Research in the Teaching of English* 40.4 (2006): 461–501. Print.

Hansen, Kristine, Suzanne Reeve, Richard Sudweeks, Gary L. Hatch, Jennifer Gonzalez, Patricia Esplin, and William S. Bradshaw. "An Argument for Changing Institutional Policy on Granting AP Credit in English: An Empirical Study of College Sophomores' Writing." *WPA: Writing Program Administration* 28.1–2 (2004): 29–54. Print.

Jolliffe, David A., and Bernard Phelan. "Advanced Placement, Not Advanced Exemption: Challenges for High Schools, Colleges, and Universities." *Delivering College Composition: The Fifth Canon.* Ed. Kathleen Blake Yancey. Portsmouth: Boynton/Cook, 2006. 89–103. Print.

Jorgensen, Susan. "Re: Exemptions from Honors 150." Message to Colleen Whitley. 27 Aug. 2007. Email.

Kearl, James. "Re: Honors Freshman Writing." Message to Colleen Whitley. 21 Aug. 2007. Email.

Laing, Susan T. "Re: Exemptions from Honors 150." Message to Colleen Whitley. 27 Aug. 2007. Email.

National Council of Teachers of English. *The Impact of the SAT and ACT Timed Writing Tests.* Report from the NCTE Task Force on SAT and ACT Writing Tests, Apr. 2005. Web. 4 Dec. 2007.

Olson, Gary A., and Elizabeth Metzger. "The Language and Composition Course." Olson, Metzger, and Ashton-Jones 116–29.

Olson, Gary A., Elizabeth Metzger, and Evelyn Ashton-Jones, eds. *Advanced Placement English: Theory, Politics, and Pedagogy.* Portsmouth: Boynton/Cook, 1989. Print.

Spear, Karen, and Gretchen Flesher. "Continuities in Cognitive Development: AP Students and College Writing." Olson, Metzger, and Ashton-Jones 25–51.

CHAPTER FIVE

From Advanced Placement Student to Concurrent Enrollment Teacher: A Personal and Professional Evolution

STEVE THALHEIMER
Fairfield Community Schools, Goshen, Indiana

A s fate would have it, the Saturday morning in May 1988 when I was to face the AP Composition exam, I woke up with a dull headache and sinus cold. I hadn't slept well the night before, yet despite the fear I would doze off during the test, I took a little cold and flu medication and a couple of aspirin, loaded my pockets with cough lozenges and number two pencils, grabbed a box of tissues, and headed to the high school library. I quarantined myself in a corner near the stacks and commenced the exam. Between lapses in lucidity, I tackled the multiple-choice portion. Later I addressed a quote from Alexis de Tocqueville and a passage from Frederick Douglass. I love history and felt I did well with these.

By the third writing sample, however, the medication and lack of sleep kicked in and I just got silly. The open response prompt required me to write about something of importance as if it were to be printed in a magazine, but to write it in a creative way so as to encourage others to read it. Slaphappy and feeling pressed for time, I turned to something I knew. I had worked in restaurants since my sophomore year of high school and loved to cook, so I chose to write about the dangers of food spoilage and the importance of cleaning out the refrigerator. I began with comic images of mysterious items in the icebox, including the "cottage cheese that ate Cleveland." I threw in enough facts about botulism and salmonella to make it real, but overall it was simply goofy. Still, once I had thrown myself over that cliff, I had to go all the way.

When I finished the test, I just wanted to go home and go to bed. As I waited for the scores, I regretted the choice I made on that last prompt, fearing that the lame article on food safety might prevent me from getting a 3, the magic number for college credit. Imagine my surprise when the score report arrived, and I had a 5. Yes, drowsy and medicated, I had scored a 5, which I really didn't deserve. Still, I rationalized that maybe the final response wasn't "that bad." If the College Board gave me a 5, it must be good enough. After a year of intense preparation, all A's in high school, and a 5 on the AP exam, I was ready for college.

I was one of the first graduates of my small town high school to go to college with AP credit, since Advanced Placement Composition had been introduced only during the 1987–88 school year. I had been a little apprehensive about this new AP "stuff," but I entered Mr. McLane's class that year confident in my writing abilities; after all, I had a 4.0 GPA after three years and was on track to be valedictorian. I especially liked the idea of getting some college "out of the way," saving my parents money, and gaining a head start on my undergraduate degree. On my first timed writing for Mr. McLane during the first week of school, I had to respond to a brief statement from someone whom I have long since forgotten. I will never forget the grade on that first piece, a C-. I was stunned. Here I was entering this new venture feeling hopeful, only to have Mr. McLane dash it all with a Jackson Pollock-esque flurry of red ink and end comments that included "trite" and "trying to sound smart." After a despondent first week, I vowed that I would not be beaten by AP Comp. I read every assignment in *Writing Well* by Donald Hall; I listened to every hint and trick from Mr. McLane. I viewed every timed writing as a chance to hone introductions and quickie thesis statements that I would deftly support and polish off with witty conclusions. Consequently, I did become adept at wrapping a topic up in a pretty package of timed writing, a skill that earned me a 5 that May. Perhaps I shouldn't have been so surprised, because we did a lot of timed writing in preparation for the AP test.

By the end of my senior year I had a very particular view of college writing—one that was grossly incorrect. After I left high school with my AP score of 5 and high SAT verbal scores, I was exempted from the W131 Elementary Composition writing requirement at Indiana University, and I was even awarded two hours of W198 English Composition credit to boot. Considering college courses as something one could avoid, I tested into fourth-semester German and tested out of a three-credit American history course. Before I even stepped foot into a college classroom, I had been granted sixteen hours of credit, some of which was conditional on my earning a C or better in that fourth semester of German. This college thing didn't seem so tough.

That illusion was shattered my first semester on campus. For my major, I enrolled in Professor William Cohen's honors history survey: Napoleon to the Present. We had lectures twice a week and met with him (instead of a graduate assistant) on Wednesdays to discuss readings and prepare for essays. For our first essay, the topic of which I have repressed (note the pattern here), I did my reading, wrote a draft, and submitted it like a Magus handing over fragrance. The next week, I received it back with a C; it was Mr. McLane all over again.

As a freshman who had performed well in high school, my whole identity was that of a good student. And now I was being told I wasn't a very good one because my writing was not as highly regarded as it had previously been. I questioned whether I had what it took to succeed, just as I had at the beginning of my senior year before AP. However, there was a difference. This time, I had been told I was worthy; I had been stamped with a 5 by the College Board.

What happened to me at this juncture in my education has been identified by Jeanne Gunner, who describes how "writing as a disembodied skill" serves merely to function as "a credential that can be impersonally produced. Students in turn can be labeled *haves* and *have nots* according to this commodified notion of writing, their worth determined by their use value: do they have good writing skills?" (112–13). I thought I had what it took to be a successful writer in college, partially because of the grades I had received in high school, but more so because AP had deemed me worthy. When I determined college writing was a "thing" I had obtained, even had mastered, in a high school setting, I personified Gunner's fear that students see college writing as merely a commodity. Entering college, I saw myself as a "have" when in actuality I was closer to a "have not."

When students and teachers see writing as a commodity to acquire in a precollege environment, they relegate it to the realm of transactions. Think about how we refer to the credits for college writing and college course work in general: we "earn" them; we "pay for" them; we "transfer" them. With these tropes, I fear we take the personality and the skill out of the writing enterprise because it becomes something outside of us rather than within us. Thus, it becomes easier for us to think we can assess writing quickly because it is either something students can know or do or it is something they cannot. I felt that since I had put in the time and labor my senior year and since I had aced the AP exam, I had "arrived," and the work was done. Yet after I was humbled by Professor Cohen's grades, it took three semesters of a history and English double major before I again felt like I had acquired college composition skills.

When I became an English teacher six years later, I reviewed those two first essays I wrote for Mr. McLane and Professsor Cohen. I laughingly placed them next to the AP test booklet that fell so incongruously in between. When I looked at those pieces together, I swore to myself that as a teacher I would do three things:

1. Temper negative comments so students would not have to feel what I felt on the two occasions when I received grades so far from what I expected.

2. Apprise students of their writing ability so that they know where they need to improve, and so they would not be set up for the feelings I experienced.

3. Teach students to think and to use writing as a vehicle for that thinking so that they would be prepared not only for the AP test but also for bigger tasks beyond. I would instill in students that they could improve their writing skills but never really master writing, for even the greatest writers find ways to revise and criticize their own work.

Much of my work with students from grades 6 to 12, summer school to college, has been to challenge students and treat them fairly in their written expression. I never wanted another student to have to go through what I did in that transition to college. In my early years as a teacher armed with the lessons I learned in college, I had a notion that writing was power and a challenge, a "game" to figure out. But I saw the game as much bigger than passing the AP test. Mastering writing was about learning to have a voice that is taken seriously in academic and public discourse. Simply, I wanted students to learn to have something to say and to say it in a way that would get it heard.

I strove to be fair and honest in teaching in those early years. Then, after a half-dozen years in the secondary classroom, I found myself back on the campus of Indiana University during the summer of 2000 as a trainee for IU's concurrent enrollment literature and composition classes, which are part of its larger initiative to link high school and college, Advance College Project (ACP). Even before arriving on campus, I intuited that courses that were connected with a prestigious university that trained teachers for a week to teach a college-level class would fit my three-pronged philosophy. After I had attended the week of literature training, I was trained along with a group of about twenty high school teachers (some who continued from the literature workshop) to teach W131 Elementary Composition, IU's required introductory college writing course, in the high school setting. During the week we looked at sample student work and reading selections that we could use to teach the five required papers—summary, critique, comparative critique, comparative analysis, and trend analysis. We familiarized ourselves with Rosenwasser and Stephen's *Writing Analytically* as a way to evolve and complicate thesis statements and provide detailed evidence without judgmental binary thinking. During the week we received a binder full of materials particular to each paper type, and we were led in our instruction by university faculty, including the director of composition. By the end of the week, we returned to our schools with draft syllabi for our courses. Professionally, it was one of the most affirming moments of my life; I collaborated with other teachers who wanted to challenge students while preparing them for the rigors of college. We wanted to teach students to think and sharpen their abilities to analyze and synthesize. And we wanted to reward students fairly for earning a grade of C or better with the college credit they deserve; we did not want that credit to rely on only one test on one day after weeks of work.

For the next seven years, I taught courses in both ACP composition and literature. I saw these courses do amazing things for students while they were in high school, but, more importantly, I heard from students how much the courses prepared them for college. One young man who attended Rose-Hulman Institute of Technology thanked me for teaching him writing so well that he could volunteer to write his group's lab papers, the "easy part." One young woman sent me an email saying that some days she had left my class crying because the work was so hard, but she had just had her college professor read her essay to the entire lecture hall with the concluding remark, "This is how it should be done." Another young woman who attended the University of Chicago felt that her preparation had put her on even footing with students who attended far superior high schools, and she was able to engage in the thinking required to master philosophy and gender studies. Because each succeeding essay in ACP Elementary Composition builds upon preceding ones and because teaching and learning each essay are supported so clearly by the textbooks and materials provided to teachers, ACP presents a most sound way to "take care of" a college writing requirement.

From what I have written so far, it would appear that I am anti–Advanced Placement, but that is not true. For certain disciplines, particularly math and science, I think AP works well, as I explain later, but for the subject of writing, it becomes complicated. The preparation I had received for the AP exam twenty years ago in a setting similar to where I taught in no way reflected what I was asked to do as an undergraduate. In contrast, the work I saw my high school seniors undertake in ACP was demanding, mature, analytical, and engaging; it treated students as writers and thinkers, not just as test takers. But as I have come to critique my own preparation for college writing, I have also analyzed my role as a teacher and administrator. Is the ACP concurrent enrollment model fundamentally better than AP? Did I truly prepare students? What was I preparing students for, and as I prepared them, did I contribute to the commodification of writing against which Gunner warns? To answer these questions, I describe my work with high school students who have chosen one or both paths—AP and ACP—to earning college credit for writing in high school, and I describe what I see as the pros and cons of both ACP and AP. I conclude by raising some other questions that I think must be answered in order to more fully develop the relationship between college writing programs and high school English courses and to better serve students.

The high school where I taught ACP is located in southeastern Indiana near Cincinnati, Ohio, right on the Ohio River. Student enrollment hovers around 525 with nearly 100 students graduating each spring. Of those, approximately two-thirds go on to college. Through 2006, fewer than 15 percent of students took AP exams, and of those about 30 percent scored a 3 or higher. Since 2001, AP exams have been offered in biology, chemistry, calculus AB, U.S. government and politics, and Spanish. The reader will note that AP composition and literature are not part of the preceding list. This high school has offered ACP English since 1987, and for the first half of that twenty-year span, students enrolled in ACP were encouraged also to take the AP exams on the assumption that ACP preparation would transfer to AP success. More recently, however, students have chosen not to take the test and instead have opted solely for credit via the ACP program. The main reason is that the ACP program has refined its focus on analysis and synthesis in expository pieces requiring all facets of the writing process, and students see this course as superior to simply practicing timed essays to pass the AP test. Another reason is the hesitancy of students to pay for an examination that may not yield credit. They think their chances are better with ACP, for if they pay discounted tuition to Indiana University as the ACP course begins and pass it with a C or better, they receive college credit that transfers to many schools across the nation. Nevertheless, there are some schools, mainly small private colleges, which do not accept the ACP credit but will consider accepting certain AP scores for credit. For students considering those schools, the AP exam is still an option, and students who express an interest in taking it are given study materials, sample tests, and assistance in preparation.

The last student I taught who considered the AP option was a young woman in the class of 2001 who was already a logical thinker and writer upon entering the ACP course. Jennifer told me early in the semester that her prospective college did not accept ACP credit, so she wanted to explore the AP exam. I provided her sample materials and told her to look over them and then come back to set up a study schedule. She returned the booklets by the end of the week and said, "I don't even want to bother with this. I would rather spend my time learning to write well and do well in this course than study for some test that I may not score high enough on anyway." She probably could have scored a 3 or a 4 easily on the exam, but she needed to score a 5 to receive exemption from the introductory writing course at her college. She doubted her ability to achieve that, particularly because she knew she was a student who needed time to crystallize her thinking. Only late in the second semester of the literature course did she master timed writing.

Jennifer's decision not to attempt the AP test might be explained in terms of David Bartholomae's notion that students doing college writing tasks have to "invent the university," that is, they have to imagine what a university audience is and attempt to discern the conventions they must follow in writing for that audience. Her comments raise the question of who or what stands as a de facto "gatekeeper" at the entrance of a university. Who is it that declares a college-level writer "proficient" and "complete," ready for the rest of college? As I taught my first few years, I came to believe any true course of study in writing should offer students the tools to access and present knowledge—the keys to power—by familiarizing them with what is expected at upper levels of college study and real-world settings. Teaching for ACP confirmed that belief for me, as I learned to "determine just what the [writing or learning] community's conventions are, so that those conventions could be written out, 'demystified' and taught in our classrooms" (Bartholomae 601). Thus, I could certify as proficient students who had learned the standards for college writing and who had grown significantly toward demonstrating them. The grades I awarded in that writing course would then reflect how well students had met expectations in terms of personal growth and growth compared to their peers. In ACP, then, I could be the gatekeeper because I was familiar with the university whose course I taught. Looking at the AP materials, however, Jennifer did not feel confident in her ability to invent the audience for whom she was supposed to be writing and the conventions she should follow, and she did not want to attempt it, even with my help. Even though AP and ACP are both intended to prepare students for college writing, their methods of evaluating writing proficiency are very different and thus affect instruction. With my intense preparation as a senior in 1988, I had learned the language of the AP exam, but not of the university. The AP evaluation appears so different from ACP that Jennifer potentially could have seen the unknowns of AP as a threat to her worth as a student; I could identify with her fear of being told she was less than a 5. She had begun to feel at ease in my writing course; she was able to invent our "university" and felt safe with me as an instructor who had worked with her as her advisor for the student newspaper. She chose to put her energy into learning the ACP model and not be "distracted" by preparation for the AP exam. Perhaps the small liberal arts schools that set a high threshold for accepting AP credit and that do not accept concurrent enrollment high school/college courses have it right. They don't want to leave it to either AP or ACP to guess what their university is, as they prefer to groom their own writers.

The likelihood that students want to engage with what they know and to avoid the unknowns of the AP exam may explain the success of ACP composition and literature in the small high school where I taught. During the period 2001–06, students there earned only 30 units of credit across five AP courses, while at the same time they earned 101 units of credit just in the composition and literature semesters—more than three times as many credits as in all the AP courses combined. More students opted for the composition credit because it fulfills the writing requirement for many programs, but about one-fourth of the 101 units were for the literature course, which often transfers as elective credit.

Some might argue that the ACP composition course grants so much credit because it is a cakewalk. My students would beg to differ. First of all, by design the course is created in conjunction with university faculty and requires students to learn to write five papers common in academia. As added instruction, I had my students write shorter practice drafts of the first four papers, resulting in my students writing two summaries, two critiques, two comparative critiques, two comparative analyses, in addition to the minimum ten-page trend analysis. Secondly, several students who took my ACP course in high school, but did not take it for credit, told me that when they were required to take the composition class at the college or university they chose to attend, their classes on campus hardly compared with what they experienced in high school. Their instructors were unavailable or distracted or did not know how to teach composition. Many lamented that they wished they could have had me back because they didn't feel like they were learning anything. The temptation to discount college writing taken in high school is unfair because there are demanding teachers in the high schools who can teach advanced composition skills, and good concurrent programs groom those instructors to create hallmark programs. The ACP program requires summer training, follow-up workshops during the academic year, and observations by college faculty. By contrast, it is interesting to note that a high school teacher who prepares students to take the AP exam is encouraged, but not required, to take AP workshop training and must submit a syllabus for an AP Course Audit only if the course is to be designated "AP" (College Board 19, 23).

So is there any way to get the best of both worlds? Can we obtain the standardization and cachet of AP with the continuous instruction, intervention, and assessment possible in a concurrent enrollment course? Might this bring some continuity to this process of earning college composition credit in high school? Some schools in Indiana that favor the ACP model feel pressure to offer AP and attempt a hybrid of the two courses. In 2007 at the high school where I taught, the high-ability broad-based planning committee, which oversees the development of programming for high-ability or gifted students, recommended that the school explore ways to combine ACP and AP into single courses offering students the option of either taking the course for ACP credit or taking the end-of-course AP examination. Many of my ACP colleagues have discussed in training workshops the difficulty in making a hybrid of the ACP and AP composition models. While the biology class for AP and ACP, for example, can use the same text and cross-pollinate well, reconciling the two models within

English proves difficult because of the different philosophies and approaches of the curricula.

The issue that makes this reconciliation most difficult returns us to the question of exactly what it is we are evaluating. How we evaluate college-level writing promotes what we value. Edward M. White reminds us that

> we need to be clear about what stage of college writing we are talking about. Do we mean writing ability at the point of entry, as with a placement exam? Or do we mean after completion of a college writing course . . . ? Or do we mean at the time of movement from lower-division, or community college completion, to upper-division work . . . ? (246)

In other words, does passing the AP exam with a 5 after preparation in an AP course equate to the grade of C or better in an Advance College Project course? Does a 5 in one AP class equal a 5 from another AP class? Does a B from one ACP instructor equal a B from another? The problem I had as a freshman after I earned a 5 on the AP exam was that I took the stamp of approval from the College Board as saying I "had arrived" when really it meant I was granted passage. When we evaluate with a final holistic score, it tends to signal that one has attained a certain standard that is different from what one really has achieved. As an entering college freshman, I saw myself as "done" with something that I had no idea how to do. An A in ACP could do a similar thing. We have to be careful when we contribute to a system that allows students to think they are ever "done" with learning.

These questions stem from other differences between Advanced Placement and the Advance College Project. Some of these differences result from the way the two models of instruction are set up, while other differences may merely be ones of perception. Nonetheless, the effects of the two models on the writing process and their audiences, the ways the models treat the skills of writing, and the consequences for students of this writing are real. Thus, the two approaches to writing make the hybrid marriage of the two very difficult. With AP composition, students are trained in different modes of writing; however, that breadth of knowledge is assessed in timed settings with limited prompts and sparse opportunity for revision. While an instructor may take time in the class to have students revise, stress collaboration, and conference with students, eventually attention has to be paid to the format of the test and ways to score well on it. In contrast, because ACP is evaluated cumulatively over the course of a semester and results in a letter grade, the writing process is not short-shrifted. ACP writing mirrors the writing in college courses; it requires days, centers on topics requiring a writer to hone a thesis, and demands revision. In fact, each successive paper type becomes more complex, demands more of students, and generally becomes lengthier. The variety of paper types in ACP Elementary Composition prepares students for myriad future writing tasks, as we address what it means to make the choices we do in our writing. We talk about our assumptions in the formation of theses, our use of (or lack of) evidence, and our view of the audience. Regarding the teaching of timed writing, I asked myself the following question: Outside of the AP exam, college blue book tests, graduate and professional school entrance exams, and maybe a job interview, where might a person need to perform well on timed writing tasks? I put my emphasis on teaching sound composition. As a result, I relegated timed writing to the second semester as we dove into literature. It seemed more appropriate to have students refine timed writing in response to literature after a semester of solid composition study, not in the midst of it.

Linked to these differing views of evaluating the writing process is the notion of audience. As Walter J. Ong famously warns us, the audience "is always a fiction" (55). Part of our attempts to "invent the university" of college writing is an attempt to successfully create the audience. Again, an AP instructor may teach process and real-world audiences for the writing, but inevitably the audience becomes the cadre of readers hired by the College Board who award the scores. I am not so naive to believe that in a college writing course or in ACP students do not perform for the teacher in ways similar to the ways other students perform for AP graders. Still, within a writing course not geared to a narrow final evaluation, the audience can more readily be expanded to include peers, academia, and other authentic audiences. My ACP students would share their trend analysis findings in a presentation to their peers at the end of the course, so they were very aware that their research would be for someone else besides me. Furthermore, to combat mere teacher pleasing, I coached students in conferences to consider choices in their writing, and I challenged ideas with questions, rather than with direct suggestions. As we saw with Jennifer, there is still this idea of writing for an authority, but the human audience in front of the students daily in ACP contrasts sharply with the impersonal and anonymous AP graders hired by the College Board. This fact is particularly important if the AP instructor is not fully in tune with what the AP graders will want. There is more to the process of learning to write than an evaluator can measure without having worked directly with the student. Students at my school chose not to take the AP composition exam, and even other AP exams, because they acknowledged that contradiction and did not wish to subject themselves to it. If students had the option and means to pay for the ACP credit, they removed that detached grading altogether.[1] By so doing, they chose to deal with an instructor and expectations they understood. As their instructor, I was less of a fiction. In my preparation for the AP exam, I came to see writing as something finite and capturable, something with an endgame to it. I sought out hints and tricks, while my practicing for timed writing conditioned me to think in limited time and space. I came to see my whole future as an undergraduate writer linked to the snapshot of my writing that one May morning. Conversely, in teaching ACP I often had explicit conversations with students, both capable and struggling, about finding a point at which they could pull their thinking together and represent it in its best possible form. I would tell students that the essays they would submit on the due dates were in no way all of their finished thinking on the points under consideration; instead, the essays submitted were snapshots of their most crystallized thinking at that point. Obviously there is a connection between ACP and AP in that *all* evaluation is a one-time impression at the moment it occurs. The difference, though, is that while AP relies on that *one* snapshot to evaluate an introductory college writer, my ACP course relied on *nine* such snapshots to come to a final determination, and students were privy to the nature of that ongoing evaluation.

Foremost, I see the problem of evaluating students with this one snapshot as an issue of skills versus content. I would not deny that Advanced Placement exams have a fitting place in areas where content is the core of the subject—such as chemistry, biology, calculus. While college classes may cover a great deal of that content, there still seems to be a finite amount of material that one is expected to take from Introductory Biology or Chemistry I. Although Jack W. Meiland suggests that all knowledge in college is treated as theory to be evaluated (10–11), the AP exam does not test students in that way in math and sciences or even in the arts and humanities. AP tests contain bodies of knowledge deemed knowable and "correct" in terms of what is established "fact"; there are right and wrong answers scattered among multiple-choice distractors. This makes sense in fields in which data and processes for solving problems can be honed. However, there is just something fundamentally different about chemical stoichiometry or mathematical derivatives compared to the rhetorical and synthesis skills in language arts. Matters of style in writing and literary interpretations cannot easily be narrowed to four multiple-choice answers or a universal rubric.

The skill of writing is not so neatly bound, and college credit writing exams do not treat writing as the messy, time-consuming endeavor it really is. Writing is a skill that beginning students must practice, evaluate, and recursively think about. It involves the slippery concepts of thesis formation, style, voice, and audience, and it involves training students for a variety of writing modes across many disciplines. Muriel Harris reminds us that college composition instruction is so hard precisely because of "the variety of programs and goals as well as the fundamental problem of lack of universally similar responses from readers" (122). Writing courses suffer from identity crises; they carry a variety of titles and subtitles as a way to ground the study of writing. There is no one way to fashion a writing course, so instructors struggle to represent and meet the demands of different disciplines and genres. English and writing courses try to be all things to all people. In contrast, how often does a course catalog or a syllabus provide an explanatory subtitle for an introductory physics course? English courses often carry such secondary titles in order to clue students in to what they can expect from such a course. The disparity in the ways students learn and are asked to produce writing renders it one of the most subjective endeavors in all of education—how can we evaluate a snippet of that work in such a way as to hand down a judgment of writing proficiency and award college credit? It would seem we would need to assess a larger chronology of work to make that judgment sound.

As a consequence of the desire for students to get writing credit out of the way and the willingness of the College Board to render that judgment, the AP test, intentionally or not, seems to be the guardian of college credit, and only those who master the shibboleth of acceptable forty-minute essays earn credit. Another view is that only the lucky can earn their way past a test that is designed so that not everyone passes. Add to this the difficulty that more and more colleges require a score of 4 or 5 to be exempt from a composition course. It seems that the target is constantly shifting, and students have a more difficult time demonstrating what they know and can do. How did my essay on the perils of spoiled food or my two meager responses to figures in American history demonstrate my mastery of college-level writing? I had worked hard all year in that first AP composition class at my high school, but I don't think I always worked in smart ways, nor did I learn what I truly needed. If I had scored lower than a 3 on that exam, I would have believed the work had been for "nothing" because I would not have earned the credit. But, perhaps, in the long run, I would have been better served by a "failing" score because I would have had to take a composition class upon entering IU. As the desire for college credit by examination grows, are we increasing the perception that those who earn it are worthy only because they are either naturally talented or very lucky?

Within a dual-credit course, there is obviously still that danger that a student will take his or her worth from the comments of an instructor or the grade received. That email from Carrie, who told me a year after my course that on many days she had left my class crying, made that clear to me. However, Carrie's self-worth rebounded by the end of course because of her ability to rise to the challenge of those nine snapshots that showed a developing thinker and writer; it was further elevated when validated at her college the next year. I took to heart the comments of Mr. McLane and Professor Cohen and numerous other history and English professors throughout my undergraduate and graduate work. Even more, I can say that I often dreaded the grade from those writing instructors less than I did the score from the AP exam or even the score report from my GRE writing sample for EdS admissions.

This drive to get college writing credit "out of the way" comes with consequences. Michael Dubson laments that students don't really care about their writing, and their lack of interest makes "a mockery of the idealism teachers bring with them into college classrooms" (96). I would proffer that part of that apathy is disillusionment from students who see themselves as "having" to take the composition course because they were not "lucky enough" to test out. Students may resent being required to sign up for an *elementary* composition course when they feel they already learned how to write in high school through college prep, AP, or dual enrollment. Furthermore, as Dubson points out, there is the irony that while the class is labeled critical for students' success in college, it is often the least desirable to teach, handed off to overburdened grad students or adjunct faculty (105–6). Perhaps that is why concurrent enrollment composition has acquired a bad reputation among some colleges, and credits are not always accepted. If low-level college faculty are stuck teaching early composition, then what kind of high school teachers must be teaching it? When we deem required introductory college writing as something students can subvert, and when it is relegated to the least prestigious corners of the college or not even accepted by colleges when completed in high school, then there is little wonder students deem it as something to "take care of" before they get to a college campus or something they want to avoid altogether.

What, then, is my summation about this business of college writing in high schools? My personal experience and my professional instincts tell me that AP cannot test students on the skills of college writing because even a sound introductory college writing class—whether ACP, AP, or one at a university, college, or community college—can never claim to teach students all they need to know. My understanding of writing forces me to declare that writing is too complex to neatly bundle it in a standardized test taken one morning. Students, in particular those from my background in smaller schools, question that as well. A critical aspect of college writing in high school is that students can be wrongly led to see the skill set as a commodity they would ideally like to acquire by testing out of or by earning the credit through concurrent enrollment. If we continue to use the language of transaction, then we must regulate our courses to combat credit laundering and students' being ill prepared for "real" college. Foremost, we cannot allow the language we use to ever let students feel that they have this skill mastered, whether with a high AP score or an A in a concurrent enrollment course. Students need to see all of their writing as an ongoing developmental process.

Additionally, we have to be sure that whatever curricular or instructional model we follow in the high schools, it is a solid one. As is the case with any subject and any institution, there will be teachers who are reflective, who make themselves aware of best practice, and who inform themselves about what it is students need to be able to do. Unfortunately, some teachers do not. Perhaps the College Board's recent steps to audit AP syllabi and their continued emphasis on training will bring that system more consistency. The oversight and training in the Advance College Project model at Indiana University provide the self-regulation necessary for it to be a rigorous and valuable experience for students. But within that there are still subtle signals we need to be aware of. Even though my ACP students did not "waste away" their senior year, for they were analyzing, synthesizing, and struggling with big ideas, I still have to wonder if my language in my own classroom devalued what it was I was trying to do when I inadvertently made college writing something to "get through." Was ACP really that different? In the end, I would have to say yes. My experience with AP established writing as a commodity, as an ore, a resource that one mines for. It is outside of us; we need to find it, so we feel very lucky when we get it. While ACP may have still commodified writing, it treated it more like verdant produce, something that we grow and feed over time; we nurture that writing talent from within, supporting and pruning when necessary, to bring out what is there.

But I would challenge writing teachers and readers of this essay to look beyond the structural differences of the AP/ACP dichotomy. Instead of asking whether there need to be checks and balances on the teaching of composition in high school for college credit and which program does it better, there should be an examination of what it is college composition is meant to do in the first place and whether the skills an introductory composition course offers can truly be "taken care of" on or off campus. What are the skills and types of writing we want college composition to teach, and how do we train high school teachers to teach them? We need to ask what the commodification of college writing does to the discipline and whether the awarding of college credit in high school does more damage than good. Just as reliance on one test as a measure of students' performance proves faulty in evaluating schools under No Child Left Behind, reliance on one writing test on one day shortchanges the abilities of students and the expectations of what preparation for college should be.

Primarily, I propose this because the opportunity for demanding, proto-college writing should not be denied students in high school. There are students who are ready for that challenge, and as we look at the need for colleges to remediate students more and more, there would be nothing wrong with college courses, as well as college-prep courses, actually preparing students for college. As I often told my non-ACP seniors in English 12, the senior year of high school should be all about next year because high school is over. College faculty and deans need to collaborate with high school teachers and administrators to clarify expectations and establish these notions of what college-level writing should be and do. Instead of some schools accepting credit and others not and the AP bar fluctuating from school to school, there should be a movement toward identifying core principles or standards of college writing that all postsecondary schools can agree on and accept. This conversation needs to alter the language so that the emphasis is on preparation, not finding a way to cheat the system or "get out of" something that simply can't be elided. Models of effective, self-regulating programs exist; they need to be improved upon and replicated to ensure students leave high school truly prepared for postsecondary study, not merely assuming they are ready, as I thought I was, armed with that AP score of 5.

Note

1. The Indiana legislature passed a law in 2006 requiring concurrent programs to remit tuition for students who qualify for free and reduced lunch. Thus, eligible students receive the college credits from the Advance College Project at no cost.

Works Cited

Bartholomae, David. "Inventing the University." *When a Writer Can't Write: Studies in Writer's Block and Other Composing-Process Problems.* Ed. Mike Rose. New York: Guilford, 1985. 134–65. Print.

College Board. *AP Program Guide 2007–08.* College Board. Web. 5 Jan 2008.

Dubson, Michael. "Whose Paper Is This, Anyway? Why Most Students Don't Embrace the Writing They Do for Their Writing Classes." Sullivan and Tinberg 92–109.

Gunner, Jeanne. "The Boxing Effect (An Anti-Essay)." Sullivan and Tinberg 110–20.

Harris, Muriel. "What *Does* the Instructor Want? The View from the Writing Center." Sullivan and Tinberg 121–33.

Meiland, Jack W. *College Thinking: How to Get the Best out of College.* New York: New American Library, 1981. Print.

Ong, Walter J. "The Writer's Audience Is Always a Fiction." Villanueva 55–76.

Sullivan, Patrick, and Howard Tinberg, eds. *What Is "College-Level" Writing?* Urbana: NCTE, 2006. Print.

Villanueva, Victor, Jr. *Cross-Talk in Comp Theory: A Reader.* Urbana: NCTE, 1997, 589–619. Print.

White, Edward M. "Defining by Assessing." Sullivan and Tinberg 243–66.

— II —

CONCURRENT ENROLLMENT: PROGRAMS AND POLICIES

CHAPTER SIX

Early College High Schools: Double-Time

BARBARA SCHNEIDER
University of Toledo

She was ushered by an administrator through the library to the back table where I had set up shop. After brief introductions and an exchange of permission forms, I invited her to sit down as I tested the tape recorder. She sat forward on the hard wooden chair, hands clasped in her lap, every one of her fifty-eight inches focused on the teacher in front of her, the very picture of the eager first-year high school student. Only this was not just her first year in high school. This was also her first year in college.

Just fourteen years old, the girl perched on the chair was one of six students selected out of the entering class to test the waters of college composition for a newly created "Early College High School" on my campus in 2006. Called TECHS (Toledo Early College High School), the high school enrolled almost 100 students in its first ninth-grade class. As they prepared for the school's third year, administrators were anticipating more than 200 students, including a new first-year class of approximately 80.[1] The six students I interviewed when they were first-year high school students would be high school juniors in the fall, and three of them would also have college standing as sophomores. The design for the high school calls for students to earn sixty college credits by the time they graduate high school. The hope is that these students will then enroll at the University of Toledo and achieve a college diploma in just two more years. If all goes as planned, those six test cases will be ready for work or graduate school by the time they are twenty.

Toledo Early College High School is just one entry in a growing trend. Initiated in 2002 with funds from the Bill and Melinda

Gates Foundation, 130 such high school–college institutions were operating in the spring of 2007, up from 46 operating in 2004. The organization expected to have 170 schools up and running by 2008, with the ultimate goal of operating a total of 240 high schools serving approximately 100,000 students. The initiative's record to date indicates that they are on track to achieve those goals. However, even when all 240 schools are up and running, the 100,000 students they will enroll constitute just a very small percentage of the approximately 16 million students enrolled in U.S. high schools (Census Bureau). The initiative takes direct aim at a high school population not usually addressed by more traditional avenues for earning college credit while still in high school, such as Advanced Placement and dual enrollment. The Early College High School initiative seeks to "serve low-income young people, first-generation college goers, English language learners, and students of color, all of whom are statistically under-represented in higher education and for whom society often has low aspirations for academic achievement," using an accelerated curriculum as the motivator (Early College). The curricular plan is organized to move students from their first year of high school through their sophomore year in college in four years instead of the usual six.

My interest in this initiative was sparked when at a social function I overheard that the university was enrolling fourteen-year-olds in our college writing courses. As director of the composition program, I had deep misgivings about the wisdom of putting fourteen-year-olds in classes with students who are, on average, four crucial years older, where the reading material sometimes warrants an R rating, and where the conversation can stray into X-rated territory. At the same time, I was more than willing to consider what may be a new solution to the enduring problem of recruiting and retaining young people whose families have not, in Deborah Brandt's terms, accumulated the literacy capital that can sustain them through four expensive years of college.

I begin here by briefly reviewing the history of the initiative as well as the claims it makes for its purposes and intended outcomes. My inquiry into those claims reveals the meritocratic assumptions that ground those purposes and claims, as well the assumptions about the relationships between race and class that inform them.

I then turn to interviews with students and teachers from that first semester in order to illustrate how those purposes play out in college writing classrooms for both students and instructors. I conclude by considering a series of questions I think this initiative raises about both our high school and college curricula: Are students who still live at home with their parents, who are not old enough to drive cars, get married, be drafted, or go to an R-rated film without a supervising adult ready to fully participate in a university education? If ninth-graders can succeed in college courses, what does that say about the rigor of our instruction? If these students do not need high school to handle the content of college courses, what does that say about the necessity of a high school education? But this initiative also raises broader questions about the purposes of education. Is the vision of the initiative consonant with the mission of the university? Should job readiness be the primary aim of a university education? Are private foundations funded by corporate gain a way to redistribute wealth to remedy social inequalities, or are they a threat to public education?

A Brief History of Early College High Schools

The concept of the early college high school grows out of an educational experiment first enacted at the Middle College High School, a New York City Public School that opened in 1974 on the campus of LaGuardia Community College and still operates there today. Then, as now, the aim was to retain students at risk of dropping out and move them beyond the high school and into college courses. To achieve these ends, the educators who first articulated the middle college model proposed structural changes to the existing secondary school organization in three key areas: size, location, and institutional integration.

First, enrollment is limited to no more than 450 students. Designated as "small schools," the limited size is intended to support better student-teacher and counselor-student ratios and to foster more intimate peer relationships. The model requires at least three professional counselors per school and provides daily peer and group counseling with the assistance of paraprofessionals.

The middle colleges are also located on college campuses. Advocates invoke this as "the power of site," arguing that locating a high school "on a college campus provides motivation and mitigates the usual teenage behavior" (Lieberman).[2] Further, they argue, putting students on campus encourages in those students a "future orientation," enabling them to see themselves as college students, something many of these students had no previous reason to imagine. The location on a college campus extends physical resources as well, giving students and faculty access to the college library, cafeteria, public lecture halls, gym, and, in some cases, media labs and other material goods. In many instances, high school faculty in middle colleges gain private offices not available to them at traditional high schools.

The third key structural change to the traditional high school model is the change from the isolation of the two institutions to a system where the two are not just articulated but overlapping and sometimes seamlessly integrated institutions. High schools shift to a college calendar and daily schedule, allowing longer class periods that accommodate both project learning and portfolio assessment. The shift to a college schedule and campus also removes high school students from an environment where their movements are constantly monitored to one where they "are treated as adults: there are no bells, no hall monitors, and no metal detectors" (Lieberman). The integration of the two institutional systems has been challenging. While the middle college model was not conceived to include the aggressive accumulation of college credit hours into its curriculum, it does encourage students eligible for dual enrollment to take college courses. Financing college credits for high school students has required coordination between funding sources for secondary schools and college financial aid offices. Bringing faculty groups from secondary and postsecondary positions together is complicated by their membership in different unions, different faculty scheduling practices, and different pay scales.

The middle college's gradual success in reducing dropout rates and increasing college-going rates garnered the endorsement of the Ford Foundation, which provided seed money to reproduce the school model at six other sites. Those six schools generated even more interest. In 2007, according to the Middle College National

Consortium (MCNC), twenty-eight middle college schools were operating on campuses across the country, with approval of four more pending. The results MCNC posts from data gathered at New York City schools from 1990 to 2000 are impressive:

- ◆ 97 percent of the students stayed in school, compared to an approximately 70 percent rate of retention in the city as a whole.
- ◆ 87 percent graduated.
- ◆ 90 percent of graduates went on to college.

MNCN claims that the schools located in other regions of the country show similar results, which "proves that the structural changes succeed in a variety of locations and under different legislative parameters" (Lieberman).

That success prompted middle college leaders to seek more funding from the Ford Foundation, this time to sponsor a second design, called the early college high school. The design builds on the work of the middle colleges, targeting the same student population and enacting the same structural changes, but incorporates a curriculum extended beyond the high school and accelerated to include sixty college credit hours by the end of the senior year of high school. The Ford Foundation agreed to support this design, but the initiative really got off the ground when the Bill and Melinda Gates Foundation stepped in as primary sponsor in 2002.[3] Now called the Early College High School initiative, the program is administered by Jobs for the Future (JFF), a national not-for-profit organization that has been integrally involved in a number of school-to-work initiatives (see *Jobs for the Future*).

As an effort to transform public schooling from grade 9 through the second year of college, the initiative participates in a long history of school reform in America. In his analysis of that reform, sociologist David Labaree proposes that there are three goals for education arising out of the tension between our political ideals of equality and our economic realities of unequal access and distribution: education for democracy, education for social efficiency, and education for social mobility. Education for democracy is designed to produce citizens capable of running the government and is therefore education for a public good. This goal demands an education system that promotes equal access and focuses on equal outcomes and participation. Education for social efficiency, he argues, is designed to prepare people to work productively within hierarchical social and economic structures. As people achieve ever higher levels of education, they exit the schooling structure horizontally and ideally occupy the work niche that corresponds to their level of academic achievement. Because it fosters economic viability and operates on a merit system, education for social efficiency is also education for the public good. Education for social mobility, alternatively, is education for private goods. Here, persons seek an education for the cultural, social, and economic goods it can deliver to them, and they relate to the school system as consumers rather than as citizens (16–32). It is this last goal of education that Labaree argues has increasingly overshadowed the other two, leading students to seek education only for the purpose of obtaining credentials that can be exchanged for economic and social rewards and undermining attempts to engage students in the actual work of discovery, learning, and contributing to the common good that inform the other two goals of public education. A cursory reading of the arguments in support of the initiative suggests that it is perhaps over-invested in pursuing this private good, a pursuit that leads everyone—students, educators, and employers—to mistake credentials for knowledge and economic positioning for education.

Analysis of the Initiative's Values and Grounding Assumptions

A publicity brochure for the Early College High School initiative argues that these new schools are both necessary and efficacious. The opening claim, visually amplified as a bold-faced subhead, "Why Early College High Schools Are Necessary," is followed by a series of economic statistics: "A postsecondary education means greater opportunities for economic and personal success. A four-year college graduate earns two-thirds more than a high school graduate does" (Early College),[4] followed immediately by statistics that compare college success rates of African American, Latino, and Native American students to white students, casting in high relief inequities arising out of racial difference. The primary claim that early college high schools are necessary because college degrees lead to substantially higher incomes is supported by additional claims for economic benefit to the students. The article points out that these schools can save tuition dollars for students who earn college credits while still enrolled in public high schools, compress the number of years between high school and college, thereby allowing students to enter the workforce and income stream earlier, and, importantly, prepare students for "family-supporting" careers.

Economic reasons, however, are not the only evidence offered for the necessity and efficacy of these schools. In "Core Principles," JFF argues that the accelerated curriculum is a primary motivator to keep students in school: "The partners in the initiative believe that encountering the rigor, depth, and intensity of college work at an earlier age will inspire average, underachieving, and well-prepared high school students to work hard and stretch themselves intellectually." In fact, being allowed to enroll in college courses is both the incentive and reward for students who work hard and accomplish objectives. In several of their publications, JFF notes the initiative's commitment to advancement based on merit rather than accumulated school hours and implicitly chides schools that promote students without ascertaining student competencies.

The argument here relies heavily on assumptions that ground an ideology of meritocracy, a system sociologists Stephen J. McNamee and Robert K. Miller Jr. describe as a myth:

> In industrial societies such as the United States, inequality is justified by an ideology of meritocracy. America is seen as the land of opportunity where people get out of the system what they put into it. Ostensibly, the most talented, hardest working, and most virtuous get ahead. The lazy, shiftless, and indolent fall behind. You may not be held responsible for where you start out in life, but you are responsible for where you end up. If you are truly meritorious, you will overcome any obstacle and succeed. (3)

This ideology, they argue, is pervasive: "Most Americans not only believe that meritocracy is the way the system *should* work; they also believe that meritocracy is the way the system *does* work" (2). The meritocratic system is one that has been criticized by many, including Harlon Dalton, who calls the myth epitomized by Horatio Alger's *Ragged Dick* stories harmful because, he argues, it perpetrates a cultural blindness to the root causes of inequality and the consequences that result from it.

Three features of the Early College High School initiative show evidence of subscription to meritocratic beliefs. First, JFF proposes that higher education leads to higher income, an equation McNamee and Miller say is more myth than reality in the present system. While the two acknowledge that income is often tied to educational achievement, they point out that there are multiple nonmerit factors not accounted for by the higher education equals higher wages equation. Most of these factors are inherited, including the social and cultural capital parents have available to hand down to students and the effects of discrimination experienced by students born into racial minorities. Numerous other studies point out how deeply embedded individual achievement is in family, regional, and cultural contexts, including Deborah Brandt's illuminating study of how literacy development accumulates across generations to produce a literacy heritage that profoundly shapes an individual's literacy accomplishments.

Second, JFF amplifies its commitment to merit-based advancement, aligning its schools with standards-based criteria and positioning early college high schools against schools that allow social promotion. Their third line of argument, that these schools are necessary to overcome the failure of our public education system to address the needs of underachieving students, reiterates the American dream that with a little more work and a bit of luck, any student can overcome the barriers he or she may face and realize the promises of equality through the acquisition of literacy. This third line of argumentation, that literacy erases difference, is reinforced when JFF collapses the difference between race and class, as it does in the opening series of statistics on the disparities in graduation rates among racial groups cited earlier:

> Only 18 percent of African Americans between the ages of 25 and 29 and 10 percent of Latinos complete a four-year degree by age 29, compared to 34 percent of whites. The numbers are

even lower for Native-American students: only three in five will
graduate high school, and of those less than 3 percent will go on
to earn a bachelor's degree. In contrast, upper income students
are seven times more likely than low income students to earn
a bachelor's degree by age 24. (Early College)

The last sentence quoted here makes sense only if one assumes
that race and class are interchangeable categories. What upper-
income students are contrasted *to* are the three minority race
categories analyzed in the previous sentences, leaving inescapable
the conclusion that those upper-income students are white and
lower-income students are members of racial minorities. Asian
students are never even mentioned. I find this collapse of race
and class unsettling, not only because it is factually inaccurate,
but because it reinforces the broad public perception that all
racial minorities are low income, all whites are upper income,
and Asian students are so exceptional they are not even included
in debates about public education. The material consequences
of race cannot and should not be ignored, and this collapse of
the two analytical categories should therefore be questioned,
especially since it occurs in arguments made to support serving
selective populations of students. What collapsing the categories
does, of course, is make it possible for a reader to assume that
increasing the literacy of minorities will allow them to overcome
the economic barriers they now face as if those economic barriers were built of their own low achievement and not systematic
discrimination based on race.

Clearly, the initiative's founders realize that the long history
of racism in this country is a key reason a meritocratic system
remains a wish rather than a reality. But a second effect of the
collapse of race and class is that it makes race important only in
economic terms, eliding the historical, cultural, and social aspects
of race in America. That focus on economics illuminates one of the
limitations of the initiative, a point to which I will return shortly.

A closer examination of the structural changes the initiative
provides and its supporting rationale, however, demonstrates that
while the initiative participates to some degree in perpetuating the
meritocratic myth and in focusing narrowly on social mobility, it
also directly addresses several of the nonmerit barriers that make

advancement based on merit a myth. In doing so, the initiative offers solutions that align with McNamee and Miller's suggestions for turning the myth into reality. One of the nonmerit barriers often cited in debates about "the culture of poverty" is the supposed present time orientation of the poor. McNamee and Miller are worth quoting at length here:

> It is one thing, for instance, to say that they have a "present time orientation" because they are hedonistic thrill seekers who live for the moment. However, it is another thing altogether to say that—regardless of one's personal value system—one is forced to focus on the present if one is not sure where one's next meal might come from. The middle and upper classes have the luxury to be able to plan ahead and defer gratification (going to college instead of accepting a low-paid service job) precisely because their present is secure. . . . In this formulation, exhibited behaviors and perceptions associated with a "culture of poverty" reflect the *effects* of poverty—not the cause. (30, emphasis in original)

McNamee and Miller propose that present orientation results as poor people adjust their ambitions according to realistic assessments of their chances. Altering that assessment is one of the aims of the initiative.

Putting these schools on college campuses, as Lieberman argues and as noted earlier, encourages high school students to develop a "future orientation." In this structural change, advocates of the initiative signal their awareness of the nonmerit barrier of poverty and offer a solution, proposing that being on a college campus makes the potential of earning a college degree seem more realistic to students who come from families and communities otherwise unlikely to consider it possible. The initiative further signals its awareness of the cultural and social change such an ambitious educational curriculum sets for students who face multiple nonmerit barriers by providing close guidance throughout the high school–college experience. The financial structuring of the high school–college is also designed to remove barriers to access and simultaneously enacts, albeit in a limited way, another solution McNamee and Miller propose as a way to level the playing field. They suggest that one "potential solution to the problem of inequality, then, would be to encourage a greater sense of noblesse oblige among the wealthy in ways that level the playing field, increasing the potential for meritocracy while decreasing the intergenerational effects of inheritance" (206). JFF also strongly advocates for a new financial structure for the high school–college, arguing that compressing the school years allows longer public funding for students most at risk of losing out on education, an advocacy that aligns with McNamee and Miller's call for greater government support of education.

The initiative's efforts to overcome the barriers that make a meritocratic system more wish than reality at the same moment that they perpetuate it underlines one of the persistent problems facing any attempt to reform our schools. In Labaree's terms, the initiative focuses its efforts on social efficiency and social mobility. It foregrounds its promise of preparing productive workers in the arguments it makes for the necessity and efficacy of its design when it addresses legislators, educators, and funding sources. It foregrounds its promise of social mobility when it recruits students into its schools. The third historical goal for public education in America, educating for democracy, is not addressed by this initiative, either explicitly or implicitly. The initiative's silence on this goal may be read as a disregard for this important public good or as a recognition of the current valuation of education. While this may be seen as a narrowing of the promise of education, it could be argued that a narrower focus allows for greater headway on the other two goals. Still, the absence of any appeals to democratic education should be a concern for educators seeking to broaden the political horizons of those who one day will run the country, whether they are ready or not.

Relying on Student Readiness

In addition to the preceding assumptions, the entire Early College High School initiative rests on the assumption that adolescents, adequately supported and properly motivated, can move through these years of schooling at an accelerated pace, that they are in fact ready to undertake university education. Lieberman claims that "important academic and institutional rationales that underlie the structure of early college high school are based on well-established theories of developmental psychology, embedded into a practical model of education reform," and include research that indicates that "intellectual maturation is a continuous process: there is little or no difference between a student at the conclusion of the twelfth grade and the beginning of college enrollment" (3). While that may be true, the initiative as it is being enacted at TECHS and other early college high schools across the nation is enrolling first-year high school students in college writing and math courses. That four-year difference between a typical first-year high school student and a typical first-year college student was the basis of my concern and the reason I insisted on participating in the placement of the first students and requested interviews with both the students and their instructors.

At my request, the administrators of TECHS agreed to work with me to integrate this new population into our program. In consultation with the English teacher at TECHS, we decided to enroll the first six students in our basic writing course, a five-credit course we call Composition I with Workshop to signal that it covers the same material as regular Composition I. Students passing Composition I with Workshop progress to the Composition II sequence just as students passing Composition I do. The Workshop course is designed to assist inexperienced writers by adding two extra hours of instructional time per week and limiting enrollment to sixteen students per class. We thought the slower pace, extra hours, and enhanced student-teacher ratio offered the best chance for student success. Administrators helped me arrange both an early and post-term interview with the selected students. In addition, the students allowed me to review samples of the writing they produced in their composition courses. Instructors were equally accessible, each providing both an interview and a written post-term reflection. I extended my engagement with the project by serving on a special curriculum committee that designed a plan of study integrating college courses with high school courses.

I interviewed the TECHS students after their first three weeks of classes, late enough for them to have their first writing assignments, but too soon to predict their success. My questions were designed to elicit responses that would offer some insight into their level of intellectual and social preparedness for college work and cast some light on their motivation for leaving the neighborhood high schools they would otherwise have attended to take up this accelerated curriculum. There was a certain uniformity to their answers, perhaps demonstrating the common themes addressed in the daily counseling sessions in which students in initiative schools participate.

All of the students were confident that they were performing the intellectual work of the college writing classroom at an acceptable level, and, indeed, a few thought they were better prepared than some of their college classmates. They did note the difference between their experience in the high school classroom and the college classroom. One student noted, "In high school, there was a lot of reading and discussion, and here there is a lot more writing."[5] Another student noticed that "when you walk into a class in high school everyone is talking, and here, people are just much more focused." The bigger difference students noticed was in the level of autonomy.

Some of that autonomy was experienced in the range of choice available in their writing assignments. "We are writing in different genres and we have to write that kind of thing, but we can choose what we want to write about," said one student, echoing an observation made by most. The expectation that they would operate independently was also noticed in the teachers' expectations. "In high school, they kind of eased you into the assignment. Here, they expect you to pay attention and just get it done," said another student. Most critically, the students observed a difference in not only the workload but also the level of accountability. Four of the six students, in their post-term interviews, said that one of the most important things they learned was time management. Coming to class prepared to discuss readings, carrying drafts for peer review, and meeting final draft deadlines challenged students in ways that surprised them. "The hardest thing I found was getting the final paper done. I just didn't have enough time to do the research. We only found out about it about a month before it was due. In high school, we got two months to do what they expect us to get done in three weeks in college," said another student.

In their initial interviews, many of the students expressed anxiety about other students finding out how young they were. Most tried to keep their age difference to themselves, and one student, who identified herself to the instructor as a high school student, was mortified when the teacher mentioned it to the entire class. Three of the six students mentioned some sense of uneasiness going into the first peer review, and again, the concern rested not on a sense of being intellectually unprepared but on having the other students discover how young they were. One student mentioned that a college classmate asked for a copy of notes from a class he missed and then remarked, "I wonder how he would feel if he knew I was fourteen." Another student noted that she had been very nervous before the first few classes, but by the third week, she said, "I don't feel like I don't belong." The instructors and I had been concerned that conversations about sexual identity, pop cultural references to drugs and sex, or other adult topics might contribute to a sense of social discomfort, but none of the TECHS students saw this as any kind of a problem, or indeed, that any of these topics were in any way startling or new.

When asked why they chose TECHS in the first place, the answers were happily diverse. One student said, "I like learning and I'm pretty smart. I thought if I came here, I would meet other people who thought like me. I also think this is a good chance to get a pretty good education." Another said, "I really wanted more of a challenge. School can be pretty boring. This sounded like a great opportunity to me." A third student admitted that when he first heard about it, he didn't really want to do it because he didn't want to miss the usual high school experience. "Now that I'm here, it's just awesome. I'm glad I'm doing this. I can get a lot of the classes I need done and out of the way so I can move on." In these interviews, one hears echoes of the values of social efficiency—a good education equals a good job. One also hears echoes of the values of social mobility—education is a way to collect credentials so that a student can move on to whatever is next, rather than an experience of exploration and learning.

In their post-term interview, every one of the students said they felt they had succeeded, and all pointed to the fact that they got either an A or B in the class as evidence of that success. All also agreed that managing their time was very challenging, but that managing the course content was relatively easy. Two students remarked that they thought the work would be more challenging. Asked what advice they would give a student new to the program, five out of the six students said they would tell the student that college was not nearly as scary as they thought it would be. All six said they would warn the student to get organized.

Teacher Preparation

I handpicked the instructors for the test semester, choosing three instructors whose teaching evaluations showed good rapport with basic writing students and whose engagement in our ongoing professional development program, the Composition Colloquium, provided evidence of sound theoretical and pedagogical preparation for teaching diverse student populations. I interviewed the instructors early in the term, and all expressed delight with the level of preparedness of the students. Two noted that because these students were in the structured program of TECHS, monitored for attendance and counseled about homework daily, their attendance and preparation tended to be better than that of students who generally populate the workshop class. All three instructors expressed some misgivings about the wisdom of enrolling such young students in the class, not because they worried about its effect on the selected students, but because of the effect they feared it would have on their own teaching practices and on the learning environment for the college students who were their classmates. One instructor's early impression was that he was altering his teaching practice in two ways: he was being more deliberate when covering new material, especially argumentative strategies, and he was conferencing more: "I feel some responsibility to make sure these students are getting what they need." He did not see these alterations as detrimental to any of the students enrolled in the course or to his own time management. The other two instructors said they were quite carefully not altering their teaching strategies or course content.

When asked to assess their experiences at the end of the term, the instructors remained rather ambivalent. Interestingly, their concerns fell into two distinct categories. All three instructors agreed that the TECHS students were certainly intellectually capable of accomplishing the writing assignments and that they were, in fact, poorly served by being enrolled in the Composition I with Workshop class. One instructor made an especially critical assessment of the placement of these students, and her comments are worth quoting at length:

> I do not think that Composition I with Workshop is designed to challenge bright students like [student]. A high school student taking her first college composition course ought to find it more rigorous than Comp I with Workshop is able to offer. [The student] was in a classroom in which most of the students have very low language, reading, and writing skills and are generally ambivalent about class attendance and participation. These factors necessarily affect the pace of the course, the length and complexity of writing assignments, and the classroom conversation. Although the other students were at least five years older than she, I doubt that she found the level of discussion and writing greatly different than her own TECHS classroom full of high achievers like herself. I think she would have had a more beneficial experience in Composition I where there would be other motivated students whose leadership in the classroom she could recognize and learn from.

All three instructors also expressed concern that having more than one or two very young students in the class would alter the class dynamic. The one instructor who had altered his practices was less concerned than the other two instructors, but even he said that he feared if the course were saturated with very young students, it would change the level of discussion. Another instructor, after noting how very gifted the one TECHS student in her classroom was, admitted that she had more questions than answers after her first semester experience:

> I question the notion that the dynamic of the classroom can remain rooted in a mature, challenging academic foundation if a child is introduced into the equation. The tenor of the class, for many, may change—subtly or obviously. . . . When it comes right down to it, I think the college classroom should remain the college composition classroom. It is a site for meaning-making through critical inquiry and discussion—importantly, based on experience and the ability to thoughtfully engage the world, the self, and the other. Can most 14-year-olds do that?

The real concern, then, is not with the intellectual preparation or capability of the students in the pilot. The writing those students produced served as evidence that they achieved course goals adequately. These students, however, were selected for their capability, and the instructors expressed concern that future students, drawn from the general population of TECHS, might not be as capable. Instructors' greater concern, however, was with the level of student experience and maturity. Writing courses often ask students to critically examine their own experience in light of broader social concerns, so very young students are potentially disadvantaged in two ways. First, young students generally do not have the miles on their tires to have accumulated much experience on which to reflect. But even when young students have a rich background on which to draw, critically examining the values, opinions, and beliefs with which they have been raised while they are still in the home and in the process of being raised is enormously difficult. The instructors' concerns, then, center on the depth of the learning experience of students rather than on their acquisition of formal skills. Assessing the depth of that learning, however, is much tougher to accomplish than assessing their ability to demonstrate discrete skills. The learning that arises from critical reflection is also not learning that automatically happens within the confines of a course. Sometimes, as we know, that learning takes years.

Early Results

My own assessment of this initial experience and my concern about the impact of an increasing enrollment of this population over the next three years, when TECHS will reach maximum capacity, prompted me to negotiate some changes in the ways we enroll TECHS students in our college composition classroom. First, we now ask that TECHS students achieve a placement in our mainstream Composition I course by taking the same placement exam all students take before enrolling in our program. We instituted this change in part to assure that the TECHS students are getting the kind of intellectual challenge designers of the initiative imagined. But we also instituted this change to reduce the number of students in a course where two of the hours are coded as remedial and where students are at risk in our state of being shipped out to the community colleges. Second, only three TECHS students will be allowed to enroll in a given section with regular college students to hedge against the possibility of shifting the dialogue and dynamic of the classroom from college level to high school level. Because we offer an average of ninety sections of this course each semester, we presently have the capacity to enact this policy and seat these students. This change also creates greater consistency with our policy for enrolling area high school students in our postsecondary option program, a dual-enrollment program where students earn college credit and substitute one of our courses for a high school English course. We enroll only three postsecondary students in a given section, and we also ask that postsecondary option students achieve placement into our mainstream course. One remaining difference is that we require that postsecondary students be at least sixteen-years-old or juniors in high school. Finally, we are continuing the arrangement we made during our test semester of enrolling the TECHS students only in sections of composition taught by full-time lecturers. We are pursuing this course out of our concern for teaching assistants who already often face a crisis of efficacy in the classroom, deeply uncertain about their ability to teach anyone and even more un-certain about their ability to flexibly respond to different kinds of needs and questions young adolescents are likely to bring into the classroom. So, because we think the age difference of TECHS students may require a teacher with more experience than our teaching assistants have at their command, we will place these students only in classrooms with full-time lecturers.

My initial engagement in this project provided a few answers. Perhaps the easiest answer is that some fourteen-year-olds can, in fact, achieve course objectives. These six students were hand-picked for their demonstrated capabilities, however, so more time will be needed to see how future students perform who are placed into the course by the same methods used to place all first-year students. Still, I do not anticipate a serious challenge to the initiative on this front.

The question of what constitutes readiness to participate in a college course as raised by the instructor who questioned how much experience and maturity a fourteen-year-old can bring to the college writing class is tougher. Assessing the integration of knowledge through a careful reading of student writing is always hard, and skill can cover a vast sea of uncertainty. For example, students in one section were assigned a problem-solving paper. They were instructed to identify a complex problem of local concern where multiple solutions had been proposed but about which no consensus had been reached. They were told to research the problem and propose a solution. They were further instructed to use both quantitative data and qualitative analysis to support their argument. One student's response, which earned her a passing grade because it did address all the formal aspects of the assignment, chose unsanitary conditions of student dining on campus as "a complex problem of local concern." She writes: "The sanitation in the cafeterias at the University of Toledo is neglected in The Crossings, International House, Parks Tower, South Dining Hall, Ottawa House, the retail venues in the Student Union, and the Scott Park Café." The sentence is well-structured, displays good word choice, and makes a strong argumentative claim—it is skillful. A closer reading of the argument that follows, however, reveals a lack of real familiarity with student dining halls and proposes solutions that are not grounded in real practice—the writer lacks experience. Further, the student's reflection on the work focuses on the production of graphs and not on solving a real and local problem. In short, the student focuses on form to the neglect of substance. The shallowness of the paper may be simply a function of the assignment, or it may be a function of the student's experience and engagement. I think only long-term qualitative and quantitative assessment of student work and self-reflection by the students after completion of the course of study will provide any strong answer to the question. However, I am also aware that chronology, experience, and guidance all affect maturity, that it develops unevenly over time, and that it can be possessed by a fourteen-year-old in the same measure as an eighteen-year-old or a forty-year-old, for that matter. Statistically, however, we might, upon further study, find a distribution of qualitative and quantitative markers that would indicate that younger students cannot fully integrate and retain the higher-order skills they should acquire in these classes, and we would therefore encourage postponement of college courses until an older age. The jury is out on that question, but I think we can afford to proceed cautiously and await the research.

So, while the initiative seems to be capable of delivering on its promises of getting at least some of these students through high school and into college on a much shorter track, a number of questions remain to be answered. Some of them are raised by the advocates for the initiative who propose that the success of this program will call into question the structure of our high schools. Following a subhead in its publicity brochure that reads, "How Early College High School Will Change Public Education," advocates propose that the initiative "represents a concrete step toward a comprehensive approach to educating all our nation's young people, from kindergarten through a postsecondary degree. It also raises important policy issues related to design, governance, and financing of the nation's education system." The authors then ask, "Should the nation offer all students a free public education through the [first] two years of postsecondary education or the Associate's degree? If so, what new configurations might serve the needs of adolescents 14 to 24 years of age?" (Early College). Initiative advocates also ask if states should consider putting K–12 and postsecondary education under the same governing board or offer financial incentives to high school students who earn college credits.

While these questions deserve our attention, they do not speak to the deeper issue of what all of this education is for but rely instead on earlier arguments that education is for job readiness. A comparison between the "Core Principles" that inform the initiative and the mission statement at my institution reveals a gap in vision. The initiative states that stakeholders in the initiative "share a common vision for student success: they value learning for its own sake and for the career choices it puts before young people" (*Jobs for the Future*, "Core Principles"). Both are reiterations of the values of social efficiency and social mobility. All of its other supporting statements, however, measure student success in terms of job readiness.

The University of Toledo mission statement, however, and that of most colleges and universities, sees broader purposes for education, including educating for democratic inclusiveness and equality. The opening line of our mission statement states that "the mission of the University of Toledo is to improve the human condition; to advance knowledge through excellence in learning, discovery and engagement; and to serve as a diverse, student-centered public metropolitan research university" (University of Toledo). It then lists six core values, offered here without the elaborations that follow each entry:

- ◆ Compassion, Professionalism, and Respect
- ◆ Discovery, Learning, and Communication
- ◆ Diversity, Integrity, and Teamwork
- ◆ Engagement, Outreach, and Service
- ◆ Excellence, Focus, and Innovation
- ◆ Wellness, Healing, and Safety

Along with many other scholars who were drawn to studies in various disciplines that can loosely be defined as the liberal arts, I see the purposes of public education as informed by these core values and Jeffersonian ideals of an educated citizenry. The goals that the University of Toledo is willing to publicly broadcast as its own—all directed in one way or another to either education for democracy or education for a brand of social efficiency—intersect only tangentially with the initiative's goals of workplace social efficiency. Nowhere does the University of Toledo proclaim to dedicate itself to helping students get a leg up on the competition, and nowhere does the initiative proclaim to dedicate itself to the formation of citizens.

In the midst of these institutionally conflicting goals, there are also the personal investments of all of the players, many of which collude and collide with the institutional goals in myriad ways. One of the insights that Deborah Brandt offers is that sponsors of literacy, which she describes as "agents, local or distant, concrete or abstract, who enable, support, teach, and model, as well as recruit, regulate, suppress, or withhold literacy," always "gain advantage by it in some way" (19). Certainly, in funding this initiative, the Bill and Melinda Gates Foundation serves as a powerful sponsor of literacy. What this foundation is offering to sponsor is a form of education that serves the goal of social efficiency, fitting workers for "family-supporting careers," with the added appeal of sponsoring education that serves the goal of social mobility. Just because the Gates Foundation, through the initiative, does not offer to sponsor education to serve the goal of democracy, however, does not mean other participants in the process cannot pursue it. In fact, as Brandt points out, there is a long tradition in which those whose literacy has been sponsored to serve the narrow interests of the sponsors take that literacy and turn to their own interests:

> [P]eople throughout history have acquired literacy pragmatically under the banner of others' causes. In the days before free public schooling in England, Protestant Sunday schools warily offered basic reading instruction to working class families as part of evangelical duty. To the horror of many in the church sponsorship, these families insistently, sometime riotously demanded of their Sunday schools more instruction, including writing and math, because it provided means for upward mobility. (20)

It may well be that the students who attend TECHS and the other early college high schools have their own ideas about what they will do with the learning and credentials they acquire. And it may be that teachers have their own ideas about what education is for and that they will layer the sponsorship in their classrooms with education to serve democracy. In the end, the challenges to public education that the initiative offers may go deeper than institutional structure. They may go all the way to the core of what education is for in the first place.

Afterword

It has now been three years since we enrolled those first six students in our composition courses. Of the six, all of whom started in the high school in the fall of 2005, one has graduated high school—in three and a half years—and enrolled in the university this semester, with more than sixty earned credit hours. A second will graduate high school this spring and will be just a few hours short of having simultaneously earned a college degree and a regular place on the dean's list. The other four students are all on track to graduate high school this spring, and all will have enough credits to start as at least second-semester college sophomores. They were hand-picked for this pilot program, and their success may not be duplicated by their fellow students. Still, their success simply makes the challenge more pressing.

Notes

1. Numbers were approximate for 2007 prior to official count dates.

2. Janet Lieberman is one of the original architects of the Middle College High Schools program and an integral member of the Early College High School initiative. The article quoted here was prepared at the request of the initiative's administrator, Jobs for the Future.

3. The Early College High School initiative is sponsored by the Bill and Melinda Gates Foundation, with support from the Carnegie Corporation of New York, the Ford Foundation, and the W. K. Kellogg Foundation.

4. The Jobs for the Future website includes access to multiple articles, books, and videos commissioned to chronicle and support the Early College High School initiative. All references to the initiative's materials point back to this site. Some name authors; others are corporately authored. When an article's author is named, I have used the name in the citation. When the material is not attributed to a writer, I use the name of the web page.

5. I elected to keep the students and instructors interviewed for this project anonymous rather than assign them pseudonyms because it makes for easier reading, and I saw nothing to gain by the latter practice.

Works Cited

Brandt, Deborah. *Literacy in American Lives*. New York: Cambridge UP, 2001. Print.

Dalton, Harlon. "Horatio Alger." *Re-Reading America: Cultural Contexts for Critical Thinking and Writing*. Ed. Gary Colombo, Robert Cullen, and Bonnie Lisle. 7th ed. Boston: Bedford/St. Martin's, 2007. 320–26. Print.

Early College High School Initiative. "Early College High School Initiative." Brochure. 2003. *Early Colleges*. Web. 23 Mar. 2007.

Jobs for the Future. Jobs for the Future, n.d. Web. 2 July 2007.

———. "Core Principles." Jobs for the Future, n.d. Web. 23 Mar. 2007.

Labaree, David F. *How to Succeed in School without Really Learning: The Credentials Race in American Education*. New Haven: Yale UP, 1997. Print.

Lieberman, Janet E. "The Early College High School Concept: Requisites for Success." Boston: Jobs for the Future, 2004. *Early Colleges*. Web. 22 May 2007.

McNamee, Stephen J., and Robert K. Miller Jr. *The Meritocracy Myth*. Lanham: Rowman, 2004. Print.

United States Census Bureau. *School Enrollment: 2000*. Web. 4 Dec. 2007.

University of Toledo. *Mission Statement*. U of Toledo, 30 Nov. 2006. Web. 9 Apr. 2009.

CHAPTER SEVEN

Round Up the Horses—The Carts Are Racing Downhill! Programmatic Catch-up to a Quickly Growing Concurrent Credit Program

JOANNA CASTNER POST, VICKI BEARD SIMMONS, AND STEPHANIE VANDERSLICE
University of Central Arkansas

In the late spring of 2006, the University of Central Arkansas announced it would grow its small concurrent enrollment program involving one high school by developing similar partnerships with all high schools in its region. A stated goal of the program was to enable students to earn many of their college-level general education credits while in high school. From the perspective of many faculty, the program's unexpected expansion over the summer of 2006 was breathtakingly rapid, as the departments were told to implement the program immediately at the beginning of the fall semester. As a former Arkansas state senator, Lu Hardin, the president of UCA, had written the original concurrent credit legislation in 1989, and he had continued to have a hand in concurrent credit legislation and policy when he served as the director of Arkansas's Department of Higher Education. When as university president he announced plans to expand the program, many felt that he just wanted to increase UCA's enrollment. However, other two-year and four-year schools were crossing traditional service boundaries to connect with high school markets in UCA's backyard. President Hardin wanted not only to preserve tuition dollars but also to continue to serve high school students in our own county. To ensure UCA concurrent credit opportunities were available to students in areas traditionally served by UCA, he initiated this concentrated effort to expand UCA courses to all high schools in the surrounding region.

In this article we blend a number of voices to tell the story of UCA's efforts to establish a concurrent enrollment program in first-year writing. The voices represent different perspectives that were gathered through literature review, survey research, and self-report. We hope our tale will be instructive to others who likewise have to implement a concurrent enrollment program quickly. Because of the hasty way we had to begin the program, in some ways we believe the cart ended up in front of the horse, and we have had to work very hard to catch up and put the horse back in front. But we have made some progress, and we analyze how well our efforts to this point have met the ideal of concurrent enrollment programs: creating better communication and collaboration between high schools and universities so students are better prepared for higher education. We believe that as high school and university teachers work together on using effective writing pedagogy, we can achieve greater understanding of one another's very different worlds, strengthen writing instruction at both the secondary and postsecondary levels, and help students make a smoother transition from high school to college.

But first a word about us. Vanderslice is an associate professor in the writing department specializing in composition and creative writing. Simmons is the concurrent credit coordinator for Academic Outreach and Extended Programs (AOEP), the office that administers concurrent enrollment and acts as a for-profit arm of the university; formerly she was the liaison between the UCA writing department and the high schools offering the first concurrent enrollment courses. Castner Post, an assistant professor specializing in composition and technical communication, is a member of the writing department, separate from the English department. In what follows, we explain why UCA established its concurrent enrollment program and what bumps, twists, and turns we encountered along the way; then we present some early results of our efforts to assess the success of our program and our plans for future growth and assessment.

The Rationale for Concurrent Enrollment

The American high school curriculum, specifically the language arts curriculum, is currently adrift in a primordial soup of education initiatives. Leading organizations, such as the Bill and Melinda Gates Foundation, have issued a call for reinventing high schools—a call that comes close to characterizing the institution as a dinosaur of education that, without visionary overhaul, is destined for extinction. Recent reports such as the National Governors Association's *Redesigning the American High School* (Warner) are in emphatic agreement with the Gates Foundation. Additional initiatives, such as the American Diploma Project, the Partnership for 21st Century Skills, Achieve, and, in our state, Next Step for Arkansas's Future (crying, "Help us save the American High School Diploma" on its website), also purport to be focused on reinventing the American high school. Many of these policy groups have determined that a successful overhaul of secondary education includes establishing dual-enrollment programs between high schools and colleges (outside the well-established AP system) so that students can earn college credits in core subjects such as writing, science, and mathematics while still in high school. Such programs, at least on paper, are said to enhance student preparation for and success in college.

Yet within this same broth swim divergent groups highlighting serious gaps between high school and college instruction. Researchers Steve Graham and Dolores Perin, for example, commissioned by the Carnegie Corporation of New York to conduct a meta-analysis of effective adolescent writing instruction, point out that nearly one-third of high school graduates are not prepared for college writing, in part because secondary writing instruction may not be current on best practices (7). The National Commission on Writing, moreover, charges that writing, the second "R," is a seriously neglected component in school reform (1). While the commission does not claim that students "can't write," it does underscore an abundance of research that asserts students cannot "write well enough . . . to meet the demands they face in higher education and the . . . work environment" (154). Assembled by the College Board, the National Commission on Writing is composed of business people, politicians, and educators, including some associated with the National Writing Project. Although the commission's concern about writing is no doubt justified, it is important to acknowledge its connection to the College Board and the ways in which its findings may also serve that organization's agenda.

Both these camps support the idea that there are serious problems with the shape and scope of secondary education in America and that dramatic change is necessary. However, the solutions they offer are dramatically different. Policy groups such as the National Commission on Writing and researchers such as Graham and Perin advocate that a sea change in writing instruction is necessary in order to enhance the effectiveness of the secondary writing curriculum and, consequently, the writing skills of high school graduates. On the other hand, Next Step for Arkansas's Future and Achieve propose dual-enrollment programs in order to raise the stakes of the high school classroom by merging it with the collegiate writing requirement.

According to Carl Krueger, writing in a policy statement for the Education Commission of the States (ECS), fewer than 20 percent of ninth graders entering high school will graduate from college by age twenty-four (1). In a technologically advanced, knowledge-based economy with ever-increasing civic demands, Krueger asserts, the United States "cannot afford human capital loss of that scale and remain globally competitive" (1). Likewise, after analyzing attempts to bridge K–12 and university divides Michael Kirst and Andrea Venezia conclude that at a time when "70% of students enter postsecondary education after high school," it is no longer tenable to claim that not all students need to meet high curricular standards because not all students will attend college. They add that "the other 30% need high level skills and knowledge to succeed in the labor market," as well as in civic life (10).

Historically, "educational change has been isolated within either the K–12 or the higher education sector" rather than focusing on the nexus between the two levels (Kirst and Venezia 2). Problems associated with this long-standing disconnect include "access to college prep courses, grade inflation," the need for remediation at the college level, and the infamous senior slump

(2). All of these hinder the transition from high school to college and ultimately limit educational opportunity and success for many students. Secondary teachers often assume they are preparing students for college courses when, often, those teachers may be completely unaware of the content of college courses. Even when they are aware of the content of each other's courses, secondary and postsecondary teachers may serve different masters, as high school teachers usually face a mandate to prepare all their students to pass standardized multiple-choice and timed essay exams, whereas college teachers often have more freedom to take time in their classrooms to help students write several drafts of papers and explore the content of reading in some depth. The disconnect in pedagogy reported by Graham and Perin bears out these differences, all of which hinder the transition from high school to college and ultimately limit educational opportunity and success for many students.

Due to this critical gap between secondary and postsecondary education in the United States, Kirst and Venezia maintain that critical to college success is "signaling," or effective communication of college performance expectations to secondary school students, parents, and educators (7). Unfortunately, for those students who don't experience rigorous curricula in high school (which is often reserved for Advanced Placement students, the majority of whom already belong to a higher socioeconomic class), college expectations are shrouded in mystery. As a result, it is often the less privileged students, according to the U.S. Department of Education, who make up 25 percent of freshmen at four-year colleges and 50 percent of freshmen at two-year colleges who will not progress beyond their first year (5).

Many organizations, including the ECS, Achieve, and Next Step for Arkansas's Future, view concurrent enrollment as the magic bullet that can eliminate these inequities and better align high school and postsecondary schools in the bargain. Indeed, their optimism is not entirely unfounded, as significant data support the assertion that participation in concurrent enrollment programs *does* ultimately lead to college success. For example, according to the ECS, 25 percent of students who earn nine or more concurrent enrollment credits not only complete college but also continue on to graduate school.

Despite these statistics, there is still controversy over concurrent enrollment programs. Disparities in quality of instruction are a concern, and assessment issues abound. Even as concurrent enrollment policies exist in some form in forty-seven states, ECS reports that as of 2001 there were few comprehensive plans for the evaluation of programs or student success. A 2007 policy brief from the Center for Public Policy and Administration at the University of Utah comes to the same conclusion: "Some states have detailed policies guiding the types of courses offered, instructor qualifications, admissions requirements, and course content, while other states provide little or no guidance" (Robinson and Jack). A related problem, according to ECS, is that even when articulation policies within states are clear, state-to-state standards of articulation are rare. As a result, students may have a difficult time transferring courses from state to state. Nevertheless, according to Kirst and Venezia, the potential for concurrent enrollment programs to stimulate curricular review and innovation in both secondary and postsecondary institutions is high (28).

Each group previously named sounds the same call for action: strengthening high school education through better communication and collaboration between universities and high schools. This collaboration will, ideally, make high school teachers more knowledgeable about what goes on in university education, and make students' transition to college smoother than it presently is. As high school teachers understand better what college writing entails and how college faculty teach writing, their own writing pedagogy should become more effective. And as college composition programs are required to articulate their expectations and values clearly and consistently for the benefit of their high school partners, they will strengthen the college composition curriculum as well. That's the hope, at least. Next we turn to an account of how well the hope was achieved in practice as UCA established its concurrent enrollment program in first-year writing.

The First Year of UCA's Concurrent Enrollment Program

Vicki Beard Simmons is the UCA liaison to high schools participating in concurrent enrollment. In 2006, she was hired to serve as the liaison between the Department of Writing and Speech and the high schools offering the first concurrent courses in writing and speech. Then in 2007 she was appointed to work for the AOEP, which existed before concurrent enrollment, administering programs such as conference services, nondegree professional development, professional institutes, extended study courses, and online classes. In her current position Simmons works with all the department chairs under AOEP's director and with every other party related to the concurrent enrollment program. She has the challenge of mediating among five perspectives, many of which seem oppositional in some way: the president of UCA, who is in competition with other Arkansas colleges and universities to recruit students and who wants to provide a better product as well; the director of Academic Outreach and Extended Programs (AOEP), who works under the president and administers the concurrent enrollment program; the chair of writing and the writing faculty, who are concerned about staffing and quality issues; the participating high school administrators, guidance counselors, and teachers; and the participating high school students and their parents. All of these people or groups have different concerns and goals. Thus, Simmons has an important inside perspective, and her observations and experiences help set the stage for understanding assessment data that are presented at the end of this chapter.

Simmons was appointed in mid-October 2006 by Dr. David Harvey, chair of the writing and speech department, to be a department liaison in six partner high school classrooms offering UCA's Writing 1310 and 1320 (first- and second-semester composition) and Speech 1300 (first-semester speech) for the first time. Courses and instructors already had been approved by the chair, but some of the approvals were provisional, based on the condition that a liaison or mentor would oversee the courses and instructors. This condition met the guidelines of the Arkansas Department of Higher Education in effect at that time, which allowed universities to provide mentors for high school faculty who lacked advanced degrees but were assigned to teach concurrent enrollment. Because of the rapid expansion of the program in summer 2006 and implementation the same fall semester, the chair did not have a chance to institute any other policies for the high schools regarding curriculum, teacher qualifications, or student readiness. (At this point, new Arkansas state laws setting standards for concurrent courses were being created but were not passed until April 2007; the new standards required teachers of college courses to have a master's degree and a minimum of eighteen graduate hours in the subject being taught.) So Simmons's job was to ensure the integrity and quality of these UCA-required general education courses, certifying that they were comparable to those taught at UCA by regular faculty. Simmons was handed a copy of UCA's textbook for both writing and speech as well as a stack of folders, one representing each partner school and containing the syllabus for each writing or speech course taught and the credentials of the teachers for each school. Students who had not yet taken the ACT exam had already been admitted into the program after passing the Accuplacer, a reading and writing test administered in the high schools by Academic Outreach staff. Upper-level, college prep–type high school courses already in existence were designated as the first concurrent enrollment courses, fulfilling both high school requirements and college general education requirements.

In addition to mentoring two speech teachers without appropriate credentials, Simmons spent time in four other schools in Faulkner County observing writing courses. Because the instructors met qualifications then in effect and because their curricula aligned with UCA's, she visited the classrooms once or twice every two months and communicated with the instructors via email or phone, aiming to make teachers feel she was not "babysitting" them but instead was partnering with them for the betterment of the students. Some teachers were a little apprehensive at first—after all, they already served many constituencies, including principals, school board members, parents, and students—but with time and open communication, they realized that they were capable of teaching the course in the way that UCA wanted it taught.

One of the biggest problems to be overcome in this first year was the mismatch between the typical curriculum of a high school English course and that of a college first-year writing course—a mismatch that created the question of what sort of college credit to grant the high school students. The typical focus of a high school English course is the study of literature, and in their writing the students typically analyze this literature. However, the UCA

English department, which focuses only on literature, felt that the high school concurrent courses required too much emphasis on writing and didn't cover all the genres of literature. On the other hand, the writing department felt the courses placed too much emphasis on literature rather than the process of writing. As a result, the writing department wanted high school students to receive credit for a literature course rather than a composition course when the high school curriculum focused on literature. But the English department at first did not allow its general education courses in literature to be offered for concurrent credit. This conflict is an issue we continue to sort through, but for the most part, it is being resolved. Laura Bowles, writing department instructor and former high school teacher, was able to analyze the frameworks for junior- and senior-level high school English and pull out the elements relevant to our first- and second-semester composition courses. She was able to use these frameworks, which are familiar to high school teachers, to explain the goals of our own courses and show how they could accomplish the college writing goals along with some of the other activities and assignments already developed for high school. We can't say that we are finished working with curriculum development for the concurrent courses, but we have certainly come a long way.

Since that tumultuous first year, AOEP has required that the departments with the highest concentration of concurrent enrollment courses—history, mathematics, writing, speech, language, and biology—must have a liaison who not only provides oversight of courses offered in high schools but who also creates a resource manual, provides professional development, and maintains contact via email, phone, or personal classroom visits. This collaboration between high school faculty and UCA creates the context for better communication between secondary and postsecondary teachers and administrators. It not only meets the new Arkansas state law but also fulfills some of the accreditation requirements of the National Alliance of Concurrent Enrollment Partnerships (NACEP). Arkansas Act 936, which set teacher certification standards, also requires that UCA accredit its concurrent enrollment programs through this national association. In accordance with the NACEP accreditation requirements, UCA faculty must provide professional development opportunities for partnering high school faculty—a stipulation that has proven to be a true asset to our program. As we explain next, high school faculty are now starting to engage in dialogue with university faculty about their disciplines and beginning collaboration between two institutions that, for the most part, did not previously communicate.

Preliminary Assessments and Plans for Program Development

As of 2008 UCA is a provisional member of NACEP, working toward accreditation, a process that takes five years. As a prelude to accrediting our concurrent enrollment program, NACEP has already begun gathering data. Here we present some data gathered from a 2007 survey created by NACEP for the purpose of understanding the attitudes of the high school participants in concurrent enrollment programs. UCA's Academic Outreach office distributed three survey types: one for high school teachers, one for guidance counselors, and one for high school administrators participating in UCA's program. We compiled the survey data submitted by the twenty teachers across the four high schools participating in 2007. Four of these teachers taught the first-semester composition course; three teachers taught the first-semester speech course, and the other teachers were dispersed among the following disciplines: chemistry, physics, math, French, Spanish, history, biology, and physical education.

The survey data (see Tables 7.1, 7.2, and 7.3 in the appendix) indicate that the experiences of the high school teachers in this study were overwhelmingly positive. Although it is important to note that we cannot generalize broadly from the limited number of surveys, the results do seem to bode well for those of us working to develop effective ways to partner with high school teachers in delivering college courses. The survey data and observations indicate that teachers may be receptive—indeed, even excited—about learning more about teaching their discipline at the college level, especially the data that address the effects of teaching college courses:

- 70 percent of teachers report being re-energized as teachers as a result of teaching concurrent courses.

- 80 percent report more satisfaction with their jobs as a result of teaching concurrent courses.

- 90 percent felt more connected to their discipline after teaching concurrent courses.

Adding to the hope that high school teachers may be eager to work with us are the findings that 75 percent of them believed that teaching concurrent courses showed parents that their students are doing challenging work and that 80 percent of them reported that concurrent courses enhanced the prestige and academic reputation of their high schools. These statistics paint a picture of teachers who feel they have been given new status rather than added and unwanted responsibilities; they are expanding their knowledge of their fields and feeling more connected: 85 percent of the teachers reported learning new developments in their disciplines; 70 percent felt that they learned new instructional strategies, and 90 percent said that they developed a good understanding of what colleges expect students to know and do. Their enthusiasm is high despite the finding that 70 percent of the teachers disagreed that they had been able to give their concurrent enrollment courses and students more time because other duties had been lightened. This response is likely due to the fact that the teachers are not teaching extra courses—they simply turned their existing courses into dual-enrollment courses offering both high school and college credit.

Despite the added responsibilities of their new role, 65 percent of the teachers reported that they did not find it more difficult to fulfill their regular duties. At first we thought that high school teachers would be unhappy about taking on a university general education program in addition to their other responsibilities, especially without extra compensation because, in Arkansas, high school teachers who teach concurrent courses are paid as usual. (The compensation UCA receives is in student enrollment—we count concurrent credit students as UCA students. Four concurrent credit students equal one full-time student, and the state compensates the university accordingly.) However, the survey results suggest that many teachers feel more excited about the program than overwhelmed. Their positive attitudes are important because we can't move on to the next phases of developing strong concurrent enrollment courses without teachers who are motivated to learn and try new pedagogies. Creating courses appropriate for both purposes, high school English and college composition, will take some time. Indeed, we are still working on a solution acceptable to everyone because of many challenges we still face —some that we are already resolving and some that will take more time.

One of our immediate challenges is to determine whether the high school students are achieving the same outcomes as regular college students. An unambiguous 100 percent of the teachers said they believed their students gained in-depth knowledge of the subject matter they were learning. This is a perception we are attempting to verify further via essay assessment. In spring 2008, the essays produced through the concurrent program were included in our department's regular assessment work. Each spring, the Assessment Committee reads 20 percent of the final essays produced in the second semester composition course. Papers are chosen from each class based on a calculation of the rank of the professor and the number of students in each class. So, for example, if tenure-track professors taught 14 percent of the students in composition courses, the Assessment Committee would make sure that 14 percent of the final essays read came from that group of teachers. Frankly, our spring 2008 assessment showed just how much work we still have to do. Our results showed that we don't have a unified vision for what college composition does; we are not on the same page as a program. As a group, including the high school teachers, we emphasize different things, and we value different elements as we assess. So we are now in the process of creating a renewed vision. To that end, we are participating in reading and discussion groups to share ideas and brainstorm, and we are meeting formally to rethink our programmatic purpose and our courses. We are including the high school teachers as often as we can. The problems that have come from concurrent enrollment have actually caused a new excitement about rethinking our practices together. It is a creative time for us, full of potential. The excitement is not as much about concurrent enrollment per se as it is about building a vision for our program. But concurrent enrollment was the catalyst for this productive rethinking.

We have also taken steps to resolve another immediate challenge, the issue of student preparedness. The NACEP survey showed that 95 percent of the teachers felt that the students developed realistic expectations of college work, and 80 percent of the teachers said that the students became more effective time managers. Because many college writing faculty are still suspicious of concurrent enrollment, we plan further assessments to see if results support the high school teachers' perceptions. Some professors in the writing department have expressed concern that students may be surprised by the rigor of upper-level college courses if they move straight from high school to a university setting and upper-level courses. In the meantime, we have taken steps to ensure that only qualified students will enroll in the concurrent courses by creating admissions standards that students have to meet first. In 2007 the University Admissions Committee approved the following policy for student admission to concurrent enrollment:

- A composite ACT score of at least 19 or an equivalent SAT score

- An ACT test score of 19 or above in reading or an equivalent SAT score

- For students enrolling in a mathematics course, an ACT test score of a 19 or above in mathematics or an equivalent SAT score

- For students enrolling in a course for which the high school will award English credit, an ACT test score of a 19 or above in English or an equivalent SAT score

- A GPA of 3.0 or above

- Classification as junior or senior

- The recommendation of the high school principal

It is true that students taking courses as high school juniors would have to take the ACT as sophomores, and yes, this is very early. But faculty on the committee wanted to make sure that only students ready to take college courses were enrolled.

In addition to the assessment data gathered at the end of spring 2008 semester, writing faculty are working with colleagues such as Simmons in AOEP to build on the initiatives begun in 2007 to ensure the quality and integrity of our concurrent credit courses. The Department of Writing was fortunate to have a chair who developed some initiatives right from the beginning of the program that will help us continue to integrate our expertise and oversight into the program. For example, he created the liaison position for our department and paved the way for other departments to do the same. Our department was also lucky to have one of its members chair a faculty senate committee devoted to concurrent enrollment issues, and that committee did a lot to clarify the role department faculty should play in the concurrent enrollment programs versus the role AOEP should play. At the end of the first year of the newly expanded concurrent enrollment program, our department had a good foundation on which to build.

The Department of Writing is continuing to work with AOEP to implement the requirements for concurrent credit courses laid out by Arkansas state law and NACEP. However, there were problems in instituting new requirements immediately, since the April 2007 law was not passed until after some legally binding agreements with high schools were already in place. AOEP calls these "articulation agreements," but they are contracts, and they did not require of schools what the law requires now and what we would have hoped. In particular, they did not require that high school teachers participate in our professional development programs and teach the concurrent courses to our standards. We had to wait until the old agreements expired to move forward with more and better collaboration with high school administrators and teachers. As the agreements are now expiring, we are engaging in new rounds of diplomacy, as some schools do not understand why the new standards and requirements are more rigorous. The writing department has a new liaison to mentor all high school writing faculty, and the department has been offering professional development for the high school faculty as well. It may be that some schools drop out of the program because they do not want to participate in these activities.

At the beginning of the second year of the concurrent enrollment program, the chair of the writing department appointed a new director and two assistant directors to run the writing center and to oversee the department's concurrent credit courses, given the tricky diplomatic environment created by the agreements with high schools already in place when the 2007 Arkansas state law came into effect. They developed two half-day professional development workshops for two different Saturdays during that fall semester and invited writing department faculty as well as our concurrent colleagues to both workshops. The second workshop was open to all faculty on campus interested in teaching writing. The first workshop covered college composition approaches and ways to develop effective assignments in keeping with a chosen approach, and the second workshop focused on expanding ideas for researched argument writing and effective feedback practices. The workshops were a great success, but only a few high school colleagues attended. The three Writing Center directors have had to work slowly and carefully to begin to open the lines of communication to high school administrators and teachers and to implement the new initiatives.

One of these directors has now replaced Simmons as the concurrent enrollment liaison. As a former Arkansas high school teacher and a PhD candidate in rhetoric, she has a foot in both worlds. She has been working with the high schools to see where our first semester composition content would best fit and how to work with the high school teachers in a way that doesn't sour their enthusiasm for teaching UCA courses. She developed a weeklong summer orientation program and invited our high school colleagues to attend. Many more high school colleagues attended this event than the workshops held in the fall and spring semesters, and we all learned a great deal from one another. The liaison's idea to pull out from the high school frameworks those elements that will fit with UCA course goals will hopefully send high school teachers the right message: that we value what they do. Ideally this message will help teachers remain open to adding new content and pedagogical practices that align with UCA's goals for college composition. In spring 2008, the same professional development workshops were offered, with the liaison making follow-up visits to the teachers at the high schools to observe courses, work with teachers to develop their syllabi, and keep the lines of communication open.

As we move forward, we are optimistic that our efforts to establish communication and collaboration between high schools and the university will adequately surmount the delicate problems caused by old agreements in conflict with new laws. Further, the NACEP survey data certainly give hope for strengthening writing curriculum and pedagogy in both the high schools and university writing departments. The high school colleagues participating in the survey and our workshops *do* want to learn more about college composition and how they can best teach it to their students. College instructors seem open to gaining fresh perspectives, learning more about secondary education, and having new colleagues. Even though we have legal oversight of the programs, the territory of the partnerships is uncharted. The mixture of old agreements and new laws is confusing to everyone, and there are many layers of secondary and postsecondary administration that make communication difficult. Perhaps the administrative buffers meant to soften anticipated communication problems may actually be creating more fear of problems than is warranted.

As we solve the problems already enumerated, however, additional ones loom on the horizon. One that must be resolved is the relationship of AP and IB courses to concurrent enrollment courses. The state of Arkansas requires all high schools to offer a minimum of four AP classes, but currently there is no requirement that high schools offer courses that are exclusively concurrent enrollment. As a result, some high schools are attempting to blend the AP curriculum and the concurrent enrollment curriculum. That is true for three out the seven high school teachers with whom we work. Another high school colleague teaches an International Baccalaureate English course that results in credit for our college composition class, just as a concurrent enrollment course would, so in effect it is a concurrent enrollment course without our curriculum. The other three teachers in our partnership are able to separate their AP courses from concurrent English or college composition courses. But several smaller schools in the state have been allowed to count their AP courses as their concurrent credit course since they lack the resources to staff separate AP and concurrent enrollment courses. The Department of Writing will be assessing the writing from the blended AP and concurrent enrollment courses and making a decision about whether they can continue as such. The writing of students in those courses will be assessed just like the writing from the regular UCA composition courses, through holistic evaluation of the final paper, an argument supported with research.

As a result of blended AP and concurrent enrollment courses in some high schools, the Department of Writing must now rethink its policy for granting credit and exemption for AP exams. The present policy allows students earning a 3 on the AP Literature and Composition test to place out of first-semester composition, and students earning a 4 on the same test are allowed to place out of second-semester composition. However, students in an AP course studying for the Literature and Composition test would not be following UCA's composition curriculum. Writing faculty are considering changing the required AP test to the Language and Composition test only and then working with instructors in small schools to blend AP Language and Composition curriculum and the concurrent enrollment curriculum effectively. Our new concurrent enrollment liaison is currently developing ideas for how such a blended course would work. The two blended courses already running, however, *are* being taught to the AP Language and Composition test, so the next evaluations should reveal how this blend is working.

As if these problems weren't complex enough, other mandates that high school teachers face complicate their work and our efforts to establish a strong concurrent enrollment curriculum. For example, an English teacher teaching a junior-level AP course in Arkansas has to prepare students for the AP exam, and that requires very specific to-the-test instruction. But that teacher also has to prepare students for the state's eleventh-grade literacy test, another exam with very different requirements. Now add to that load UCA's first-semester composition course, which stresses rhetorical flexibility rather than a specific writing style for test taking. In short, neither the AP curriculum nor the eleventh-grade literacy test aligns with our first-semester composition course. High school teachers have always had to listen to principals, school board members, and parents; now they have to deal with us!

Another consideration is the difference in curricula designed for different levels of student maturity and independence. As UCA brings the high school curriculum in alignment with its composition courses, and high school teachers begin to use our textbooks, we can foresee problems resulting because the acceptability meter for subject matter is very different in high schools and universities. Some readings that are commonly used in our UCA course may not meet with the approval of parents of high school students; and those parents may complain to the school board, the principal, and the teacher. Because their children are minors, parents are used to having much more control over what is discussed in high school classrooms, and we believe such a skirmish over the curriculum of concurrent credit courses is bound to happen. Another concern is that some of the high schools can't provide the students access to technology required to do the assigned work. For example, our second-semester composition course calls for argument essays supported with research. Some high schools have only a few computers in the library, and library time is limited. Students must have adequate time and tools to conduct research effectively, or their work and preparation for college will suffer a great deal.

Despite all the problems, after the first year and a half of the expanded program, we are optimistic that we can still get the horse before the cart and, given enough time and resources, turn our program into an increasingly effective one for students. For example, the popularity of the concurrent enrollment program could very well lead to more technology for high school students, as well as more writing instruction that focuses on rhetorical flexibility rather than on standardized-for-a-test templates. Communication with our high school colleagues has already helped us understand better the writing experiences with which our students come to college and why they come with those specific experiences rather than others. As we move forward in this collaboration, we have some important strengths on our side:

◆ A writing department chair committed to improving the quality of the concurrent courses.

◆ A liaison in Academic Outreach committed to building on the high school teachers' strengths and continuing to work for the quality and comparability of the concurrent courses.

◆ A new writing department liaison who understands both the high school and the university cultures.

- ◆ AOEP administrators who are enthusiastic about our ideas for ensuring the quality of our courses.

- ◆ Colleagues on admissions and faculty senate committees who have been able to get important quality-control policies passed.

Is the jury still out? Absolutely. We have a great deal of assessment and program research to complete. Stay tuned.

Acknowledgments

We would like to thank the following colleagues who read drafts and answered questions: Laura Bowles, concurrent enrollment liaison; Francie Bolter, Faculty Senate Committee; Lynn Burley, Admissions Committee; David Harvey, chair of the writing department; Marcy Tucker; and Hui Wu. We also thank Dean Kim Bradford for her review and thoughtful insights.

Appendix

TABLE **7.1.** High School Teachers' Rating of Students' Development in the UCA Concurrent Credit Program (percent)

Teachers were asked to respond to the following question about their students.

As a result of taking UCA Concurrent Credit courses in my high school, students have:

	Disagree strongly	Disagree	Neutral	Agree	Agree strongly	Does not apply/ Don't know
a. Continued rigorous learning in their senior year			5	35	60	
b. Developed realistic expectations of college work		5		60	35	
c. Considered, for the first time, going to college		15	25	30		30
d. Developed a better understanding of their academic skills			5	55	30	10
e. Gained in-depth knowledge in the subject area				50	50	
f. Developed effective time management skills			15	60	20	5
g. Developed effective study skills		5	15	45	25	10

Note: N=20 teachers. A few of the questions were left unanswered, thus some percentages are based on fewer than 20 responses. The numbers of teachers at each school break down as follows: four from "School V," five from "School S," two from "School CC," and nine from "School G."

TABLE 7.2. High School Teachers' Rating of Their Development in the UCA Concurrent Credit Program (percent)

Teachers were asked to respond to the following question about themselves.

As a result of teaching UCA's Concurrent Credit courses, I have:

	Disagree strongly	Disagree	Neutral	Agree	Agree strongly	Does not apply/ Don't know
a. Learned about new ideas and developments in my academic discipline		5	5	65	20	5
b. Learned new instructional strategies			30	50	20	
c. Found my job more satisfying			20	35	45	
d. Taken leadership positions within my department, school, district, or professional association			26	47	16	11
e. Been reenergized as a teacher		5	20	45	25	5
f. Found it more difficult to fulfill other school responsibilities	15	50	10	10	10	5
g. Benefited from the support of and contact with colleagues in other high schools and with UCA's Concurrent Credit liaison		5	45	35	5	10

continued on next page

Table 7.2. continued

h. Been released from other school duties, enabling me to give courses and students more time	25	45	10	10		10
i. Developed a good understanding of what colleges expect students to know and be able to do in the academic discipline of my CEP course			5	65	25	5
j. Felt more connected with my academic discipline			5	75	15	5
k. Found content and/or pedagogy of the CEP course useful in non-CEP classes		5	10	60	20	5
l. Established higher standards for student work		5		65	25	5
m. Felt supported by the CEP liaison/ mentor		5	5	68	11	11

Note: N=20. In rows where percentages are not multiples of five, only nineteen respondents answered the question.

TABLE **7.3.** High School Teachers' Rating of Their School's Response to the UCA Concurrent Credit Program (percent)

Teachers were asked to respond to the following question about their school.

As a result of offering UCA's Concurrent Credit courses, my high school:

	Disagree strongly	Disagree	Neutral	Agree	Agree strongly	Does not apply/ Don't know
a. Progressed in meeting its goal of offering rigorous classes for students			5	65	30	
b. Offers prerequisite courses for CEP courses that are appropriately rigorous			20	60	10	10
c. Raised expectations for student performance in courses preceding CEP courses			5	70	10	15
d. Demonstrated to parents that their students are doing challenging work as juniors and seniors			10	50	25	15
e. Enhanced its prestige and academic reputation			15	55	25	5

Note: N=20.

Works Cited

Achieve. Home page. Achieve, n.d. Web. 8 Apr. 2009.

American Diploma Project. *Ready or Not: Creating a High School Diploma That Counts.* Achieve, Feb. 2004. Web. 2 Feb. 2008.

Arkansas. General Assembly. *House Bill 1730.* Arkansas Code 6-16-1204(c). 86th General Assembly, Regular Session, 2007. Web. 8 Apr. 2009.

Bill and Melinda Gates Foundation. *High Schools for the New Millennium: Imagine the Possibilities.* Seattle: Bill and Melinda Gates Foundation, n.d. Web. 2 Feb. 2008.

Education Commission of the States. "Dual/Concurrent Enrollment: Quick Facts." *ECS.* Mar. 2006. Web. 6 June 2007.

Graham, Steve, and Dolores Perin. *Writing Next: Effective Strategies to Improve Writing of Adolescents in Middle and High Schools—A Report to Carnegie Corporation of New York.* Washington: Alliance for Excellent Education, 2007. Web. 8 Apr. 2009.

Kirst, Michael, and Andrea Venezia. "Bridging the Great Divide between Secondary Schools and Postsecondary Education." *Phi Delta Kappan* 83.1 (2001): 92–97. Print.

Krueger, Carl. *Dual Enrollment: Policy Issues Confronting State Policymakers.* Denver: Education Commission of the States, Mar. 2006. *ECS.* Web. 6 June 2007.

National Commission on Writing in American's Schools and Colleges. *The Neglected "R": The Need for a Writing Revolution.* Princeton: College Board, Apr. 2003. Web. 31 Jan. 2007.

Next Step for Arkansas's Future. Next Step for Arkansas's Future, n.d. Web. 2 Feb. 2007.

Partnership for 21st Century Skills. Partnership for 21st Century Skills, n.d. Web. 20 Feb. 2007.

Robinson, Jennifer, and Tricia Jack. *Concurrent Enrollment in Utah: Access and Quality.* Center for Public Policy and Administration, University of Utah, 26 Sept. 2007. Web. 2 Feb. 2008.

Warner, Mark. *Redesigning the American High School.* 2004–2005 National Governors Association Chairman's Initiative, n.d. Web. 2 Feb. 2008.

CHAPTER EIGHT

Concurrent Enrollment in Rural Minnesota: Addressing the Needs Caused by Shifting Demographics, Economics, and Academics

RANDALL MCCLURE
Georgia Southern University

KEVIN ENERSON
LeSueur-Henderson High School, LeSueur, Minnesota

JANE KEPPLE JOHNSON
United South Central High School, Wells, Minnesota

PATRICIA LIPETZKY
Minnesota State University, Mankato

CYNTHIA POPE
Rasmussen College

Rural colleges and universities are aggressively remaking themselves. Decreases in funding, demands from government and industry, and, most strikingly, demographic shifts that have led to unstable and, in some cases, rapidly declining enrollments have forced many rural institutions of higher education to adopt wider, more diverse missions. They are developing global perspectives, forming community partnerships, and offering online and other forms of distance learning. Perhaps most significantly, they are forming close-knit partnerships to foster enhanced learning in surrounding high schools, to which they were once only loosely connected by geography, student teaching programs, and admissions and advising offices. Partnerships have been attempted before; however, they now involve ways for high school students to earn significant college credit, thus bringing colleges and high schools together in new and exciting ways. These new partnerships go far beyond passing curricular experiments or access initiatives having a one-directional feel or effect; they are bilateral and mutually beneficial.

One increasingly popular partnership for rural universities, including those in rural Minnesota, is concurrent enrollment college courses taught by high school teachers as part of the regular high school day. In this chapter, we argue that concurrent enrollment is the superior postsecondary education option for all involved parties in rural areas, especially students, and for reasons beyond dollars and cents. Speaking from our positions as high school teachers (Johnson and Pope), a high school principal (Enerson), an academic dean (Lipetzky), and a writing program administrator (McClure) who have participated in a concurrent enrollment program, this kind of partnership uniquely addresses the demographic, economic, and academic needs of rural schools, both secondary and postsecondary.

Our decision to form a concurrent enrollment partnership in 2004 came as a result, albeit delayed, of the 1985 Postsecondary Enrollment Options (PSEO) Act enacted by the Minnesota state legislature. The purpose of this statute was to "promote rigorous academic pursuits and to provide a wider variety of options to high school pupils" (MN Stat. 124D, art. 09, sub. 2). Joe Nathan, Laura Accomando, and Debra Hale Fitzpatrick note that "Minnesota was the first state to give high school juniors and seniors the right to apply to colleges and universities, and if accepted, to take courses, full or part time, with state funds following them, paying tuition and book charges." They add that many states have copied the Minnesota model because "PSEO programs can help deal with several important policy challenges: (1) the rising cost of higher education for families and states; (2) the importance of students not only entering, but graduating from some form of postsecondary education; and (3) increasing the number and percentage of students fully prepared for college when they graduate from high school" (3).

Higher education institutions and high school districts implement the PSEO statute in two ways. The first is called Postsecondary Enrollment Options programs. In such programs, high school–age PSEO students typically travel to one or more college or university campuses in order to take classes, similar to fully matriculated students. The second method of implementation is concurrent enrollment (CE). In Minnesota, CE is generally implemented by establishing programs that allow select high school students to take college-level courses in their high school buildings during the regular school day, courses that are offered through partnering colleges and universities in the state. Unlike courses in PSEO programs, however, these courses are taught by high school teachers as part of their regular teaching assignments. The high school teachers, courses, curricular materials, and students must meet criteria defined by each participating college or university in compliance with state and system policies.

The PSEO Act is now more than twenty years old, and while most colleges and universities in the state have offered PSEO programs for more than a decade, until recently only a few institutions in Minnesota had ventured into CE. The obvious reason for the prevalence of PSEO over CE programs is one of resources. In PSEO programs, high school students meeting the university's admission criteria simply apply for PSEO status and begin enrolling in courses. As long as the students continue to meet the university's criteria for PSEO status, they can continue to take classes. Enrolling high school students in college courses might be slightly more work for a few offices; otherwise, the college or university remains unburdened as enrollment numbers increase. In CE programs, however, additional resources are required as programs must be set up inside high schools. Since each high school contact is different, the participating college or university must extend itself, often requiring the participation of several offices and departments. In many cases, forming CE partnerships requires additional staffing with little guarantee of solidifying agreements and enrolling students.

Recently, however, there has been renewed interest in CE and other postsecondary learning opportunities in the state of Minnesota for two reasons: government-led initiatives and notable shifts in demographics, academics, and economics. The governor's office proposed an increase of 7.7 percent in the state's education budget, or more than $700 million, for the 2008 fiscal year in order to fund initiatives such as "World-Class Students"

(Minnesota Department of Education). In this initiative, formally announced in April 2007, the governor's office envisions "one year of post-secondary education for every Minnesota student" in what is described as "a system of education for the 21st century, preparing Minnesota students to compete with students from anywhere around the world" (Pawlenty, Foreword). The "World-Class Students" proposal calls for every Minnesota student "to take at least one year of postsecondary education while in high school" with the students earning "dual credit" for both high school and college (Pawlenty, "World-Class Students"). Slated to begin in 2010, this initiative has been on the radar of public school districts as well as colleges and universities in the state for a few years. With more than $700 million possibly behind the initiative, the financial implications alone of postsecondary learning opportunities in the state are clear and significant, especially for rural areas that face severe demographic and economic challenges.

In fact, the governor's proposal states, "High schools must offer programs that support postsecondary access that may include: Advanced Placement (AP), International Baccalaureate (IB), Post-Secondary Education Options (PSEO), College in the Schools (CIS), Concurrent Enrollment, and College Level Examination Program (CLEP)" (Pawlenty, Foreword). This impending requirement is one among many recent national calls to create postsecondary programs for high schools. In fact, several influential studies have cited the need for increased attention to college access, preparation, and transition in order to address problems of rising attrition, failure, and remediation of students entering colleges and universities (Nathan, Accomando, and Fitzpatrick 6). These academic concerns have been sounded urgently not only in the Minnesota governor's claim that the "current high school format is not designed to meet the demands of a new global reality" but also in the Spellings Commission Report, which cites concerns over the future of American higher education (Spellings), and in David T. Conley's *College Knowledge*, which emphasizes the rift between postsecondary and secondary schools. Initiatives such as "World-Class Students" and postsecondary learning opportunities—and especially, as we argue, CE—can help bring, in the governor's words, the "rigor, relevance and results" (Pawlenty,

"World-Class Students") not common to high school curricula, particularly in rural areas.

Rural Minnesota high schools, presumably like those in other rural areas of the United States, are remaking themselves for reasons of demographics, academics, and economics. Many of these schools are losing students, some at exponential rates, and losing the funding that comes with them. Others are faced with staffing shortages, often leading to limited curricula and few or no extra- and co-curricular opportunities for students. As a result, schools are actively seeking relationships that can provide what they cannot. Occasionally, these relationships come from local business and industry, perhaps in the form of sponsored programs, vocational training, or internships. In most rural communities, however, especially those with largely agrarian economies, such relationships are few and far between. Thus, high school teachers and administrators are looking at neighboring colleges and universities differently than in years past, seeing them no longer as the point where their work ends but as partners in their work. CE is a prime example of such a partnership.

Much more than their college and university partners (and many high schools have more than one), rural high schools struggle to meet the academic demands made by government agencies and policies, let alone to meet expectations in their own communities or to launch new initiatives. Because PSEO programs provide the advanced and diverse course work not typical in the common high school curriculum, they can help students and teaching staff meet academic demands. For example, teachers can enroll in workshops, training seminars, or courses for professional development. Students can sometimes enroll in correspondence courses, but since the human contact is limited, this type of postsecondary partnership has failed to gain favor. Many rural high schools, however, do not have access to PSEO programs because the geographical distances between potential partner schools are just too far to travel. Moreover, many rural high schools that do offer access to PSEO programs are facing dramatic demographic and economic challenges that threaten the viability of those programs. In a nutshell, when students leave schools to participate in PSEO programs, their precious funding dollars leave too.

For this reason and many others, high school administrators and teachers see PSEO and CE as radically different options. Both PSEO and CE programs offer increased curricular range, rigor, and engagement for high school students, and both focus on quality and accountability, clearly points of emphasis in today's educational climate. Given their largely different levels of impact on public funding dollars, however, the "costs" of offering PSEO programs can be debilitating for rural high schools. Further, high school administrators who steward PSEO programs face magnified issues of school and curricular integrity, student safety, and transportation costs. Most rural high schools will continue to offer PSEO programs to their students, mainly due to local pressures for maintaining access to the breadth of curriculum available on college campuses. However, because PSEO programs drain state funds away from high schools and because initiatives at the state level are now encouraging development of CE partnerships in rural areas of Minnesota, we believe more of these partnerships will be formed.

It may seem counterintuitive for colleges to offer high school students courses for dual credit and, in most cases, at discounted tuition rates during a time of declining enrollments, fiscal constraints, and fierce competition in higher education for students and their education dollars, especially in rural areas. One simple justification for doing so, however, can be found in the literature that discusses the perceived gap between high school learning outcomes and college and university learning expectations (see Conley). Whether real or imagined, this perceived gap between high school achievement and readiness for college-level work weighs heavily on the minds of teachers in both institutions, and it is possible that misperceptions abound. Not only is it the case that most college professors have not been in a high school classroom since they were teenagers, but high school teachers make assumptions about college preparation based on their own undergraduate days. Bringing high school teachers and university professors together over real issues of curricular alignment and student achievement can help bridge the perceived gap, resulting in greater understanding and appreciation on both sides. The two groups can also work to define clearer pathways for students to enter college. CE involves a partnership not just at the institutional level but, perhaps more importantly, at the human level. For these reasons, we believe that CE can be superior to PSEO for rural high schools, as we explain and illustrate next.

MSU Mankato's Design for Concurrent Enrollment

Since its inception as Mankato Normal School, Minnesota State University, Mankato—a regional comprehensive university located in southern Minnesota, two hours south of Minneapolis and Saint Paul—has been involved with primary and secondary education. Following enactment of the PSEO Act, MSU Mankato began admitting high school students as on-campus PSEO students. Partly because of local concerns regarding quality, accountability, and implementation, the university's CE program did not begin until 2004, when an outreach unit, under the leadership of an academic dean, helped to create a favorable climate for CE. Contributing to this climate were predictions of decreased enrollment in higher education because of demographic shifts and changing economic trends. MSU Mankato is now a member of the National Alliance of Concurrent Enrollment Partnerships (NACEP) and is in the process of receiving accreditation from this organization. While future plans for MSU Mankato include developing more partnerships with high schools at greater distances, the university now serves only those districts within the immediate geographic area because of requirements for direct involvement of university professors with high school teachers and for the provision of some services, both discussed below.

MSU is part of the Minnesota State Colleges and Universities (MnSCU) statewide system of thirty-two two- and four-year public colleges and universities. MnSCU Board Policy 3.5 defines a CE course as "a college or university course made available through the PSEO program, offered through a secondary school, and taught by a secondary teacher." Further, the policy establishes minimum standards for student participation, although the partnering university can define more rigorous standards. Currently, MnSCU defines admission standards for juniors as a class rank in the upper one-third or a test score at or above the 70th percentile on a nationally standardized, norm-referenced test; for seniors, the standard is a class rank in the upper one-half or a test score at or above the 50th percentile on a nationally standardized, norm-referenced test. Students who want to participate in CE are formally admitted to the university following high school counselor recommendations that admissions criteria have been met and that students are ready for and have the ability to perform college-level work.

In our design, which has more rigorous standards than those set by MnSCU policy, high school teachers must also meet criteria to participate in the CE program. While the minimum requirement is not defined by MnSCU policy, MSU Mankato requires all participating high school teachers to hold at least a master's degree in an appropriate field. After identifying eligible teachers, the partnering academic department at our university ultimately makes the decision to offer a CE course or not. Once the decision is made, a university faculty mentor meets with the eligible high school teacher to review and approve the teacher's depth of subject knowledge, course syllabus, and instructional materials. Following this step, the university faculty mentor presents the high school teacher and his or her credentials to the mentor's academic department for approval.

This procedure for starting a CE partnership, while time consuming, has had some positive (though, in some ways, unintended) benefits. The decision to both accept the high school CE teacher as a member of the university faculty and verify the course materials involves and engages the department. Through this process, the department accepts "ownership" of the course and thus bucks the trend of driving the college curriculum down into high schools. CE provides us at the college level with opportunities to examine our curriculum by looking at it alongside our partnering high school principals, teachers, and especially their students. In the college composition course discussed later in this chapter, for example, the writing program administrator collaborated with principals and high school teachers to propose to the university department a course that meets the needs and outcomes at the high school and college levels. In both cases, changes to the existing composition course as it had been taught at the college level were minimal and included only small shifts in the reading-writing balance. Specifically, the high school teachers in our CE partnerships assigned more reading than writing before our collaboration. More emphasis on revision in the writing process was also added to the course, and the number of major writing projects was increased from three to five. Still, both teachers already relied heavily on pedagogy common in the college course, such as an investment in the writing process, peer review, composing with computers, composing arguments, and visual rhetoric, to name a few. In fact, the high school teachers in our CE partnerships were both already well informed on composition theory and pedagogy, likely due to our requirement that the teachers hold a master's degree in the field.

In should also be noted that students are asked to provide regular feedback on the course design, and the input from students is used to refine the course. We believe such involvement from students and close discussions of curriculum between secondary and postsecondary professionals remain the exception in public education today; therefore, we argue that CE partnerships can accomplish what many other initiatives have attempted and failed to do in establishing meaningful dialogue between high schools and colleges. Our CE partnerships have allowed our university departments to gain tremendous insight into high school curricula and teachers, resulting in opportunities for curricular alignment and refinement in our own programs.

For example, our university English department has amended three of its graduate-level courses, including its composition theory course, to include more content on teaching writing in high school. This change better prepares our large cadre of teaching assistants by informing them about the curriculum common to secondary schools in our region, the same schools that provide us with the majority of first-year students we encounter. In fact, two high school teachers from the region have also participated in the revised composition theory course. Thus, high school teachers who have participated as CE instructors have not only gained knowledge of our academic departments but have also opened up avenues for their own professional growth.

Participating college faculty and high school teachers in our program collaborate closely. After the course and teacher are formally accepted, the high school teacher and university faculty mentor work together in the concurrent course a minimum of three times each semester. While each mentoring relationship is unique, types of classroom participation include team teaching, guest lecturing, co-planning of lessons and assignments, and dual grading. They also communicate via phone and email, ensuring ongoing engagement. Finally, participating high school teachers are provided with inservice and other professional development opportunities at the university. In fact, MSU Mankato's commitment to professional development of CE teachers was recognized in June 2007 at the state level, when the newly formed Minnesota Concurrent Enrollment Partnership held its first statewide workshop, "Inspired Practice," for English composition faculty and high school English teachers in CE partnerships.

Our CE courses are not offered solely for outreach purposes; in fact, they serve more as early introductions to the university experience. Because that experience involves more than just attending classes, other support offices are also included in our version of CE, enriching the experience for all involved—students, teachers, guidance counselors, and administrators at the high schools along with faculty, admission officers, administrators, and other staff at the university. For example, our university's distance learning librarian meets with CE students in their high schools to provide instruction on accessing the university's online research databases. Concurrent students are also invited to participate in the university's new student orientation, where university policies and expectations are explained and student identification cards are distributed to permit students access to on-campus experiences and events. This approach is particularly advantageous for rural high schools that have few students, minimal resources, and limited course offerings. But recruitment is a goal of the CE experience as well. MSU Mankato is like many other universities that recruit most of their first-year and often first-generation students locally and regionally, and the recruitment opportunities created by CE partnerships should not be underestimated.

Two Cases

MSU Mankato formed two of its initial CE partnerships with two small rural high schools, LeSueur-Henderson (LSH) and United

South Central (USC). For Kevin Enerson, principal at LSH, the chief motivation to enter the partnership was offering expanded and rigorous academic options for students without requiring them to travel to a college campus. For Cindy Pope and Jane Kepple Johnson, English teachers at LSH and USC, respectively, the leading motivation was to assist students in making the transition from high school to college. Pat Lipetzky and Randall McClure, administrators at MSU Mankato, wanted to encourage high school students to see themselves as future college students by experiencing and succeeding in a college course in high school; they also wanted to work with high school teachers to develop a rigorous curriculum. The strong mutual commitment of all the actors in this partnership helped us meet the challenge of ensuring quality and rigor while working within the state university system and with local policy.

Although LeSueur-Henderson is a small two-city school district about an hour south of the Minneapolis–St. Paul metropolitan area, LSH retains its small-town feel. The district is largely an agrarian community with just more than 18 percent of its residents holding a bachelor's degree and more than 47 percent of its residents living on a household income under $50,000 (School Matters, *LSH*). Still, this rural area has its benefits. Currently, LSH students in grades 6–12 are housed in the same building, and teachers get to know students early on in their high school careers, even if it is just at lunch, in the hallways, or at extra- or co-curricular activities. The similarly rural, economically depressed, agrarian community of Wells, Minnesota, more than two hours away from a major metropolitan area, is home to the United South Central (USC) School District. In this district, the high school serves students from several surrounding communities: Bricelyn, Easton, Freeborn, Kiester, Walters, along with Wells—a combined geography encompassing 370 square miles (School Matters, *USC*). The area is clearly economically disadvantaged, with a median household income of $33,060 (the state average is $49,158), a fact that qualifies nearly 46 percent of the district's 829 students to receive free or reduced lunch (Public School Review; School Matters, *USC*).

Both high schools originally ventured into CE in part because of local pressures to offer their dwindling numbers of students the opportunity to earn both college and high school credit. Otherwise, opportunities to earn such credit are few, given the limited course and AP offerings for high-achieving students as well as the schools' locations, which prevent most students from participating in PSEO programs on college and university campuses. Both schools have now offered CE courses with MSU Mankato as their partner for three years. Besides composition, the districts offer CE opportunities in biology, sociology, and psychology through MSU Mankato, with opportunities in math and speech communication now in the planning stages. In these two districts 38 percent of the students have taken more than one concurrent class ("MSU"), yet CE has resulted in larger benefits for students, the district, the community, and the university.

Benefits for Students in Rural Schools

Students cite various reasons for choosing to take the composition course through CE. Of the students recently enrolled in USC's CE course in composition, 97 percent reported on an exit survey that they took the course to earn college credit while still in high school. Given the depressed economy of the area, this response makes sense, especially since the participating school districts pay tuition and book costs for students in CE courses. The credits students earn from successfully completing college courses such as first-year composition while still in high school allow many to bypass the typical general education requirements at their future colleges, a fact that not only allows them to save tuition dollars but may also set them on the path to completing a college degree in less time ("MSU"). While some students like the thought of saving time and money by completing some college work in high school, others appreciate the challenge of higher academic standards. Thirteen percent of those currently enrolled in the CE composition courses at USC and LSH indicated they enrolled because they wanted the "challenge of college course work." Though the high school's curriculum meets state standards, these standards are not geared toward high-achieving students, those who are ready for a more demanding curriculum.

Benefits can be of a more personal nature as well. At both LSH and USC, students are not just numbers or names on rosters, as bonds are formed early between students and teachers in these rural schools. When students sign up for their junior- or senior-level high school classes, they already have strong relationships with their teachers. Imagine the connection and the comfort level a junior-level student, a student typically sixteen- or seventeen-years-old, feels when he or she realizes the first college course taken through CE will be taught by a familiar instructor. In fact, we believe that teachers who are familiar and trusted may be more able to help rural students in the depressed agrarian economies of Minnesota see themselves as college material. Because learning is an affective as well as a cognitive process, first-generation students who are cognitively ready for college-level learning may benefit from the boost provided by a teacher who knows them and cares about them enough to encourage them to step out of their comfort zone, persevere, and imagine themselves as capable of achieving more than the generations preceding them. We don't view this as coddling or lowering the achievement bar for students; rather, it provides them the comfort, security, and motivation they often need to leave rural Minnesota and pursue a college education.

Perhaps the greatest benefit of CE to rural students is a smoother transition to college and greater success once they are on campus. Without CE, many of these students would be unwilling or financially or logistically unable to attempt to earn college credits for which they are academically prepared, and many would not have the clear starting point for matriculation into college that CE provides for them. In fact, Nathan, Accomando, and Fitzpatrick report in a statewide study of all postsecondary options that 97 percent of students were either "satisfied" or "very satisfied" with their experience (3). This statistic reflects students enrolled in several postsecondary options including CE. Monica Martinez and Shayna Klopott find that students with credits earned through some form of postsecondary option who matriculate at colleges and universities earn more credits and have a higher grade point average and graduation rates than do students without such credits (29); however, these findings might be due more to the type of student enrolling in postsecondary options than to the options themselves. Given the short length of our CE partnerships, our local data on student satisfaction and persistence to college graduation do not yet provide an adequate sample size for us to report findings with confidence. But our anecdotal data supports our impression that when students understand and experience the greater rigor of college-level as opposed to college-preparatory courses, as they do through CE, it only benefits them in their transition to life as part- or full-time college students.

Finally, CE students receive a very high level of support. In our model, participating high school teachers and university faculty mentors are selected based on their interest in CE and their expertise in the subject matter. School visits from mentoring faculty members and inservice opportunities on the university campus ensure high school teachers' engagement with their mentors and solidify their partnerships with both the university's academic departments and the university itself. Students are also closely monitored so that difficulties can be identified early and, when needed, appropriate university resources are made available. This level of support, some may argue, is actually a negative because students, when fully matriculated, may not receive such close attention. Our response is that resources for success are available to all university students, but CE students who need help are more readily identified because their high school teachers are more engaged with the students as well as the university. Therefore, we argue that the support teachers and students gain from CE is just another feature that makes it the superior postsecondary option for students in rural districts.

Benefits to Rural Schools and Teachers

CE partnerships benefit rural school districts as well as their students. As mentioned previously, out-of-the-district enrollment that is common in most PSEO programs carries a hefty price tag, not just for individual high schools but also for their entire communities, particularly in rural areas. To counteract the potential loss of revenue, school districts that partner in CE initiatives typically offer courses to their students for nominal fees. These districts understand that having students remain in their classrooms translates into education dollars remaining in their communities, and the financial implications certainly have played a role in the decision of some school districts in rural areas of Minnesota to pursue CE partnerships.

CE helps rural school districts by offering a higher caliber of instruction and a richer and more coherent curriculum that, in turn, helps maintain student enrollment. In Minnesota, students are allowed to enroll in schools outside of their districts of residence through open enrollment, so most rural school districts in Minnesota need to offer as many courses as they can in order to remain competitive, even for their own students. In fact, some districts enroll more students who live outside their districts than students who live in them, and the districts with fewer course offerings often lose students to those whose courses include more enrichment and rigor. Though only 13.8 percent of the USC district's residents have earned a bachelor's degree (School Matters, *USC*), many residents still want challenging, rigorous opportunities for their children. Therefore, students in rural districts like USC and LSH are often encouraged to take advantage of open enrollment to pursue course work not available in their own districts. In such cases, not only are public funding dollars lost, but the reputations of the home district's schools are also seriously affected. Add in the dwindling student populations in most rural areas, and open enrollment only compounds the PSEO problem for rural school districts. Offering CE courses revitalizes rural school districts with slender curricula by providing more course options and more rigorous course work within their existing budgets. The Minnesota State Legislature has recently boosted this revitalization effort by providing school districts with $150 for every student enrolled in a CE course. In addition to these financial rewards, students who are academically talented remain in the school district, frequently serving as role models and school leaders for their peers and lending to the integrity of their schools.

Professional development is another benefit of CE partnerships. As discussed earlier, the professional link between USC and LSH teachers and MSU Mankato faculty is a step toward bridging the expectation or achievement gap between high school and college by alleviating both postsecondary instructors' frustration at the number of underprepared students and high school teachers' confusion as to what colleges and universities expect. In our partnership, professional development seminars for CE instructors, mentors, advisors, and administrators are regularly offered. For participating high school teachers, these seminars

provide opportunities to learn about current theories and pedagogies from their university colleagues, to network with them, and,
in many ways, to better understand their expectations. Not only
does CE enable a level of conversation well beyond that typical
between university faculty and high school teachers, but it also
promotes development well beyond that commonly associated
with the continuing education units that high school teachers are
required to complete in order to maintain certification. Take, for
example, the following passage Cindy (now a faculty member at
a local technical college) wrote in reflecting on her role as a high
school teacher:

> Frequent feedback from university English professors assures
> me that my methodology and content are at a caliber level.
> I'm pleased to offer rigor to high-achieving students who seek
> more than mediocre achievement. I'm also satisfied to show
> my community that our high school administration's vision is
> progressive and able to serve its youth well. Lastly, to teach
> concurrent enrollment courses ensures my professional develop-
> ment will not diminish. I, and all other concurrent enrollment
> teachers, will undoubtedly take more classes to keep current
> on issues and to learn more specialized content. We will seek
> continuing workshops often times implemented by our univer-
> sity partners, and we will grow into more than we thought we
> could be for our students.

The benefits Cindy mentions are only magnified when one considers this teacher's life without CE. If she were in a district with
only a PSEO option, then she would likely lose her high-achieving
students to the university and would perhaps be less motivated
professionally. If she were in a district without any postsecondary
opportunities, she again would likely be minimally motivated in
terms of her professional development as many of her students
would leave via open enrollment. Only CE partnerships in many
rural school districts make it possible for both teachers and
students to actively pursue their fullest development. Otherwise,
both are often limited by the similarly limited curricula common
in rural districts. Cindy's participation as a CE instructor and as
a member of the university faculty at MSU Mankato has clearly
inspired her.

The CE arrangement benefits students and teachers, and by doing so, these rural south-central Minnesota communities. How satisfying it would be for all involved if every student were able to say, "my concurrent English course improved the level of my writing and helped me gain confidence so that I could compete with other students in a collegiate setting" (Mueller). In comments such as this, we learn that students involved in CE not only start to complete college requirements but also benefit from the college-level course work itself. Providing this concurrent "leg up" benefits the students academically, the districts economically, the teachers professionally, and the universities demographically. It is no wonder that 82 percent of Minnesotans support postsecondary options for high school students, 86 percent of students enrolled in some form of postsecondary option would participate again (Nathan, Accomando, and Fitzpatrick 3), and 100 percent of our CE first-year composition students felt their districts should continue to offer such courses ("MSU").

Conclusion

Concurrent enrollment is a marvelous idea, a boon for rural universities and school districts. More important, CE significantly benefits teachers and students, perhaps more poignantly in rural areas. In CE partnerships, teachers are challenged to develop professionally, and students realize the challenges of college course work with familiar faces and in comfortable settings, where they can begin to see themselves as capable of succeeding in college. Sure, CE does not reflect all the challenges of attending college as full-time students. As we have designed and implemented it, however, CE exposes high school students to the rigor and relevance of higher learning, and this exposure is critical to the recruitment, retention, and success of students, particularly in rural areas. It is our experience that no student leaves a CE class without something gained. It gives students a chance to see what they are really capable of and to assure them of what a college course entails. It provides a glimpse of one possible future. In rural areas bound to depressed agrarian economies, this glimpse is critical. We assert that CE is an important part of the vision of our collective educational future. Now if it could only solve homesickness when students leave home for dorms, we would have the answers for everything.

Works Cited

Conley, David T. *College Knowledge: What It Really Takes for Students to Succeed and What We Can Do to Get Them Ready.* San Francisco: Jossey-Bass, 2005. Print.

Martinez, Monica, and Shayna Klopott. *The Link between High School Reform and College Access and Success for Low-Income and Minority Youth.* Washington: American Youth Policy Forum and Pathways to College Network, 2005. Web. 27 July 2007.

Minnesota Department of Education. *United South Central.* 2006. Web. 20 Oct. 2006.

Minnesota Postsecondary Enrollment Options Act. Stat. 124D.09. 2008 (revised). Web. 27 July 2007.

Minnesota State Colleges and Universities. "Board Policies." Minnesota State Colleges and Universities. 2009. Web. 5 Nov. 2009.

"MSU English Concurrent Enrollment Student Evaluation." Unpublished survey, 2007.

Mueller, Kerri. Message to Jane Kepple Johnson. 20 May 2007. Email.

Nathan, Joe, Laura Accomando, and Debra Hale Fitzpatrick. *Stretching Minds and Resources: 20 Years of Post Secondary Enrollment Options in Minnesota.* Minneapolis: University of Minnesota, Hubert H. Humphrey Institute of Public Affairs, Center for School Change, 2005. Web. 22 July 2007.

Pawlenty, Tim. Foreword. *Governor's Budget Agenda: Education Budget Released for FY 2008–2009.* Minnesota Department of Education, 2007. Web. 27 July 2007.

———. "World-Class Students: From Nation Leading to World Competing." *Governor's Apr. 2007 Agenda,* 2007. Web. 20 May 2007.

Public School Review. *United South Central High School.* Public School Review, 2009. Web. 9 Feb. 2009.

School Matters. *LeSueur-Henderson Middle/High School*. School Matters, 2008. Web. 9 Feb. 2009.

―――. *United South Central Senior High School*. School Matters, 2008. Web. 9 Feb. 2009.

Spellings, Margaret. *A Test of Leadership: Charting the Future of U.S. Higher Education*. Washington: U.S. Department of Education, 2006. Web. 27 July 2007.

Chapter Nine

Contesting the Territoriality of "Freshman English": The Political Ecology of Dual Enrollment

Miles McCrimmon

J. Sargeant Reynolds Community College

Part One: Mapping the Territory

Dual enrollment, the practice of using the twelfth grade as a site for introductory college-level course work, has developed into a widespread cultural phenomenon, reaching more than a million high school students annually. Immensely popular politically, it's here to stay, with local, state, and national pressure being placed on colleges and high schools to offer it up in greater volume and variety. It tends to operate at the margins of secondary and postsecondary education, with 74 percent of students taking dual-enrollment courses on-site at area high schools, taught either by part-time college faculty only loosely affiliated with either educational institution or by high school faculty with at most a nominal relationship with the college granting credit. Factors such as geographical proximity and affinities in educational mission have traditionally led community colleges to be natural partners with high schools, with 77 percent of dual-enrolled students receiving two-year college credit.[1] While skeptics of the practice can be forgiven for wondering who's minding the store, recent substantive calls for better oversight, communication, accreditation, and peer review across educational cultures should give them reason to take another look. As a community college professor who's been involved with dual enrollment, teaching twenty-one sections at three different high schools over the last fourteen years and managing the program for my department for five of those years, I have come to believe in its unique potential to challenge some of the persistent binaries that shape the daily work of our profession—between secondary and postsecondary institutions, between two-year and four-year colleges, and even between commerce and pedagogy.

Opinions about the legitimacy of offering college-level composition to high school seniors often pivot around the definition of "Freshman English," a commodity that has been undergoing a significant identity crisis for some time now. I use the now-antiquated phrase in my title because I want to foreground how thoroughly problematic both its adjective ("Freshman") and its noun ("English") have become. Dual enrollment, like other credit-bearing alternatives (AP, CLEP, IB, experiential learning credit), demonstrates in massive numbers that a significant percentage of the work of introductory composition is no longer a "Freshman" (or first-year) enterprise. We know too that "English" is hardly a sufficient container for the variety of fields and channels being used in introductory composition courses, regardless of when or how they are taught. Even "College Composition" is proving to be a slippery phrase, as Kathleen Blake Yancey points out: "college—if defined by its students and the places it delivers instruction—is no longer a specific place, if indeed it ever was. Rather, college occurs in multiple sites—physical and virtual, informal and formal, official and just in time—that are defined explicitly or function de facto as collegiate" (4). And yet, in the minds of the legislators and administrators who champion dual enrollment, and just as much in the minds of faculty who are often its fiercest critics, these phrases—"Freshman English" and "College Composition"—function as powerful cultural texts that still evoke largely unchanged connotations.

And what are those associations we still carry with us, even if we have moved beyond these old-fashioned phrases? It's a question admirably asked and variously answered in the 2006 NCTE collection edited by Patrick Sullivan and Howard Tinberg, *What Is "College-Level" Writing?* Sullivan's opening attempt at definition in his introduction (17) serves as an editorial gambit, a challenge to contributors to challenge and deepen the list. For all the noble efforts that follow, it's the contrarians of the collection (Jeanne

Gunner, Edward M. White, and Sheridan Blau) I find most useful as I think about the daily practices of dual enrollment. White
wonders, "Why is this question so hard to answer, so hard to
deal with?" (244). Viewing the question rhetorically, he makes
the point that "the term *college-level writing* is meaningless in
itself, ignoring as it does the enormous variety of institutions,
rhetorical situations, levels of education, and fields of study of
college students" (266).

After applying his dry wit to a review of two wildly divergent
attempts in California to define the concept two decades apart,
the first (*Statement of Competencies* in 1982) quite narrow, the
other (*Academic Literacy* in 2002) extraordinarily ambitious,
Blau finally calls it "a discipline of mind that makes writing
the most effective tool for discovering and clarifying thought
and thereby the principal instrument for intellectual discourse"
(375). Blau readily admits that in most high schools "education
is focused largely on training students to standards of behavior
and academic performance that are determined less by a tran-
scendent commitment to liberating and refining thought than by a
parochially defined and politically expedient interest in transmitting a given ideology and sustaining whatever happens to be the
dominant bureaucracy of power" (375). But he also reminds us
that "colleges do not own and are not the only sites for cultivating intellectual discourse" (374). His work for many years with
the National Writing Project has demonstrated to him that K–12
teachers, working in concert with postsecondary practitioners,
can form "the kind of intellectual communities that colleges and
universities themselves have always claimed to be . . . but in their
modern corporate and bureaucratized incarnations have often
failed to become" (374).

Gunner's contribution, "The Boxing Effect (An Anti-Essay),"
like Blau's, illustrates how powerful ideological, cultural, and
economic forces encourage us to emphasize our differences. While
she does not explicitly mention dual enrollment, Gunner's thesis
could be placed into service as either a critique or a defense of
the practice. On one level, as critique of the "container model"
of education, in which "teaching becomes a matter of boxing,
bundling, and otherwise delivering learning packages through a
writing process that standardizes all products" (113), it speaks

to the most reductive and dangerous impulses behind dual enrollment (as a method of "taking care of" or "outsourcing" first-year requirements as cheaply and as antiseptically as possible, preferably off-site). But if we take up her challenge to think about "college writing" more creatively, as something other than "a formulation that reifies a system of nonporous institutional boundaries" (111), we can begin to resist its "commodification" (119) and in the process build a more compelling defense of dual enrollment as a way to subvert what she calls the "linear notion of relationship: two-year school education precedes university education, a temporal frame that discourages serious attention to what happens in the two-year school, just as has been the pattern of relations between secondary schools and colleges" (117). If dual enrollment is already causing the borders between educational territories to become blurred and porous, secondary and postsecondary institutions would do well to consider how to take advantage of this liminal space and jointly inhabit it.

Part Two: Surveying the Stakeholders

In my community college's English department, eight of our eighteen full-time faculty members have taught dual enrollment as part of their regular five-course-per-semester workload at some point in their careers. In a given term, one to three full-timers are joined by five to seven part-timers and five to seven high school teachers to offer fifteen to eighteen sections of dual-enrollment English classes on-site at eight to ten area high schools. And yet, despite the relatively high profile of dual-enrollment at my college and the significant level of full-time faculty involvement in it, I dare say that most of my colleagues would be surprised to learn that dual-enrolled high school seniors (more than 2,300 students) make up nearly one-seventh of our student body.[2] I get the distinct impression that many of my colleagues don't really think of the members of this population as being integral to our educational mission, especially because so many of these students seem to be on their way to a four-year college. And yet, how different are they, really, from those masses of students from four-year colleges who take our courses in the summer when they are home with their family or, for that matter, from those masses of other students who matriculate with us for one or two semesters before moving on? Some of my colleagues seem troubled by the prospect of expanding our discipline's territorial claim into high schools. They argue that college writing is situated and context-based, but they often seem decidedly less bothered by its application to other alternative situations and delivery systems. The only demographic enrollment increase from 1999 to 2004 in my state's community college system more dramatic than that in dual enrollment (+81%) was in distance education (+105%). However, remarkably to my mind, faculty members by and large resist expanding these distance education offerings far less than they resist the expansion of our dual-enrollment program.

What is it about setting foot in a high school that gives so many of my colleagues in postsecondary education pause? Why and how do they think of this population differently? How might they regard the shared space where college and high school overlap? Who is best qualified to inhabit this space? Curious to study further how stakeholders from different academic cultures view these questions, I asked thirty-six colleagues (twenty-four employed by my college, twelve employed by the county school district where we have delivered the most instruction in dual-enrollment English) to respond by email to the following survey about dual enrollment:

1. On a scale of 1 to 10 (1 being not well, 10 being very well), how well do you think the cultures of high school and college fit together through dual enrollment? Feel free to explain your response.

2. What do you see as the biggest obstacles to understanding across the two educational cultures?

3. What remedies or solutions can you suggest to bring the two cultures together?

4. Considering the question generically, from most to least desirable (1 to 3), rank the following three types of instructors for teaching dual enrollment on-site at a high school:

   Full-Time College Faculty (FTC)   _____

   Part-Time College Faculty (PTC)   _____

   High School Faculty (HS)   _____

5. Explain the rationale for your ranking.

I received twenty responses, seven from the high school district (from an assistant superintendent, two principals, a counselor, and three experienced teachers), and thirteen from my college (from higher-level administration through middle management to full-time and part-time English faculty).[3] College respondents gave the cultural fit (Question 1) an average rating of 5.5, while high school respondents were a bit more sanguine (7.3). Both populations shared a number of the same assessments of the obstacles to cross-cultural understanding (Question 2): poor mechanisms for communication and few opportunities for meaningful collaboration were most commonly cited. High school students themselves were characterized by both populations as obstacles. One principal put the issue diplomatically—"high school students are still learning to balance freedom and responsibility"—while a college faculty member labeled the syndrome more bluntly as "senioritis." The greater level of parental involvement in high school students' lives was also cited as a problem to establishing a collegiate atmosphere. Skepticism emerged slightly more often from respondents in the trenches actively engaged in delivering or closely supervising the instruction (administrators rated the cultural fit as a 6.7, while faculty and counselors rated it at 5.9).

Because we employ a mix of three distinct teaching populations to teach dual enrollment on-site at area high schools, I was especially interested in the answers to Question 4, which asked respondents to rank teachers of dual enrollment from most to least desirable. The three teaching populations received the average rankings shown in Table 9.1:

TABLE 9.1. Respondents' Ranking of Three Types of Instructors for Teaching Dual Enrollment On-site at a High School

Teaching Population	Average	First-Place Votes	Second-Place Votes	Third-Place Votes
Full-Time College	1.75	10.5	3	5.5
High School	2.05	7	5	7.5
Part-Time College	2.20	2.5	10	7

Note: N=20

The slight majority of respondents (10.5 of 20) expressing a preference for a full-time college faculty member was made up of eight faculty, two high school counselors, and our college's dual-enrollment coordinator. On the other hand, the seven first-place votes for using high school teachers were cast by a "super group" of the seven highest-ranking administrators among the survey respondents: the top four from my college and the top three from the high school district. This pattern would seem to suggest that the closer respondents are to the daily management of the dual-enrollment classroom, regardless of their institutional affiliation, the more likely they are to express a preference for putting a representative of the college in it.

I hadn't expected that four of seven part-time college faculty respondents would rank full-time college faculty above their own constituency, but as one said, "given my argument above about full-time faculty and continuity, I have no choice but to rank full-time faculty highest, even if it means less stability for us part-timers." Another gave a more pragmatic rationale for avoiding over-reliance on her own constituency of part-timers: "I am not aware that any extra compensation is given for travel time and gasoline costs, which have become more of a consideration as gas prices rise." A third part-timer gave a slight nod to full-timers on the basis of "Teaching quality" and "tighter control of students" while granting that part-timers carried "economic benefits" to "both schools."

The counselors both pointed to the benefits of having a full-time college presence on the high school campus in order to "instill that college mentality" and to support the "parental perception . . . that the college staff is 'giving them what they pay for.'" The college coordinator gave the most pointed rationale for ranking high school faculty last: "they are 'caught in the middle.' There is a challenge in verifying that they are adhering to all college standards, with respect to course instruction and classroom policies."

Nor had I expected that all three high school teachers surveyed would rank full-time college faculty above their own constituency. Their reasoning varied. One made the distinction as follows: "A full time instructor knows more about the typical community college student; the high school faculty knows the specific dynamics within the high school." A colleague at the same high school made a similar but not identical distinction: "I think that the full-time college faculty are better prepared to give the students a realistic view of the classes. Their expectations are usually higher, and the students get a wonderful introduction to college." However, this respondent went on to add that "high school faculty members . . . probably have a better view of the students themselves." A third high school teacher argued in a similar vein that while "high school teachers are more in tune with the high school students and can provide a better transition," full-time college faculty "have more autonomy, and I do feel that would be better for the students." Interestingly, all three made distinctions in their rankings or comments, or both, between full-time and part-time college faculty, preferring the more stable collegial relationships made possible by working alongside a consistent representative of the college.[4]

The justifications from the "super group" of higher-level administrators for putting dual enrollment in the hands of high school teachers were laced with caveats about "ensuring college-level instruction, culture, and standards" through a robust program of professional development and orientation for the high school faculty engaged in teaching on behalf of the college and the program. One high school administrator moved from a "logistical" argument about the convenience of "schedules, calendars, discipline issues, etc." to a more ambitious point: high school teachers, she said, "have the potential for becoming genuine advocates of dual enrollment as a valuable option for high school students" and thus "may have tremendous impact on individual students in their goal setting and career planning." These seven administrators were roughly split about their second choice (full-time or part-time college faculty), with three preferring full-timers for ease of staffing and level of college continuity and commitment, and the other four attracted to the cost-savings of using part-timers; but all seven preferred high school teachers over either type of college faculty for ease of delivery of instruction:

- ◆ Principal: "High school people better understand the psyche of the 18-year-old while in high school."

- ◆ Dean: "High school faculty understand this type of student better."

◆ Assistant dean: "They best know their students, their capabilities, and their limits."

Overall, rankings in Question 4 and the subsequent rationales in Question 5 were shaped by the nature of respondents' primary investment in the program, usually expressible as a matter of convenience (ease of staffing, scheduling flexibility, volume of offerings, or cost effectiveness) or control (ease of supervision, assessment and assurance of quality, reputation, or responsiveness).

Over the years, our college's dual-enrollment coordinator and various academic program heads have developed practices (including professional development activities such as faculty mentoring, syllabus and document review, calibration sessions, workshops on pedagogy) to make it more likely that that this cadre of teachers offers an educational experience to twelfth-graders that is the equivalent to what they would receive if they were matriculating on our college campuses. But while we have these systems in place, the "warts and all" responses from those in the trenches show that we would be remiss in painting too rosy a picture of how we're doing. Make no mistake—dual enrollment, when properly managed, is an exceptionally difficult way to deliver education. Are its rewards worth the cost in time, effort, and resources? Most of the respondents to this survey seemed to think so. What's more, this modest effort at research ended up affecting those surveyed. After I shared the results with respondents, our subsequent cross-cultural conversations, both formal and informal, have been more honest, richer, and deeper, suggesting that administering a survey like this one annually to all stakeholders would be in order.

Part Three: Resolving the "Pollyanna versus Doomsday" Binary

While my "convenience sample" was made up mostly of champions of dual enrollment, the loaded questions in my survey probably reinforced and exaggerated clear-cut distinctions about educational cultures and identities. The nuanced cultural divides in my small sample hint at a much more dramatic chasm in general public opinion about the prospect and desirability of building bridges between secondary and postsecondary education. The most adamant critics of dual enrollment and other early college options, regardless of their institutional affiliation or professional status, generally tend to be the most insistent about the importance of preserving boundaries between educational cultures. Their skepticism, which sometimes slips into doomsday cynicism, is a direct reaction to the Pollyanna discourse used by promoters of cross-institutional partnerships—governors, legislators, chancellors, superintendents—who are politically invested in their success and growth, but not directly involved in their daily operations. Turned off by such Pollyanna rhetoric surrounding the program, many potential faculty participants might blind themselves to its possibilities out of a well-meaning, but finally counterproductive, stance of resistance. The National Alliance of Concurrent Enrollment Partnerships (NACEP), an important advocacy organization, clearinghouse of resources, and accrediting body founded by colleges and universities, is beginning to play a key role in articulating national standards in an effort to weed out less scrupulous forms of dual enrollment. By setting and insisting on these rigorous standards, NACEP holds the potential to act as a hedge against both overly idealistic and pessimistic claims.

I'm tempted to associate some of the criticisms of dual enrollment with other misgivings harbored in the higher educational elite that Phyllis Van Slyck has identified:

> Resistance to the scholarship of teaching, to learning communities, and to the voices of community college faculty members comes down to the same thing: it is all about professional and intellectual status. Those opposed to learning communities claim that these structures are a way of dumbing down the curriculum and turning a college or university into a high school just as those opposed to rewarding the scholarship of teaching claim that it does not require the same level of rigor as academic scholarship in one's field of expertise. (173–74)

But resistance to dual enrollment doesn't come only from the elite. Brian Huot, in the context of an otherwise sensible and scathing critique of No Child Left Behind and the Spellings Commission Report, takes what seems to me to be a gratuitous swipe at dual enrollment, in lumping it together with Advanced Placement and arguing that such "early college options . . . only widen the gap between poorer students and those from more affluent communities and better-supported schools" (515). I'm hard-pressed to imagine how the presence of dual enrollment in a public high school is not patently an opportunity for college exposure that might not otherwise exist for significant segments of the population. In fact, statistics coming out of Texas, Florida, and New York indicate that college success, persistence, and completion rates are positively affected by exposure to dual enrollment. In a study that followed a cohort of students who took dual enrollment in 2000, "32 percent of Hispanics who took dual credit graduated with baccalaureate degrees versus 11 percent who did not take dual credit in high school" (*Study on Dual Credit* 9). Among the general population, the completion rate comparison was 43 percent versus 19 percent.[5]

Huot goes on to lament that "the quality and value of these early college programs are uneven and dependent upon a further emphasis on proper and realistic alignment between high school and college" (515). But one of the very objects of his critique here—dual enrollment—may hold the key to reform. Improving and refining dual-enrollment partnerships—rather than abandoning them—will surely take us further toward "proper and realistic alignment." Writing in a more general context, Kathleen McCormick suggests in the appendix to *What Is "College-Level" Writing?* that high schools are currently too broken to be taken seriously as equal partners in the cultural project of writing instruction: "If the teaching of writing in most high schools will ever truly become more obviously 'college preparatory,' we would need a thorough overhauling of the material realities of high school English teaching—class size, testing, textbooks, and, of course, a change in how writing is addressed in schools of education" (385). While I share McCormick's skepticism about the likelihood of such an overhaul, I would encourage her to explore how dual enrollment—in which college textbooks and curriculum are required, standardized testing is often waived, and class sizes are frequently smaller—might assist in this endeavor.

To probe our understanding of dual enrollment further, to work toward tailoring a possible pedagogy for it, and to help to forge a resolution of the Pollyanna versus doomsday binary, I want to borrow from the disciplines of cultural geography and political ecology, specifically the concept of "territory" (a defined, owned area) versus "territoriality" (the status, occupation, and defense of a territory). If, in the "deeply ingrained notion of hierarchy in education" Gunner describes, "[e]ach institutional faculty is boxed into its own institutional container"(118), I wonder how it serves the purpose of those of us who teach introductory composition, especially in community colleges, to defend our own territory too fiercely, when that territory is already being contested in both directions (from secondary schools through dual enrollment and from senior institutions through an interdisciplinary emphasis on the "first-year experience"). Rather than defending what little territory we call our own, shouldn't we be expanding our notions of territoriality?

If my strategy here sounds a bit too martial and imperialistic, let me temper it to avoid making the same kinds of essentializing gestures toward high school made so frequently by senior institutions toward community colleges. When those of us in postsecondary education succumb to the temptation of turning "high school" into a static cultural text, we close off the potential to create a fruitful bicultural ecology, such as that laid out by Lawrence Buell in *The Environmental Imagination*. In this canonical text of ecocriticism, Buell describes how humans are locked into a crippling and alienated orientation toward the natural world, because they view "the nonhuman environment . . . merely as a framing device," they fail to see that "human history is implicated in natural history," and they believe that their interest in the environment is the only one that matters. Buell suggests that until humans view the "environment as a process, rather than as a constant or a given," they will be unable to develop an "accountability" or "ethical orientation" toward texts about it (7–8). Analogously, I argue that postsecondary teachers, in viewing "high school" as a "constant or a given" and assuming that our interest in what goes on there is the only legitimate one, fail to take an ethical orientation to the dual-enrollment partnership.

In a similar vein, David Mazel has pointed out that the word "environment" is a noun formation of the earlier, now nearly archaic verb "environ": "thanks to a nominalizing process that effaces both act and actor, we no longer speak of what *environs* us, but of what our environment *is*" (138–39; his emphases). Our own postsecondary biases conspire with mainstream culture to make us think of the "high school environment" as a noun, rather than a verb. But the history of higher education—even more so, its future—is "implicated" in the history our high school graduates bring with them. What goes on in high schools "environs" those of us in higher education, whether we like to admit it or not. High school culture, intractable and insoluble though it may seem to us, is not static; its assumptions about education are not constant. (For one thing, it seems likely that *without* the involvement of postsecondary institutions, high schools will become even more reductive and standardized.) To throw up our hands in despair at what's going on in the high schools and divest ourselves of the opportunity to collaborate in a way that advances our mutual interest not only is foolishly petulant but also shows a lack of "accountability to the environment" with which we are all implicated.

Part Four: Toward a Hybrid Species of Dual-Enrollment Instructor

Those who prosper teaching dual enrollment manage to transform their comfortable notions of territory and professional identity into more complicated, productive, and provocative realms of territoriality and bicultural identification. They develop a liminal conception of territoriality that opens more pedagogical avenues to them. Like a hybrid species, they must learn to adapt to the new environment in order to survive and ultimately thrive in it. High school dual-enrollment teachers can be particularly adept at this technique. Their work lives have already forced them to adopt a more natural understanding of the fluidity of territory and territoriality, interrupted as they are constantly by one stakeholder or another over the course of their day. When assigned to teach dual enrollment, they are often more positively focused on the possibilities of carving out pedagogical differences between the approach they take to this class versus the rest of their workload (where they are much more likely to be under the thumb of state and national standards), though they are often less well attuned to the subtle impact of the supervising college's territorial claims on their work.

As the primary brokers for dual enrollment, we who teach community college English could use our role in the process much more opportunistically. Because, as Howard Tinberg puts it in his introduction to his book *Border Talk*, we "live on the borders" and "work in the space between the schools and the universities" (x), we are in a special position to use dual enrollment to help shape the future of first-year composition and, ultimately, to transform our place in the postsecondary landscape. One of the hoariest clichés in education is that college faculty are content experts who aren't really trained to teach, while high school faculty are master teachers with limited content expertise. Community college teachers' own pedagogical practices tend to muddy this stereotype; due to the nature of our students, by necessity we find ways to wed content expertise with a heightened sensitivity to what works in the classroom. What's more, the binary distinction between content and pedagogy is further blurred in composition, perhaps more than in other disciplines. So a community college composition teacher could also be said to be especially primed for the liminality required in dual-enrollment teaching.

That said, we need to take great care in how we dispatch college faculty to high school sites, since they are much more likely to focus (and even fixate) on the blatant environmental differences between this alien territory and their own workplace, often at the expense of appreciating and leveraging cultural differences between the two populations. Their usual starting point, voiced by dozens of college faculty I've advised, supervised, and dispatched over the years, is the idea that "This will be a college course implanted in a high school," as if a sacrosanct collegiate territory, a closely guarded and defined occupation, a Coalition Provisional Authority (one pictures L. Paul Bremer showing up in combat boots) will be established, fifty minutes a day, three days a week, in room 211 at the local high school. Students (and, to some extent, their parents) respond quite differently to the two types of teachers. After all, it's their territory that's being occupied, if only for 150 minutes a week. As a rule, they likely overestimate the difference between college and high school pedagogy when taught by college faculty, while they underestimate the difference when taught by one of their own.

Instead of reducing our understanding of the dual-enrollment curriculum to the few things that the cultures of twelfth-grade English and first-year college composition might have in common (using a discourse of deficit surrounding terms like "articulation," "agreement," and "alignment"), I'd like to pose the question differently, asking how we might we take full advantage of the merging of contexts to expand the reach of composition, thus putting ourselves in a position to draw from the best practices and features of both settings. Fundamentally, I am arguing against the common perception that dual enrollment must be seen as a form of "outsourcing," by questioning the increasingly contested territoriality of the now thoroughly decentered notions of the "twelfth-grade year" and "the first-year experience." When the enterprise is really conducted dually, who is really outsourcing what to whom?

By dodging the tempting lurch into doomsday rhetoric, I am calling for the creation of a more positive and reciprocal pedagogy of surplus tempered by careful negotiation between the two cultures. What if college-level writing truly extended its territoriality into high school? What if we truly claimed dual-enrolled students (and their high school–based teachers) as our own? What if high school teachers involved in dual enrollment truly leveraged their "affinity" with college-level pedagogy? While the high school setting is more "nurturing," the content doesn't have to be "safe." Here, then, are some practical, pedagogical suggestions about what could happen if we traded on the hybrid qualities of dual enrollment:

- ◆ Teachers and students alike could take full advantage of the unique context of the high school setting, rather than pretending they're not squarely where they are. High school, after all, is a prime location for examining how social construction works; a "short-timer" senior with one foot out the door and an instructor who is "neither fish nor fowl" are the perfect hybrids to conduct such an examination, at a postsecondary level of sophistication.

- ◆ Students could be assigned prospective and reflective essays on college, workplace, and family dynamics, leveraging (rather than ignoring) their heightened anxiety about all three subjects in hopes that they will glean unusual and useful insights.

◆ The phenomenon of "senioritis" (currently seen as a bane and impediment) could be interrogated and explored, placing the burden of proof on high school seniors to show why they're "too cool for school." Further, seniors could be invited to argue for and demonstrate their maturity, relative to their older friends and siblings matriculating in the ostensibly more responsible collegiate environment.

◆ Because dual enrollment often draws roughly equally from "advanced" and "standard" English student populations, not only is it one of the few opportunities late in the high school experience for both populations to be sharing the same classroom, but it also presents an excellent platform for student-initiated reflection about the assumptions and implications of tracking in K–12 education.

◆ Under the protection of the mandate of college equivalency, dual-enrollment instructors, regardless of their institutional affiliation, could explore readings, writing assignments, and assessments that eschew the cultural regimentation and infantilization of the adolescent experience.

◆ Writing program administrators at four-year colleges and universities could engage in triangular partnerships with community colleges and area high schools, providing graduate teaching assistants (GTAs) with opportunities to teach dual enrollment as part of their assignment.

◆ Community college faculty could partner with high school faculty in disciplines other than English to design linked courses and learning communities, taking advantage of much more stable and predictable class rolls. (Pairing a teacher of twelfth-grade U.S. government, a course usually mandated for high school seniors, with a college English faculty member is a particularly promising way to deliver twelve credits of college course work over two semesters and to cement lasting cross-curricular and cross-institutional partnerships).

◆ High school dual-enrollment faculty could teach composition on campus at their partner college, either at night or in summer sections. One of the better models for how the two species of teachers can inhabit a shared space is described by Christine Farris, who describes how Indiana University invites high school teachers to take and teach courses on its college campuses, in an effort to break down barriers, cross-fertilize, and collaborate.

- ◆ College faculty teaching dual enrollment could conduct meaningful research about high school writing practices and disseminate the results widely on campus.

- ◆ Assessment projects, including e-portfolios and other measures of exit competencies, could be piloted with the captive audience of high school seniors and later implemented more widely in the college environment.

While the educational landscape is littered with evidence of abuse and malpractice in dual enrollment, the concept of using the twelfth-grade year to engage in college-level writing still holds great promise, when administered effectively and fully incorporated into the respective missions of the institutions dually engaged in offering the course. Dual enrollment is only just beginning to live up to its unique position as a lever of educational reform at both educational levels in both directions. For high schools it has begun to establish itself as a hedge against standardized testing and tracking, as well as an opportunity to reinstate academic rigor in reading and writing in the final grades. Its potential for revolutionizing college education is more subtle, but a few of the ideas above suggest avenues for further exploration. Above all, both populations should use dual enrollment to create a shared territoriality to begin to understand their collective mission and explore the possibilities inherent in this peculiar species of institutional biculturalism.

Notes

1. The most comprehensive nationwide study of dual enrollment to date, from which the statistics in this paragraph are taken, was conducted by the National Center for Educational Statistics in 2002–3.

2. Dual enrollment as a share of total FTE's at my college has risen steadily from 4.8 (in 2000–1) to 9.1 percent in 2005–6, and as a share of total headcount from 7.4 to 13.1 percent.

3. I thank the participants for the candor and insights they provided in their responses.

4. Full disclosure: my own answers on this survey would put me squarely in the majority, ranking full-time college faculty first, high school faculty second, and part-time college faculty third, though the rationales behind my responses might shift depending on my relationship with the program. When I was managing it and actually responsible for finding faculty to teach in the high schools, I felt a wave of gratitude every time a high school provided a qualified teacher of its own.

5. For compelling statistics from Florida and New York, see Melinda Mechur Karp et al., *The Postsecondary Achievement of Participants in Dual Enrollment: An Analysis of Student Outcomes in Two States,* esp. 55–63.

Works Cited

Blau, Sheridan. "College Writing, Academic Literacy, and the Intellectual Community: California Dreams and Cultural Oppositions." Sullivan and Tinberg 358–77.

Buell, Lawrence. *The Environmental Imagination: Thoreau, Nature Writing and the Formation of American Culture.* Cambridge: Belknap-Harvard UP, 1995. Print.

Farris, Christine. "The Space Between: Dual-Credit Programs as Brokering, Community Building, and Professionalization." *Delivering College Composition: The Fifth Canon.* Ed. Kathleen Blake Yancey. Portsmouth: Boynton/Cook, 2006. 104–14. Print.

Gunner, Jeanne. "The Boxing Effect (An Anti-Essay)." Sullivan and Tinberg 110–20.

Huot, Brian. "Consistently Inconsistent: Business and the Spellings Commission Report on Higher Education." *College English* 69.5 (2007): 512–25. Print.

Karp, Melinda Mechur, Juan Carlos Calcagno, Katherine L. Hughes, Dong Wook Jeong, and Thomas Bailey. *The Postsecondary Achievement of Participants in Dual Enrollment: An Analysis of Student Outcomes in Two States.* St. Paul: University of Minnesota, National Research Center for Career and Technical Education, 2007. Print.

Mazel, David. "American Literary Environmentalism as Domestic Orientalism." *The Ecocriticism Reader: Landmarks in Literary Ecology.* Ed. Cheryll Glotfelty and Harold Fromm. Athens: U of Georgia P, 1996. 137–46. Print.

McCormick, Kathleen. "A Response to Peter Kittle, Sheridan Blau, and Milka Mosley." Sullivan and Tinberg 384–85.

National Alliance of Concurrent Enrollment Partnerships. "Benefits of Dual Enrollment." NACEP, n.d. Web. 15 Apr. 2007.

National Center for Educational Statistics. "Survey on Dual Enrollment." NCES, n.d. Web. 17 Apr. 2007.

Study on Dual Credit Programs in Texas: A Report to the 80th Legislature from the Texas P-16 Council. N.p. Jan. 2007. Web. 27 June 2007.

Sullivan, Patrick. "An Essential Question: What Is 'College-Level' Writing?" Sullivan and Tinberg 1–28.

Sullivan, Patrick, and Howard Tinberg, eds. *What Is "College-Level" Writing?* Urbana: NCTE, 2006. Print.

Tinberg, Howard B. *Border Talk: Writing and Knowing in the Two-Year College.* Urbana: NCTE, 1997. Print.

Van Slyck, Phyllis. "Learning Communities and the Future of the Humanities." *Profession 2006.* New York: MLA, 2006. 163–76. Print.

White, Edward M. "Defining by Assessing." Sullivan and Tinberg 243–66.

Yancey, Kathleen Blake, ed. *Delivering College Composition: The Fifth Canon.* Portsmouth: Boynton/Cook, 2006. Print.

Yancey, Kathleen Blake. "Delivering College Composition: A Vocabulary for Discussion." Yancey 1–16.

CHAPTER TEN

Syracuse University Project Advance: A Model of Connection and Quality

Patricia A. Moody and Margaret D. Bonesteel
Syracuse University

First-year composition is a course so common on college campuses that it has become a rite of passage for many first-year college students. Perhaps because first-year writing courses are ubiquitous among collegiate offerings to first-year students and because writing courses are often taught on campuses by the least credentialed of the collegiate faculty hierarchy, composition courses were among the first to be offered when early college credit programs such as dual-enrollment programs first came into being. The rationale behind choosing these courses to offer through precollege programs was that if students took "freshman comp" early, before they arrived on campus, not only would they have three easily transferable credits to jump-start their college careers, but also the courses would teach them writing skills and proficiencies that would allow them to be successful in their other college courses. Since full-time on-campus faculty, busy with teaching their content specialties and with research and publication, didn't have the time such courses demand, the writing courses on campus were often relegated to inexperienced teaching assistants and part-time faculty, leading to (or perhaps the result of) the notion that "anyone can teach writing." Indeed, the thinking was that these courses could as competently be taught by experienced high school teachers as they could be by teaching assistants. Thus "freshman comp" courses were among the first to be offered through early college programs.

As the field of composition itself has changed from the early one-size-fits-all skill model, however, first-year writing has been increasingly seen as a course that is important in its own right, making it more problematic in the precollege setting. In addition, precollege programs, including Advanced Placement (AP) courses, vary considerably in content and quality from school to school and from program to program; thus there is concern among some colleges and universities about the level of rigor and even about the appropriateness and desirability of offering such courses before students matriculate at a college or university. We argue that college courses can be offered successfully in high schools, but only if certain conditions are met, institutionalized, and maintained. Careful teacher selection, regular professional development, the availability of supportive resources, and, above all, close relationships between the instructors teaching in the high school and the collegiate academic departments are among the conditions that are vital for a program that offers truly collegiate courses in the high schools. Here we offer as a model one program that has met these conditions.

Syracuse University Project Advance: History, Scope, and Mission

Syracuse University Project Advance (SUPA) is a concurrent enrollment program that enables high school students to take introductory Syracuse University courses in their high schools as a part of their regular school day. The courses are taught by carefully selected and trained high school teachers as a part of their regular teaching load. The program began in 1972, offering Freshman English and psychology courses in seven Syracuse area schools. Conceived to address the problem of "senioritis" that often afflicts the best and brightest high school students, it was thought to be a local answer to a local problem. As teachers and administrators moved from school to school and wanted to bring the program with them, however, word about Project Advance spread. Currently, the program offers Syracuse University courses to approximately 6,600 students in 140 selected high schools in New York, New Jersey, Maine, Massachusetts, and even one school in

Michigan,[1] and is one of the oldest and largest concurrent enrollment programs in the United States. More than 500 high school teachers currently are certified as adjunct Syracuse University instructors offering SU courses in biology, calculus, chemistry, college learning strategies, composition, computer engineering, economics, English, forensic science, French, information technology, Italian, psychology, public affairs, sociology, Spanish, and statistics. Project Advance has served as a model for other concurrent enrollment programs such as those offered at Indiana University, the University of Pittsburgh, the University of North Carolina at Greensboro, and the University of Connecticut. It has been honored by the National Commission on Excellence in Education, the National Institute of Education, the Carnegie Foundation for the Advancement of Teaching, the American Association of Higher Education, and the New York State Assembly.

The program's mission is threefold: to provide Syracuse University introductory courses to qualified high schools students, to provide ongoing professional development to high school instructors involved with the program, and to provide ongoing evaluation of the program and research into the articulation between high school and college experiences. The program is thus conceived as a means both to strengthen the rigor of high school course offerings and to allow students to jump-start their college careers. It also seeks to form a professional bond between high school and college faculties, and it serves to provide a platform for research into the little studied area of the high school-to-college transition.

Despite the acclaim Project Advance and its sister programs have earned, concerns about concurrent enrollment programs bring into question some of their basic premises. Can courses offered in the high schools be taught with sufficient rigor and sophistication to qualify as college courses? Should college courses be taught to high school students? Can high school instructors offer college-level instruction in the high school? Our answer to all those concerns is yes, but with some major stipulations:

1. The driving force behind the courses is the collegiate academic department. College faculty and the departments in which they teach must be the first and final word in terms of the curriculum for the courses.

2. High school instructors working with the program must be academically qualified to teach the courses and must be skilled and experienced classroom teachers.

3. College faculty and the high school instructors must work closely and collegially as the courses are implemented and taught.

In what follows, we speak from our own experience with two courses offered through Project Advance, the writing/English courses (hereafter referred to as WRT 105 and ETS 142), which we administer.

WRT 105 and ETS 142

First-year composition courses have long formed the backbone of Project Advance offerings, and these courses have, until quite recently, had the largest enrollments of all the courses the program offers (at this writing, a forensic science course, offered through the chemistry department, has recently overtaken the composition and English courses as having the largest enrollment). Initially, the program offered the two-semester composition sequence required of all incoming Syracuse freshman. In 1989, however, a departmental reorganization occurred on campus that established the Writing Program as an academic unit in its own right. WRT 105, Writing Studio I, a one-semester composition course, became the required freshman writing experience, with WRT 205, Writing Studio II, offered in the sophomore year. Because there was concern about offering high school students collegiate sophomore-level courses, the program looked to the English department for a 100-level course to pair with WRT 105 as a second semester offering in the high schools. The course that was chosen was ETS 141, Reading and Interpretation: From Language to Discourse, an introduction to contemporary literary and cultural theory.

In recent years, still more changes have occurred regarding these courses. WRT 105 is now called Principles and Practices of Academic Writing,[2] and the course content of ETS 141 has been moved to a sophomore-level course; the first-year course has been renumbered, and the program currently offers ETS 142 Narratives of Culture: Introduction to Issues of Critical Reading in the spring semester.[3] The courses are offered from two different departments, writing and English, and are not linked on campus in any way, so the tie between the two courses in the off-campus sections has always been somewhat artificial. But the school districts, in the interests of easy scheduling and of keeping students engaged through the end of their senior year, have asked the university to link the two courses administratively in the off-campus sections so that students register for and take both courses sequentially. In light of this linkage, the course content of WRT 105 is slightly changed in the off-campus sections to provide a bridging unit in discourse analysis at the end of WRT 105 leading toward the ETS course students take second semester.

This course modification represents an added element to the course and does not compromise the course's content or rigor. Campus faculty who work with the program and the high school instructors who teach the courses off-campus work diligently to see to it that the rigor and expectations of both courses are the same as they are on campus.

Program Administration and Funding

Project Advance is completely tuition-driven, although the tuition the students pay is approximately one-seventh of the full Syracuse University tuition. Students register and pay for the courses on a schedule adapted to the high school academic year, and they observe add and drop dates just as they would if they had registered for the courses on campus. The program offers emergency tuition assistance to students who can demonstrate a financial need. A percentage of the income the program brings in goes to the university for office and resource overhead costs, but the remainder of the income goes back into the program to support professional development, travel costs for school visits and meetings, and resources. Faculty members who serve as course coordinators are paid a consultant's fee for every school visit they make. Additional costs to the program include faculty and administrative travel to the schools (program administrators occasionally accompany the faculty members on the visits to handle any administrative issues that arise) and providing resources for the faculty and occasionally for the schools and teachers.

To date, the program has had the good fortune to be able to reinvest most of its tuition revenues back into the program, making possible the payment of faculty fees and resources, travel costs, and professional development costs. Project Advance operates on the premise that a solid financial investment is crucial to providing the human and material resources to make such a program viable. As a faculty member working with the program stated in an interview in 2005, "I think SUPA is good because so much money is invested in it. Lots of money. It's just a shame that the rest of the academic world isn't what this is."

Teacher Selection and Professional Development

The relationship between the university and the high schools in Project Advance begins with careful selection of teachers for the program—an ongoing priority. The prospective instructor must be academically qualified to teach the same course on campus, which means, in most cases, that the instructor must hold a master's degree, preferably in the subject area of the course. The instructor must also be an experienced and skilled teacher. Because school administrators presumably know the teaching strengths of the people on their staffs, school administrators first nominate high school teachers to become SUPA instructors based on their proficiency and experience in the classroom and their willingness to take on the additional intellectual effort, paper grading, and course planning that college courses demand. Once nominated, teachers officially apply to enter the program, filling out an application form and sending the university their graduate and undergraduate college transcripts. The faculty coordinator, a university faculty member who assumes academic responsibility for the courses offered through Project Advance on behalf of the department, evaluates these credentials and decides if the candidates are academically qualified to teach the courses. If they are, the program officially invites the teachers to the Project Advance Summer Institute.

The Summer Institute

The Summer Institute is an intensive two-week workshop during which the faculty coordinators and the instructors take up the philosophy, content, and pedagogy of the courses. The prospective instructors wear different "hats" at different times throughout the workshop. At times they are students, completing assignments just as their students will in their WRT 105 and ETS 142 classes. At times they are learners, increasing their own store of content knowledge; at other times they function in the workshops as teachers, facilitating class discussions, helping their classmates with difficult concepts, and planning course curriculum.

In the Summer Institute workshops the relationships between the campus faculty and the high school adjuncts begin to form, as teachers learn the content of the courses and become acculturated to the university intellectual community. The instructors of the workshop model the sessions both on teaching practices used in the courses and on the collegial interaction among professional educators, each of whom is presumed to bring experience and expertise to the table. As the collegiate faculty plan the Summer Institute workshop, they are conscious of walking a fine line between "sage on the stage" and professional collegiality. On the one hand, content information needs to be delivered. On the other, faculty recognize that all members of the workshop are teaching professionals and that all have worthy input into the conversation.

In reflective essays that new instructors write about their Summer Institute experience, teachers often mention an unexpected level of rigor in the workshops that is at odds with much of the professional development they participate in elsewhere. This rigor, though sometimes overwhelming, also reinforces the notion that the teachers are considered intellectual colleagues, and it helps them see themselves as college instructors. One teacher wrote in a reflective essay at the 2007 workshop:

> The workload was challenging. When I received my syllabus for the summer workshop in the mail, I let out an internal gasp. It had been a long time since I was in an intense course like this. I felt nervous that I was out of touch, especially with the critical

theory. When I realized the lack of comfort level I had with the material, I knew I would have to reintroduce myself to a more scholarly approach. I also realized that this material can really make a person focus not only on material to present, but material to incorporate into one's own journey. I am excited about immersing myself in this material with my students. The work may be challenging, the theory difficult, but it is worth it when all of a sudden you hear yourself say, "I never thought of it that way." This workshop has provided me with a template of how I hope my class runs.

Another goal of the Summer Institute workshops is bonding. Bringing teachers to campus for two weeks of intense study and class participation creates a cohesive force that bonds them to each other, to the university, and to the program. Another participant in the 2007 workshop wrote:

[The instructors] have a great sense of balancing instruction, discussion, warmth, humor, and compassion. Without them, I can't imagine this training being half of what it meant to me. Beyond [the faculty facilitators of the Summer Institute], my fellow classmates and teachers became more than SUPA colleagues. I really look forward to keeping in touch with them and seeing them each year when we get together.

Thus the selection and initial training of the new instructors not only gives them instruction in what the courses are all about and materials and resources to teach the courses, but it also serves to begin to change the teacher's mindset from high school teacher to college instructor.

The Seminars

The teachers earn Syracuse University adjunct instructor status upon successful completion of the Summer Institute workshops, and they maintain their adjunct status by teaching the courses and attending daylong professional development seminars each semester planned by the faculty coordinators. The seminars serve as both faculty meetings and professional development workshops. In an effort to hold down travel costs for school districts, Project Advance schedules these workshops in regional locations:

on campus for those schools located in relative proximity to the university, at the university's Manhattan facility for schools in the New York City area, and at a location in southern Maine for the New England schools.

The seminars typically provide a speaker from the discipline, some curriculum development work, and perhaps some paper grading and grade-norming activities. The seminars also provide an opportunity to address problems and concerns that have arisen, either on campus or in the high schools, and an opportunity for teachers to come together to talk, work, and share ideas. Of all the activities offered by the seminars, the latter is perhaps the most important, giving teachers from various schools and from both secondary and postsecondary levels the opportunity to work together and learn from each other as they address issues related to courses they are all teaching simultaneously. Brainstorming activities and the sharing of best practices represent true collegial interactions where campus faculty often get ideas and resources as surely as high school teachers gain from their campus colleagues' contributions. For example, recent workshop discussions addressed pedagogical strategies for helping students to read difficult texts. The campus presenter modeled some approaches by having the teachers read "Representation" by W. J. T. Mitchell (in Lentricchia and McLaughlin). The teachers gained a new critical text to use, and the campus presenter gained added classroom strategies. Other examples abound: one teacher suggested the Warner Brothers Daffy Duck cartoon "Duck Amuck" as a way to introduce the issues of the spring course, and quickly the cartoon became "standard operating procedure" both off and on campus.

Special Topics Workshops

In addition to the seminars, the Project Advance English/Writing program offers voluntary special topics workshops in the summer, through which teachers can deepen their content knowledge. Based on areas of teacher interest, these workshops currently take place in a retreat format at Minnowbrook, the university's Adirondack Mountain conference facility. Either teachers or their school districts pay a program-subsidized tuition fee for this week-long retreat, during which courses or independent study options run concurrently, while the conference center provides food, housing, and recreational facilities. Faculty from Syracuse University and from other institutions lead these workshops, and participants can earn SU graduate credit for the experience or simply take the workshops for their own professional development. In recent years a popular independent study option allows a participant to work on a curricular or subject-specific project one-on-one with the faculty coordinator. Offerings in past years have included writing workshops, as well as courses addressing plagiarism, U.S. consumer culture as reflected in literature, the child in Victorian literature, analytics of power, Arthurian literature, and various courses in film, storytelling, and writing workshops. Although these workshops are voluntary and attended by a small percentage of the Project Advance teachers, they also provide a time for teachers to come together to learn from each other.

Conferences

The English and writing arm of the program also sponsors an academic conference held every fifth year on campus, where faculty from both on and off campus join with colleagues from other institutions to present their ideas and practices in a conference format. Many instructors in the program have presented sessions sharing their teaching practices or their intellectual projects at the conferences, which function as an academic meeting where academics share their own work and learn from others. Robert Scholes, professor emeritus from Brown University, the late Neil Postman of New York University, and David Miller, religion professor from Syracuse University, have been past keynote speakers.

The English Cabinet

Help in planning for and implementing all these professional development activities comes from the English Cabinet, made up of ten high school instructors, elected by their peers, who meet twice a year and act in an advisory capacity to the English faculty coordinator and the English administrator. This group suggests topics for the special topics workshops, helps plan the five-year conference as well as regular seminars, and helps troubleshoot problems as they arise in the program; it also provides a sounding board for curriculum change and the review and development of new materials.

The Summer Institute, seminars, workshops, conferences, and the cabinet provide comprehensive professional development that teachers often characterize as the best they experience in their professional lives. In addition to these Project Advance–sponsored professional development opportunities, the program offers instructor scholarships that will pay up to half the cost of tuition for course work related to the courses the high school instructors are teaching through the program, even if the course work is offered at institutions other than Syracuse University. Syracuse University graduate work sponsored by the program is offered at a heavily discounted tuition rate.

In addition to faculty mentoring and professional development, the program offers teachers and students taking the courses through Project Advance access to the university library (both in person and electronically), course materials, and resource-sharing Internet sites. Through all these professional development opportunities and resources, the program hopes to encourage teachers toward constant improvement of their knowledge base and their pedagogy.

Relationships between University and High School Teachers

If concurrent enrollment programs such as Project Advance profess to administer courses having intellectual integrity, the academic basis of that integrity must rest firmly within the university academic department. Courses offered through Project Advance are, first and foremost, Syracuse University courses—the same courses that are offered regularly on campus, and the academic department has the final say in curricular issues that arise. That said, the program is also dependent on close relationships between the academic departments on campus and the high school instructors to ensure that the courses are implemented and taught with integrity. Often the high school instructors bring activities and teaching ideas to the table that get taken up by instructors of both on- and off-campus sections, so that the courses become sites for mutual professional sharing of ideas and expertise.

Each discipline has a faculty coordinator on campus who is responsible for oversight of the content of the courses, for seeing that campus faculty visit each section of each course once a semester, for planning professional development activities for the high school instructors to keep them abreast of new developments in the field and in the courses, and for cultivating a strong connection between the teachers in the high school and on the campus.

A crucial contributor to a strong connection is, of course, the relationship between the faculty coordinator and the teachers. While university faculty bring a wealth of content knowledge and expertise to this relationship, the high school instructors also have expertise to contribute, especially in the area of pedagogy. Thus the tone and affect of the university–high school adjunct relationship are important. The university personnel have oversight responsibility, but they stand to lose important opportunities to improve their own teaching practice if they come across *only* as overseers. Instead, we believe that collegiality and mutual respect are critical. The program works best when the campus faculty regard themselves as fellow teachers, rather than policing overseers of teaching practice. They thus enable high school teachers in the program to value what professors have to offer, but they equally afford the opportunity for the campus faculty to learn from their secondary colleagues.

Individual instructors who teach Syracuse University's writing (WRT 105) and English (ETS 142) courses, both on and off campus, design the particulars of their own courses around common intellectual "moves." Neither course is taught from a "canned" syllabus given them by the academic departments, a circumstance that adds to the importance of close ties between faculty off and on campus. Both Syracuse's writing program and English department have articulated for themselves and their constituencies the underlying philosophies and pedagogies, as well as the range and scope of these two introductory courses (see http://english.syr.edu/ETS/Major.htm; http://wrt.syr.edu/pub/handbook/ldlearninggoals.html). In the sections of the courses taught through Project Advance, the faculty coordinator, working from a clear sense of what the courses are and what place the courses have in the structure of the campus curricula, the majors, and the discipline, works with the secondary teachers to develop courses adapted to the high school setting. This adaptation does not impact the course content but may affect course pacing, delivery, and choice of materials. For example, the high school academic year begins after Labor Day and goes, in New York State, until almost the end of June; the campus academic year, by contrast, begins in late August and concludes in early May. So the pacing of the course is adjusted for the high school schedule, just as it is to accommodate schools on block scheduling and schools whose classes meet for forty minutes every day. Course materials that provide the theoretical core of each course are either provided or required, whereas what we might call "application" materials may be selected by the teacher. (Sometimes, of course, the exchange means that the high school teacher may offer alternative materials for the theoretical core and the campus faculty offer suggestions for "application" materials.) Thus each high school instructor in the program develops his or her own syllabus for each course, working within guidelines and with mentorship offered by the campus faculty. The campus faculty role is that of guide, mentor, and resource to this process and to the ongoing process of course or curriculum revision. This close mentoring relationship provides not only tacit oversight for the quality of the courses but also a window of opportunity for growth and development of faculty on both sides of the institutional divide. The points of contact between campus and high school adjuncts include one-on-one help planning course syllabi, faculty visits to the school once each semester, required professional development seminars offered at a campus site for the faculty twice a year, plus access by phone and email as issues arise. Through these points of contact, professional and often close personal relationships develop as teachers bring their various talents together to ensure the integrity of the courses.

The faculty coordinator's work with the program involves time and energy, and support structures, both from the department and Project Advance administration, are vital. Coordinators for Project Advance are paid a consultant's fee each time they visit a school and are paid for teaching the workshops, but these finances are only a part of the equation. The faculty coordinators are also full-time faculty members of their individual departments, with all the responsibilities for teaching, research, and service those positions entail. Thus, the work they do for Project Advance must fit in the seams of the rest of their personal and professional lives. It is the work of the Project Advance administrative staff to help make the extra work possible, by making travel arrangements, handling the nuts and bolts issues of student registration and related matters, and by providing resources (laptops, cell phones, etc.) that will make the work easier.

Research and Evaluation

Because a program that doesn't test how well it is doing or what effect it has on its constituencies operates in a self-knowledge vacuum, research and evaluation play an important role in virtually every activity of Project Advance. Its research staff is headed by one of the associate directors of the program and consists of two graduate assistants whose sole job is research and evaluation. The research team conducts a student evaluation of each course the program offers each semester, an evaluation of every program professional development activity, and a general survey of recent high school graduates who have taken SUPA courses, asking the students about the efficacy of their total Project Advance experience and about the transfer of credit to their colleges and universities. The team also surveys students four years after their high school graduation to see how the courses affected their total college experience.

The team or a team member also conducts special research projects as the need or impetus arises. In the early years of the program special research projects compared work of the students in high schools to the work of their counterparts on campus. These studies consistently indicated that students in the Project Advance sections performed at least as well as their campus counterparts on college examinations and assignments. Studies were also conducted comparing grading standards in the off-campus and on-campus sections. These studies indicated that grading standards were comparable in on-campus and off-campus sections of the same courses. Recently, a study was undertaken to determine whether English instructors' attitudes toward teaching and their subject area were changed substantially due to the professional development offered to the teachers. Indications from this study were that teachers' attitudes toward teaching have been transformed as a result of the professional development offered by the program. One teacher's response is representative of the kinds of change engendered by the program's professional development efforts:

> The Syracuse program has caused me to question and alter my approach to the teaching of literature and writing. Regarding literature, my assumptions about where meaning is to be found and how it gets there have been revolutionized by my exposure to contemporary literary theory through various courses and seminars offered by Syracuse. This has led to a willingness to broaden my ideas about what may be worth teaching as well as what may be worth discussing while studying text. (Serumola 139–40)

Both the evaluation and the research studies are vital in showing the program where it is strong and where it needs to improve, as well as possible directions for future growth. The studies also yield important information about the transitional space between high school and college teaching, learning, and social interaction.

Relationships between Project Advance and NACEP

As high schools began offering more and more college-level programs to their students, colleges became concerned about the integrity of such programs. Some seemed to offer a great deal of connection between the high schools and the colleges involved. Others seemed to be simply "cash cows," more concerned about adding to collegiate coffers than doing the hard work necessary to truly bridge secondary and postsecondary teaching and learning. In an effort to create standards in the face of this disparity and bring concurrent enrollment programs across the country into conversation with each other, Syracuse University Project Advance spearheaded the formation of a national organization, the National Alliance of Concurrent Enrollment Partnerships

(NACEP), to accredit and support concurrent enrollment programs. In order to be accredited through NACEP, concurrent enrollment programs must meet standards involving curriculum, faculty selection and training, student support, assessment, and program evaluation. NACEP also is involved in program development, national standards, research, and communication. On a federal level, NACEP has met with officials to promote a national agenda for strengthening accelerated learning programs. According to the NACEP website (www.nacep.org), the organization's accrediting standards accomplish the following goals:

◆ Serve as a guarantee to students, policymakers, and other post-secondary institutions that the accredited CEP meets rigorous national standards.

◆ Distinguish a CEP, thereby enhancing its ability to recruit new partners and students.

◆ Aid CEP alumni and families when they seek credit recognition for their CEP-earned college credits.

In addition to identifying programs of quality, NACEP provides concurrent enrollment programs with a voice on the national stage of educational policy. In the past, policy concerning pre-matriculation college course opportunities has been driven by the College Board's Advanced Placement program. In fact, AP has been the default term for such programs for years. With the voice of a national organization and its political efforts, concurrent enrollment has slowly been able to add its voice to the conversation of K–16 education.

Conclusion

Project Advance Writing/English is but one example of a program that successfully bridges the gap between high school and college. The bridge is one of relationship and mutual support taking the form of training—rigorous by any standard—and an ongoing supportive professional relationship between campus faculty and high school teachers. This supportive relationship is, to be sure, enabled by the way the program was set up fiscally from the outset, with the majority of the tuition dollars generated going back into the program instead of into the general university fund. Because the program has the resources, it can provide guest speakers, materials, training opportunities, and conferences; it can provide scholarship assistance for qualified needy students and for ongoing advanced education for teachers. It can bring high school adjuncts and college faculty together to learn and grow from one another. Without these resources and dedication from the campus faculty, high school teachers, and administrators involved in the program, the quality and scope of this program couldn't happen.

Project Advance has set the bar high, challenging everyone involved to provide continuous teacher and program development. We believe—and the evidence supports our belief—that the program is indeed a model of connection and quality.

Notes

1. While it is a distance for teachers to attend professional development events, the Michigan school has robustly maintained the partnership with Syracuse. As a historical footnote, in the early days of the program, there were a number of participating Michigan high schools; decisions by the University of Michigan and Michigan State not to grant transfer credit (while simultaneously looking favorably on SUPA credits as indicators of students' taking the most rigorous courses offered by their high schools) led to withdrawal of all but one school, which has remained an enthusiastic participant. The Syracuse University Project Advance program made efforts to get a local university to provide a comparable program, with no results.

2. The course currently is composed of a brief jump-start unit, followed by longer units in analysis and the documented argument, ending, in the off-campus sections, with a shorter unit on "discourse analysis." Fuller description of the campus program can be readily found on the Writing Program's website at http://wrt.syr.edu.

3. As with other 100-level ETS courses, ETS 142 introduces students to the discipline of English and textual studies, stressing not what is read but how (and why) it is read. The goal is not only to show how meanings are created through acts of critical reading but also to demonstrate the consequences of pursuing one way of reading over another. Each

section of ETS 142 takes up a number of major issues of concern in contemporary literary and cultural studies. These issues may include authorship, language, reading, subjectivity, ideology, space/time, history, and difference. As the course explores each area among those selected for a particular section, students are introduced to the issues at stake and then examine those issues as they arise in a wide range of cultural texts.

Works Cited

Lentricchia, Frank, and Thomas McLaughlin. *Critical Terms for Literary Study*. 2nd ed. Chicago: U of Chicago P, 1995. Print.

National Alliance of Concurrent Enrollment Partnerships. Home page. NACEP, n.d. Web. 28 Mar. 2009.

Serumola, Patrick. "Improving Performance in Higher Education: An Investigation of Perspective Transformation in Teacher Professional Development Programs." Diss. Syracuse U, 2008. Print.

Syracuse University English Department. Home page. Syracuse University, n.d. Web. 28 Mar. 2009.

Syracuse University Writing Program. Home page. Syracuse University, n.d. Web. 28 Mar. 2009.

CHAPTER ELEVEN

Absentee Landlords or Owner-Tenants? Formulating Standards for Dual-Credit Composition Programs

CHRIS M. ANSON
North Carolina State University

Dual-credit composition programs (hereafter DCCPs) had their genesis in a variety of interests, such as recruitment (attracting students from area high schools into a sponsoring university); profit (garnering college tuition even from those who do not end up matriculating at the sponsoring university); cost reduction (foisting a required course onto another system); and articulation (creating ways for high schools and colleges to scaffold their curricula). In the broader educational context, some of these interests are more principled than others. For example, universities motivated to outsource what they perceive to be burdensome, remedial writing programs by offering cheap ways for high school students to "get the requirement out of the way" do not view composition as an enterprise essential to students' transition to college or understand its full developmental potential and importance as a base for further, more complex writing experiences in the disciplines (see Jolliffe and Phelan). In structure and operation, DCCPs also range from well-coordinated courses taught by fully supported teachers to untended, shameful, "slapdash" curricula that exploit high schools and do a disservice to aspiring students (Farris 104). But without the benefit of clear, theoretically principled standards, we also judge DCCPs subjectively, leveling unfair criticisms at some and letting others off the hook. In the context of the rapid growth of dual-credit programs—now enrolling well over 500,000 students per year (Lazar)—quality-based standards are essential not only to certifying existing and future programs but also to engaging in ongoing formative evaluation and continuous improvement.

This chapter proposes a preliminary set of standards for DCCPs similar to those used in writing program assessment. Categories for the standards include *pedagogical integrity, programmatic integrity, student needs, faculty development, economic fairness,* and *fairness in labor practices.* My hope is that in the process of exploring these standards as they apply specifically to DCCPs, we will be in a better position to evaluate programs both formatively and summatively. After discussing each standard in terms of its application to DCCPs (including one in which I was administratively involved for eight years at the University of Minnesota), I suggest ways that it can be applied systematically, using key indicators and methods of assessment that go beyond those that have been reported in the literature.

Toward Dual-Credit Standards

Much controversy surrounds the idea that high school students can take a composition course deemed to be equivalent to a college version before they actually matriculate full-time on a college campus. Several approaches exist: a college course can be taught by a high school teacher in the high school; high school students, commuting to a college campus, can be mainstreamed into an existing course; college teachers can commute to a high school and teach a college course there; or students can take a high school course not designed *as* a college course but thought to be equivalent to one (see Townsend and Twombly 150).[1] At their core, however, all of these approaches assume that some high school students are intellectually, experientially, and emotionally ready to do college-level work, and it is this assumption that drives controversy on a theoretical level. For example, during their national emergence, David E. Schwalm urged resistance to dual-credit writing courses, arguing that "college writing courses are designed to help students cope with the increasingly difficult writing tasks presented to them in the intellectual and social context of college," a context "impossible to replicate in a high school senior English class" (53). Others claimed that some brighter students who might disengage from a high school course taught to the middle range of student ability could benefit from the rigor and intellectual challenge of a college-level course. (One of the earliest dual-credit programs, Syracuse University's Project Advance, started when seven area high school principals and superintendents became interested in offering courses that would challenge high school students who had already competed all their graduation requirements by the end of the eleventh grade; see Edmonds, Mercurio, and Bonesteel; also Moody and Bonesteel, this volume). In an article published alongside Schwalm's, Michael J. Vivion wrote that dual-credit programs can "offer students quality college-level instruction and . . . unite teachers at both levels in a mutually beneficial professional undertaking" (60). At base, these conflicting beliefs about the viability of dual-credit composition emerge from different ideologies of learning: one sees student development as a single social and intellectual trajectory in which students move through a system together, while the other values individual developmental trajectories for each student that are not necessarily tied to the social and intellectual spaces defined by our current system of education.

It is not the purpose of this chapter to weigh arguments for or against the assumption that some high school students are prepared to take college-level courses. Dual-credit programs are already firmly established in the U.S. educational system and are growing in popularity, especially as the costs of college tuition continue to rise disproportionately to income and as postsecondary institutions look for ways to reduce their own curricular and staffing burdens. Instead, my analysis assumes a de facto reality of dual-credit courses and a probable increase in both their demand and supply. Echoing earlier calls for greater quality control of such programs, I want to urge a more thorough inquiry into what national standards for DCCPs might look like. In turn, applying, assessing, and discussing these standards can lead us to (re)consider the underlying rationales, structures, and positive and negative effects of DCCPs.

Broad standards have already been articulated for dual-credit programs (which include courses in many areas of college-level general education). The National Alliance of Concurrent Enrollment Partnerships (NACEP) accredits programs through the application of a set of standards that focus on curriculum, faculty, students, assessment (of students), and program evaluation.[2] Although the NACEP standards and accreditation process provide crucial oversight for dual-credit programs, they must remain generic to accommodate the range of courses and disciplines that dual-credit programs include. More specific standards for the teaching of writing must be articulated within the field of composition studies. For example, NACEP's only standard concerning the content or delivery of a course—that "college or university courses administered through CEPs reflect the pedagogical, theoretical and philosophical orientation of the colleges and universities [sic] sponsoring faculty and/or academic department"—will not be interpreted the same way for introductory calculus as for first-year composition. A discipline-based rubric for assessing the quality of a dual-credit program will borrow from such general standards but will ask more specific questions about a course's goals and outcomes, instructional methods, materials, and the like. Furthermore, while NACEP's standards are generally unidirectional (everything associated with the high school course must conform to everything associated with the college course), a more discipline-specific rubric should also question the nature of the curriculum at the sponsoring university.

Although no national standards exist specifically for DCCPs, several compositionists have proposed or implemented local- or state-level standards. Concerned about the rapid increase in DCCPs in Missouri, Jane Frick and Nancy Blattner created a set of standards for DCCPs on behalf of the Missouri Colloquium on Writing Assessment (Missouri Colloquium; see Frick and Blattner). Because these standards were created amid a gold rush of DCCPs in the mid-1990s, they are necessarily regulatory, ensuring, for example, that student teachers not be assigned to dual-credit courses, that only students admitted to the dual-credit option be allowed in the class, and that the liaison at the sponsoring college or university make at least three site visits per year to each school offering the course. No provisions are included for ongoing assessment of the program or course, with the exception of the credentialing of students, teachers, and the college liaison before the program begins.

In her analysis of a DCCP offered through Indiana University, Christine Farris describes a ten-year process of improvement designed to avoid "the dual-credit arrangement composition specialists fear, in which a university merely signs off on the curriculum of high school teachers it believes are doing a good enough job teaching 'the basics' that professors would like to see addressed before students come to college" (106). Underlying this process are various standards Farris articulates through her experience working with schools and teachers and creating a "community of peers" through intense collaboration and the co-involvement of the campus and the schools. To ensure adequate articulation between Indiana University and the schools, for example, she hired several of the best retired teachers from the program to teach a section of the course at the university and contribute to site visits at the schools. Although these and other innovations helped to create an excellent program, they represent a specific case of how standards emerge from felt difficulties and localized problems, rather than from broader principles that should apply to all programs.

Focusing on another variation of DCCPs—those offered through distance education—Alan Blackstock and Virginia Norris Exton also offer a critique based on local experience. Citing the work of several researchers, they raise questions about the effectiveness of the delivery mode and propose several standards by which such long-distance dual-credit courses should be taught. Among those relevant to the integrity of DCCPs, they concur with Phyllis Surrency Dallas, Nancy Bishop Dessommes, and Ellen H. Hendrix that the college instructors should visit the remote site at least once a month. To this they add their own provisions that high school students be carefully screened to ensure that "only those with advanced writing skills and a high degree of motivation and self-discipline are enrolled in the course" (385) and that there be adequately trained facilitators at the remote high school site.

While these and other recommendations help to raise awareness about the pitfalls of DCCPs, they largely confuse the activities of implementation and assessment and often leave standards implicit and goals or outcomes unstated. Site visits to a program may be a kind of data collection on the way to formative evaluation, but in Blackstock and Exton's discussion they are presented as a programmatic criterion. Left unsaid are what happens in the site visit, what questions drive the need for such a visit, and how information collected there is to be used to improve the program. Similarly, Missouri's Metropolitan Community Colleges *Dual-Credit Enrollment Handbook* prescribes "class observations" by supervising administrators, but the evaluation form is clearly designed to be summative in nature, prompting responses to questions such as "How well does this instructor perform responsibilities related to management of the classroom? (Deals with disruptive or dominating students effectively; arrives on time prepared to begin class; brings the period to conclusion in a timely manner.)" (A concluding page asks the observer to evaluate the teacher as "satisfactory—unconditional," "satisfactory—conditional," or "unsatisfactory," with checkboxes indicating follow-up intervention.) A more effective evaluative model would begin with discipline-based questions anchored in concerns about the quality of a program, consider what characteristics of the program would provide ways to answer those questions, and then offer specific, reliable methods to collect and assess information about those characteristics.

Assessment-Based Standards for Dual-Credit Composition: A Preliminary Rubric

Dozens of standards could be proposed for DCCPs on the basis of the experiences and opinions of many teachers, administrators, parents, and students. Some high school teachers, for example, believe that swapping a college course for the high school requirement results in a net loss of writing experience by "waiving opportunities for students to write more and blurring the delineation of grade levels in the process" (Listoe). Such a concern might suggest a standard that no DCCP will result in a decrease in writing experience in either high school or college. But because students attend many colleges after high school, it would be impractical or impossible to assess such a standard in any meaningful way, even if "writing experience" could be quantitatively determined. Instead, we need a set of generalized standards or principles manifesting themselves in specific ways that can be assessed using a variety of appropriate methods.

The matrix in Table 11.1 is based on common practices in educational program assessment (see Palomba and Banta; Wolf) but borrows as well from the evaluation of service-learning programs, which, because of their multiple contexts for learning, pose similar pedagogical and administrative complexities as DCCPs (Feldman et al.; Gelmon et al.). Core standards take the form of questions that emerge from concerns about the quality and integrity of a program (these can be stated as outcomes, but for heuristic purposes they are somewhat broader and more diffuse). How do we know that a DCCP is well managed? Is there parity between versions of a course taught in very different educational contexts by teachers with different training to students who are at different social and intellectual locations in their lives? Are teachers treated fairly? Are costs and expenses equitable? How well are students supported beyond the class?

Each set of questions can be answered, in part, by "key indicators," or ways by which we will know that the core standards are being fulfilled. Left alone, these generalized indicators are meaningless; they must be assessed using appropriate tools and methods, some of which (but by no means all) are suggested in the final column. Taken as a whole, the matrix is designed as a point of departure for further discussions about how we would recognize an excellent DCCP (and by extension what it means to create such a program), as well as a possible rubric for assessing individual programs and suggesting ways that existing programs can be improved through a continuous cycle of review and implementation.

Pedagogical Integrity

Of crucial importance to the success of any dual-credit writing course is its *pedagogical integrity*, which refers to the principles on which the course is founded and the educational methods it employs to help students to write at the college level. In many ways, pedagogical integrity depends on programmatic integrity

TABLE 11.1. Preliminary Assessment Matrix for Dual-Credit Composition Programs

Core Standards		Indicators	Assessment
Pedagogical Integrity	Does the course adhere to national standards for the teaching of writing?	Articulation and realization of appropriate outcomes and writing experiences Theory/research-based approaches	External reviews of both the college and high school courses; examination of all course artifacts; observations of all teachers; examination of teaching portfolios; etc.
	How can we ensure that the courses are equivalent?	Alignment of all course goals, outcomes, syllabi	Examination of all course artifacts; formative cross-observations; etc.
	How can we ensure that the instructional methods are consistent—that the learning experience is the same?	Application of consistent philosophy, approach, and instructional strategies	Class observations; teacher interviews or focus groups; studies of response/grading practices; student surveys; student course evaluations; etc.
	How well does the course prepare students for college-level writing across the curriculum?	Subsequent student success in writing	Alumni surveys and interviews with ex-DCCP students; self-reports of grades; etc.
Programmatic Integrity	How do we know teachers are prepared? How are they selected and certified? How do we know the program is managed effectively? What articulation efforts bring the sites together?	Selection criteria and appointment process in both contexts; site-visits and observations Administrative structures in both sites; directors with sufficient credentials	Periodic reviews of instructors' credentials; reports of site visits; etc. Periodic program review; full-scale reviews for appointments of administrators; etc.
	How can we be certain that the high school students are qualified to take the course?	Application of fair, carefully constructed criteria for admission	Continuous assessment of performance rates in both contexts (e.g., portfolio assessment, data on failure rates, etc.)

continued on next page

Table 11.1. continued

Student Needs	Is there sufficient student support? What provisions are made to create a college-like intellectual environment? Does the teacher-student ratio allow for adequate individual mentoring?	Writing centers or tutors; online support; availability to high school students of college resources such as libraries and appropriate technology	Periodic review of all support systems; data on usage and effectiveness; analysis of optimal class size for student success; surveys and focus groups with students and alumni of the DCCP; etc.
Faculty Development	How are teachers in the program prepared to teach the course? What ongoing teacher development exists? How does this relate to similar opportunities on the college campus? How are reflective practice and reflection-in-action woven in and supported? What incentives exist for teachers to engage in ongoing faculty development?	Both entry-level and ongoing training and development	Teacher surveys, interviews, and focus groups; internal and external reviews; exit interviews with retiring teachers; etc.
Economic Fairness	Is there equity in the costs to teachers, schools, and students?	Direct costs (tuition, personnel, etc.); indirect costs (shifted labor, class size, infrastructure, etc.)	Full account of all costs and benefits; analyses of indirect costs; annual account summaries; etc.
Fairness in Labor Practices	Is the allocation of work to teachers fair and consistent between sites?	Class-size controls; rewards for participation	Anonymous surveys; focus groups; reports of data such as class sizes; self-reports of workload; etc.

(discussed later) because, although the high school course may not exactly replicate the college course in every respect, it must maintain the same educational standards, teach to the same general outcomes, and provide the same sorts of intellectual experiences as the college course. Furthermore, certain factors can exist in the high schools, such as curricular mandates or state-imposed testing programs, that shape the curriculum through teacher accountability and may interfere with or subvert the goals of the college course. These and other pedagogical concerns are usually the responsibility of the program administrators to study and address.

A poorly designed college course is no better when delivered to high school students. Standards for pedagogical integrity apply as strongly to the college course as to the version taught in the schools—a principle conspicuously absent from existing dual-credit policies. A dual-credit high school course that "reflects the pedagogical, theoretical and philosophical orientation" (NACEP) of a college-level counterpart by teaching formal grammar as writing is less healthy than if it deviates from the college version by engaging students in the practice of revising complete texts based on various kinds of reader response. At the same time, various methods used in the college course, such as peer-group sessions that help students learn how to revise their prose effectively and internalize discourse processes, may take on additional challenges of social maturity and classroom management in the high schools. Simply replicating a college course, reading for reading and assignment for assignment, may not be enough to realize its underlying goals in a different context.

A discussion of what principles should inform first-year composition courses would take us far beyond the scope of this chapter, but in general the concept of pedagogical integrity is tied to scholarship and best practices in the field of composition studies (see Jolliffe and Phelan for some general suggestions). Courses that significantly deviate from national guidelines such as the *Statement of Principles and Standards for the Postsecondary Teaching of Writing* (CCCC), the "WPA Outcomes Statement for First-Year Composition" (Council of Writing Program Administrators), the CCCC *Position Statement on Teaching, Learning, and Assessing Writing in Digital Environments* (CCCC), and *Writing Assessment: A Position Statement* (CCCC), or that ignore widely accepted, foundational research (such as the results of George Hillocks's meta-analysis concerning the deleterious effects of the direct and sustained teaching of grammar) should not be candidates for dual-credit offerings in the high schools, especially because such courses are designed, in part, to introduce students to the ways of thinking, knowing, and communicating that characterize postsecondary education and beyond (Bartholomae; Carter). In practice, applying "two-way" evaluation in DCCPs—questioning the progenitor course as strongly as its high school offspring—may be difficult because of the widespread assumption that an accredited college or university already offers sanctioned courses, and that a dual-credit initiative simply makes those courses available to high school students. In addition, few stakeholders (particularly the administrators of the college course) will call for a discipline-specific review of the college course before it is made available in the high schools. Yet the test of pedagogical integrity needs to be applied equally to both settings. Assessment methods include external reviews or impartial internal reviews, reviews of all curricular documents, observations of teachers at both sites, selected small-group instructional diagnoses (Coffman; Lenze), and focus groups with students. Combined external review teams that have expertise evaluating both college and high school curricula could ensure the pedagogical integrity of both course versions.

Because the college course is not specifically designed to be delivered at the high school level, there is additional responsibility to assess the effectiveness of the high school version. The goal of all DCCPs is to prepare advanced high school students to perform well as writers in college—especially if by virtue of taking a dual-credit course they are exempted from a standard first-year composition requirement. Yet too often "assessment" is based on successful completion of the high school course with a passing grade, which high school teachers may award based on an imperfect understanding of the college standards or on the standards that apply in their own high school setting. Continuous assessment of pedagogical integrity, therefore, should involve ongoing surveys of the DCCP's alumni after their first and subsequent years of college to determine how well prepared they felt to meet the demands of college-level writing. Focus groups could compare the students' experiences in the dual-credit course with what they are experiencing in college and provide additional data useful in the ongoing improvement of the DCCP. Such data could continue to emphasize a developmental view of college writing and subvert that "most problematic misperception" that DCCPs share with Advanced Placement courses—that they are "a method to *avoid* college writing courses rather than a means to *place into* a writing course that is appropriately challenging for a student's level of reading and writing ability" (Jolliffe and Phelan 95).

Maintaining the pedagogical integrity of the DCCP I administered at the University of Minnesota accounted for a significant amount of administrative time. The College-in-the-Schools Program (CIS) was founded in the early 1980s. Operated by the university's College of Continuing Education, CIS provides opportunities for high-ranking high school students to enroll in courses taught by their own teachers, on site, that are equivalent in content and delivery to the same courses taught on campus by university faculty. Currently, 104 high schools in the state of Minnesota participate in the program, but they do not all offer the same range or numbers of courses. Schools with the highest number of student registrations are mostly located in the ring suburbs of Minneapolis and St. Paul. The thirty-three University of Minnesota introductory courses offered in the program represent six general curricular areas: Agricultural Education, English and Communication Studies, Mathematics, Post Secondary Teaching and Learning, Social Sciences, and World and Classical Languages. According to the most recent annual statistics, CIS offered thirty-one courses from fifteen disciplines and received more than 6,900 student registrations.

The University of Minnesota's first-year composition course, WRIT 1301, is required for most entering freshmen, and it is this course that participating high school students take through the CIS program (a Writing Studio course designed for English language learner, or ELL, students is administered separately from WRIT 1301). The semester-long course—both on campus and in the CIS schools—carries four credit hours that are automatically displayed on a University of Minnesota transcript and can be transferred to other institutions that will accept them or allow exemption from their own required writing course.

At different stages in its existence, WRIT 1301 has under-gone curricular review continuously or only periodically. During my administration of the CIS composition course, the college course was the subject of nearly constant discussion among a core staff of administrators. Changes in the course were woven into the teacher-development workshops we held with high school instructors, but those changes tended to lag behind in implementation. Because there were four times the number of college teachers—most of them PhD students with fixed-term teaching assistantships—the college curriculum tended to be more diverse in approach than the high school version. With sufficient resources, more robustly assessing the nature and quality of the college course and its relationship to the high school version could have provided greater symmetry and ensured that our goals of pedagogical integrity were realized.

Programmatic Integrity

Just as effective writing program administrators (WPAs) engage in program assessment, so must coordinators of DCCPs, above and beyond the generalized assessments conducted by any higher-level dual-credit system to which those writing courses belong programmatically. Among the most important programmatic standards for dual-credit courses is the assurance that the high school students bring similar writing abilities and levels of intel-lectual maturity as the college students to their work. For this reason, the selection of students for the high school course must be based on carefully and systematically applied standards. Re-quiring high school students to demonstrate the skills, maturity, and intellectual curiosity to take a college-level course provides one way to avoid the elision of distinctions between high school and college education, or, as Schwalm puts it, to ensure we don't confuse "the awarding of credit hours with the acquisition of knowledge or skill" (52).

In the CIS program at the University of Minnesota, for ex-ample, students who want to enroll in the dual-credit high school course must meet stringent standards based on class rank, GPA, and teacher recommendations. Only high school juniors or seniors are eligible to apply.[3] Blackstock and Exton's description of the dual-credit course offered via distance learning in Utah offers a contrasting case in point. One of the sites, a small rural school in southwestern Utah, had neither selective registration nor anyone to coordinate the course on-site, resulting in the "disaster" of high failure rates. "Practically the entire student body" had reached the criterion of a 3.0 GPA, which allowed any of them to take the course. A more carefully designed screening and selection process, accompanied by ongoing outcomes assessment—part of what a good program does—would help to alleviate these kinds of problems.

Program assessment should also compare the performance of students enrolled in the high school and college versions of the course. A carefully conducted review of portfolios from both groups, devoid of identifying information, might reveal the need for more faculty development and better alignment between the courses and their teachers. In the College-in-the-Schools program, our periodic assessment of students' work showed that the high school group outperformed the college group, a finding clearly the result of the standards for high school acceptance to the program. (Many of those high school students ended up attending high-ranking colleges and universities, a fact that demonstrated the program's interest in success for all students in spite of its underlying desire to attract the CIS high school students to the University of Minnesota. In our case, the strengths demonstrated by the high school students helped to inform some of what we were doing in the college course.)

Although these basic dimensions of programmatic integrity almost go without saying, dual-credit courses also represent additional layers of complexity requiring special administrative attention. A single course is taught to two cohorts that, although they usually differ in age and education by just one year, bring a different collective ethos to their studies resulting from the social and intellectual spaces they inhabit. Different expectations, rules, and even legal provisions apply to the two contexts. For example, most high school teachers must comply with state reporting regulations if they see warning signs in students' writing, while college teachers have no such legal requirements. High school teachers are mindful of a parental audience (and authority), while college teachers are barred from disclosing information to parents. In organizing their lives, college students are generally free to do what they want around their classes, while high school students have their time and movements monitored and must adhere to an imposed schedule. For educational purposes, college teachers can assign, display, or have students view material that is off-limits in high school (see Bodmer 122–23). These and many other differences between the two contexts require not only savvy administration but savvy administrators, which suggests that the process of selecting the college coordinator of the writing course(s) should involve considerable scrutiny of his or her credentials and training. If no one else is available—a situation Farris documents in her description of a dual-credit program—then provisions should be made for a national search for a coordinator, regardless of the expense to the sponsoring college or university.

Since the early 1980s, the dual-credit course in the University of Minnesota's CIS program has been overseen by scholars of composition.[4] The CIS version is guided by the methods, goals, and principles of the on-campus version, which admits some variety of course readings, writing projects, and emphases. However, because there are many more teachers of the on-campus version than the CIS version, somewhat greater symmetry is found among the syllabi of the latter. The CIS teachers also have greater longevity—some have been teaching the course for over twenty years—while the large numbers of graduate students who teach the college version typically teach for a maximum of five years. Because the CIS composition course director has usually been the director of the college composition program, such disparities were obvious and could be dealt with in training and curricular review, but some DCCPs may not be administered by the same person centrally involved in the college course. One indicator of programmatic integrity, then, is how closely and consistently the two (or more) administrators work together. For example, it is common for the DCCP director to make site visits to the schools to observe teachers, meet with students and other administrators, and look at various materials and support services. That director needs to be engaged in similar review processes on the college campus.

Student Needs

Today, the outcomes of most college composition courses include enhancing research skills, especially online and in the library; becoming more effective at using digital technologies in the service of writing; and recognizing varying rhetorical and discursive conventions in the writing of different disciplines. The conditions to support such outcomes will vary significantly between a college campus and a high school. To meet the needs of students enrolled in a DCCP, all the resources associated with the college course need to be replicated in the high school setting or else students need external access to those resources. Most high school libraries, for example, have a fraction of the holdings of a college or university library. The library staff will be better trained to help high school–level students with their research than college-level students, and their own reference resources will be more limited. Technologies (and technological support staff and services) ubiquitous on college campuses will be scarce or nonexistent in many or most high schools.

Additional student support needed in a high school will also depend on its proximity to the sponsoring college or university. Students who can easily commute to the campus can visit a writing center, use computer labs, and spend time in the library, while those in more remote locations will need to rely on what may be available in their high school or community. In such cases, assessment of student resources will be important to create a successful DCCP. If no tutoring opportunities exist, some provisions should be made for additional teacher time. If technology is lacking, resources should be used to provide it, especially so that students can conduct library research digitally. If on-site library or other staff are not able or trained to orient students to college-level work, students should make field trips to the college campus or specialists should provide training through interactive TV or teleconference.

The majority of students enrolled in the CIS program attended schools within a reasonable drive from the University of Minnesota campus, and many made use of its facilities. However, as the program expanded to include schools beyond the outer suburbs of the city, it became more difficult for students to use campus facilities and services routinely. We set aside time for the students to visit the library during their field trips, and as the curriculum began paying more attention to discipline-based discourse, we set up opportunities for students to sit in on other college classes during those visits. But a thorough assessment of the differences between student support on campus and in the high schools—especially using student surveys and focus groups to determine their own experiences—would have helped us to identify areas of weakness in student support.

Faculty Development

Regardless of their experience, teachers can't be handed a course from another context and asked to teach it effectively without fully understanding its goals, outcomes, materials, and underlying pedagogical approach and theoretical rationale, and without getting support to strategically adapt the course to meet the needs of a different group of students at a different developmental stage. Like most good college composition programs, faculty development in DCCPs should include a thorough introduction to the course and the curriculum for newly appointed teachers and frequent, ongoing workshops and other opportunities for existing teachers. The challenges are not only course or content related; they concern the complex interrelationships arising from the social, interpersonal, academic, situational, and institutional spaces the students inhabit—spaces defined by public ideologies of "high school" and its socially determined rules and behaviors. As difficult as it is for inexperienced college teachers to teach something as complex as college-level writing to first-year students, for high school teachers to do the same in their own schools requires intense, sustained focus and a disposition—amid many other competing responsibilities—of continuous reflective practice (Schön). These are not accomplished or encouraged through only an occasional workshop and once-a-year site visit.

Most DCCPs separate faculty development for the college and high school teachers, perhaps assuming that the groups have different needs. In addition to the burdens of redundancy, this approach loses opportunities for the kind of articulation that supporters of DCCPs often tout. To reach a standard of effective faculty development, it may be insufficient for the program administrators simply to "align" dual-credit high school teachers to the pedagogical demands and routines of the college course. The best programs will engage all teachers in both separate and merged faculty development. In the CIS program, this was rarely the case, usually because of practicalities such as the teachers' schedules. With some advanced planning, joint development sessions could have been organized for the exchange of ideas among teachers in the two contexts.

Beyond individual site visits (which teachers can mistakenly interpret as summative evaluations of their performance), DC-CPs commonly use workshops and presentations to provide the bulk of faculty development. However, the logistics of planning and delivering workshops and getting time off for teachers force most administrators to arrange only one or two per year, hardly enough to provide ongoing faculty development. Emerging technologies offer some useful new ways to keep teachers connected and provide opportunities for reflective practice, including wikis and blogs, podcasts, listservs with RSS feeds, and synchronous conferencing. Discrepancies in technologies at the high schools should be evened out with appropriate funds for the program, a subject discussed under fairness in labor practices below.

During my administration of the CIS course, high school teachers were added to the program in very small numbers each spring, usually for replacement but also as the program slowly grew to include more schools. New teachers met with me and the associate director (a fifth-year PhD student) for a thorough, multiday orientation to the program and the course. They then joined the full group of teachers at the first workshop, timed to coincide with the start of fall classes. Individual meetings continued with these new teachers as needed. Although the entire group of teachers acted as a single collective and developed excellent rapport, many tended to socialize more strongly with certain members, which made it difficult for new teachers to know which groups to join. A more systematic effort to create learning communities for purposes of more intense collaboration and idea-sharing might have helped. At the time, digital technologies had not advanced enough to support ongoing connections with the group, which limited opportunities for continuous faculty development.

Like the course it supports, faculty development in DCCPs also must undergo continuous evaluation. How effectively do introductory workshops and orientations introduce new teachers to the course? What outcomes drive ongoing development, and how do teachers act on the principles, methods, and strategies they learn? How successfully do teachers work with each other, and what do they derive from their collaborative experiences? Typical methods for assessing faculty development include paper-and-pencil evaluations following a workshop experience, but these are often written hastily and don't always provide sufficient information. Online, formative evaluations and periodic surveys of teachers' needs or concerns can yield information useful for subsequent workshops. Substantive exit interviews should be conducted with teachers who leave the DCCP or retire; these can provide honest information about the quality of faculty development that is more difficult to collect when teachers are being evaluated and reappointed.

Economic Fairness

No dual-credit program is free. Even if a dual-credit program costs nothing to the students enrolled in the high school variation of the course, costs are always associated with the (re)allocation of labor and the administration of the program. Although it might be argued that the high school students take up no more of the on-site costs (instructional, infrastructural, etc.) than they normally would in the regular high school English course that the dual-credit section replaces, differences in class size, the need to hire substitutes when teachers must participate in training and development sessions, and the costs of administration and ongoing assessment all require additional funds. On the college campus, release time must be given to tenured faculty to administer the program and make site visits. To be financially equitable, a program must not disproportionately tax any party, and all must be agreeable to the allocation of resources and the fair sharing of costs.

Inequities can arise, for example, when a university with a dual-credit writing program profits from parents who believe that paying college tuition for their son or daughter to take a college course will save them money later. Yet if the university's tuition is based on a fixed amount for a full course load per semester, the students who have taken the dual-credit course may save nothing. They might be exempted from the university's composition requirement but will take some other required or elective course in its place. Additionally, as taxpayers, the parents have already supported the delivery of the high school course that the dual-credit course replaced. The university pays a fraction of its usual instructional costs when a "no-cost" high school teacher delivers the instruction, even when administrative costs are factored in.

The kind of assessment needed to ensure economic fairness will require budgetary transparency and scrutiny. The high school should calculate the direct and indirect costs associated with teaching the course. As Blattner and Frick point out, even if the high school course is offered for free or for reduced tuition charges, "colleges and universities make substantially more profits than on-campus offerings because the instructional facilities and teachers' primary salary and benefits are provided by participating high schools" (47). Ideally, tuition for the course should offset only the costs associated with the program, so that the sponsoring university is not profiting from the delivery of its course by the high school. Students should receive additional benefits for participating.

Student tuition in the CIS program is subvened by the state of Minnesota for all publicly funded high schools, so students take the course for free. Several times a year, students are bused to the university campus for a presentation and workshop given by a renowned writer or scholar, and this visit is carefully integrated into their course work. Students have access to university email and Internet resources, libraries, and physical facilities. The university's Division of Extension, which oversees the entire CIS program, provides support to the academic departments that administer the various courses. High school teachers in the program receive the same access privileges as campus faculty (for email, library cards, etc.), their time for training and development is covered by their schools, and their CIS classes are capped at lower numbers than their regular high school sections. All financial data, then, suggest equity among teachers, parents, and schools, in part because CIS is a state-funded program in which all funds ultimately come from the same source.

Fairness in Labor Practices

To ensure that no dual-credit program is motivated by interest either in profit or cost savings, the criterion of fairness in labor practices should never be overlooked. If a program meets or exceeds the criterion of faculty development, high school teachers will be engaged in significant activities beyond what they must already do under the terms of their employment. Although coordinators of dual-credit composition programs often point to high school teachers' desire for the "privileges" that come with being in an elite group of instructors—such as having adjunct faculty status and teaching a limited-enrollment course to high-ranking seniors (Farris 107)—their enthusiasm may mask the reality that they are putting in far more time and energy than if they were teaching standard high school courses.

Although many of the rewards for participation in a DCCP are intrinsic, some measure of additional, tangible benefit should accrue to its teachers and administrators. The responsibilities in a writing program for coordinating a DCCP will be heavy, and no director of composition should be assigned to shoulder them without additional pay or release time. For high school teachers, strict enrollment caps on DCCP courses can serve as a form of compensation for their additional work, along with access to all of the college campus' usual benefits to instructors (computer technology, library and recreational privileges, and the like). If faculty development requires teachers to give up time during summer or other breaks from their usual responsibilities, the program should provide them with a reasonable stipend for attending.

Fairness in labor practices also work both ways in a DCCP. It is important to recognize that most high school teachers are fully employed, salaried individuals with health and retirement benefits. Many school districts provide opportunities for a kind of de facto tenure for teachers, as well as "rung" systems or "fast lanes" that allow them to increase their status and salaries. Participating in a DCCP may actually garner them additional income, prestige, and status while also enhancing their professional credentials. On the sponsoring college campus, however, teachers of the same course may be underpaid, non-tenure-track, part-time, contingent faculty who receive no benefits and can be hired and fired by the semester. In such a situation, it is not the conditions of employment for those teaching the dual-credit course that deserve scrutiny but the conditions on the campus that the DCCP is supposed to "emulate." And although it may be tempting to argue that the existence of the DCCP reduces the reliance on poorly compensated instructors on the college campus, no DCCP should ever be used as the "remedy" for the abrogation of responsibility to treat college instructors fairly.

Assessment of fairness in labor practices requires the participation of all teachers and administrators. Some data-gathering methods include anonymous surveys of teachers, focus groups with teachers and administrators, self-reports of teacher workload, and frequent examinations of all data (both from the schools and the college or university) about teacher compensation and benefits over time.

Conclusion: Toward Continuous Improvement

Clearly, many of the standards in the proposed matrix overlap. Good faculty development is also about encouraging good pedagogy and about managing a healthy program. Fairness in labor practices is tied to student support, to the extent that teachers have time and incentives or remuneration to work individually with students needing additional help beyond what they typically can provide. These overlaps suggest that dual-credit programs cannot be run on the cheap; nor should they be vulnerable, once established, to repeated budgetary reductions just because they have reached a point of smooth operation.

The matrix in Table 11.1 suggests some broad categories within which we can ask quality-based questions about the nature of DCCPs, each of which needs to be answered through specific indicators that lend themselves to data collection and analysis. These data, in turn, provide crucial information about how well we are achieving the general standards of the DCCP, leading more directly and systematically to plans for improvements and their implementation.

Finally, the results of both formative and summative assessment of dual-credit programs using an expanded and refined version of the rubric presented in this chapter will suggest fruitful directions for broader (and much needed) educational research. What effect, if any, does the physical, social, and instructional context of high school have on students' intellectual readiness to engage in college-level work in writing? Do students construct their culminating high school experience, regardless of instruction, differently than they construct their beginning college experience? Steeped in the assumptions and experiences of their context, how do high school teachers interpret "college-level teaching" and operationalize it in the high school version of the course? How much knowledge of the college curriculum and experience do high school teachers need to have to teach the course effectively? Absent college-level writing experiences in other disciplines, how well can students learn variations in the genres and expectations of writing in other college courses? What are the best indexes of student readiness for a dual-credit course: GPA? Scores on standardized tests such as the SAT or PSAT? Prior performance in English or writing courses? Teacher recommendations? How do other aspects of students' cross-curricular and extra-curricular experiences affect their performance in either the high school course or the college course? What are the effects on high schools of offering college-level courses—such as effects on retention, graduation rates, and college acceptance? Exploring questions like these will not only help specific dual-credit administrators to create the most informed and principled programs but will also challenge us to keep revisiting the question of whether offering college courses at the high school level enriches the educational options for some students or simply confuses the needs of writing in two entirely different contexts, diminishing both in the process.

Notes

1. This chapter focuses on college courses taught in the high schools by high school teachers; it does not consider national, institutionalized programs such as the College Board's Advanced Placement English Program, which has a robust internal system of evaluation and accountability (see Jolliffe and Phelan).

2. NACEP defines CEPs (concurrent enrollment partnerships) only as those programs in which college courses are taught by certified high school teachers at the high school "during the normal school day" (2); other kinds of dual-credit programs are not included.

3. As an administrator of the CIS writing course, I often questioned the logic of allowing high school juniors to enroll in the program. It should be the purpose of dual-credit writing courses to strengthen *preparation* for college (an argument for restricting the course to seniors), not *admission* to college (an argument for including juniors). Assessment data showed that juniors did not score statistically lower than their senior counterparts in the course, but this was clearly an issue that required far more investigation than our resources allowed.

4. For a while, the course was co-administered by a faculty member and one of the high school teachers, who had decades of instructional and administrative experience and had been heavily involved in the National Council of Teachers of English and the National Writing Project.

Works Cited

Bartholomae, David. "Inventing the University." *When a Writer Can't Write: Studies in Writer's Block and Other Composing Problems.* Ed. Mike Rose. New York: Guilford, 1985. 134–65. Print.

Blackstock, Alan, and Virginia Norris Exton. "'Drive-by English': Teaching College English to High School Students via Interactive TV." *Teaching English in the Two-Year College* 32.4 (2005): 379–89. Print.

Blattner, Nancy, and Jane Frick. "Seizing the Initiative: The Missouri Model for Dual Credit Composition Courses." *WPA: Writing Program Administration* 26.1–2 (2002): 44–56. Print.

Bodmer, Paul. "Is It Pedagogical or Administrative? Administering Distance Delivery to High Schools." Yancey 115–26.

Carter, Michael. "Ways of Knowing, Doing, and Writing in the Disciplines." *College Composition and Communication* 58.3 (2007): 385–418. Print.

Coffman, Sara Jane. "Small Group Instructional Evaluation across Disciplines." *College Teaching* 46.3 (1998): 106–12. Print.

Conference on College Composition and Communication. *CCCC Position Statement on Teaching, Learning, and Assessing Writing in Digital Environments.* CCCC, 2004. Web. 20 Dec. 2008.

———. *Statement of Principles and Standards for the Postsecondary Teaching of Writing.* CCCC, 1989. Web. 20 Dec. 2008.

———. *Writing Assessment: A Position Statement.* CCCC, 2006. Web. 20 Dec. 2008.

Council of Writing Program Administrators. "WPA Outcomes Statement for First-Year Composition." *WPA: Writing Program Administration* 23.1–2 (1999): 59–63. Print.

Dallas, Phyllis Surrency, Nancy Bishop Dessommes, and Ellen H. Hendrix. "The Distance Learning Composition Classroom: Pedagogical and Administrative Concerns." *ADE Bulletin* 127 (Winter 2001): 55–59. Print.

Edmonds, Gerald S., Joseph Mercurio, and Margaret Bonesteel. *Research Report: Syracuse University Project Advance and the Advanced Placement Program: Comparing Two National Models for Curricular Articulation and Academic Challenges.* Syracuse: Syracuse University, Project Advance, 1998. Print.

Farris, Christine. "The Space Between: Dual-Credit Programs as Brokering, Community Building, and Professionalization." Yancey 104–14.

Feldman, Ann M., Tom Moss, Diane Chin, Megan Marie, Candice Rai, and Rebecca Graham. "The Impact of Partnership-Centered, Community-Based Learning on First-Year Students' Academic Research Papers." *Michigan Journal of Service Learning* 13.1 (2006): 16–29. Print.

Frick, Jane, and Nancy Blattner. "Reflections on the Missouri CWA Surveys, 1989–2001: A New Composition Delivery Paradigm." *College Composition and Communication* 53.4 (2002): 739–46. Print.

Gelmon, Sherril B., Barbara A. Holland, Amy Driscoll, Amy Spring, and Seanna Kerrigan. *Assessing Service-Learning and Civic Engagement: Principles and Techniques.* Providence: Campus Compact, 2001. Print.

Hillocks, George, Jr. *Research on Written Composition: New Directions for Teaching.* Urbana: ERIC/RCS and NCTE/NCRE, 1986. Print.

Jolliffe, David A., and Bernard Phelan. "Advanced Placement, Not Advanced Exemption: Challenges for High Schools, Colleges, and Universities." Yancey 89–103.

Lazar, Mary. "Dual-Enrollment and Its Impact on Composition Programs." Annual Convention of the Conference on College Composition and Communication Convention. Palmer House, Chicago. 23 Mar. 2006. Address.

Lenze, Lisa Firing. "Small Group Instructional Diagnosis (SGID)." *Practically Speaking: A Sourcebook for Instructional Consultants in Higher Education.* Ed. Kathleen T. Brinko and Robert J. Menges. Stillwater: New Forums, 1997. 143–46. Print.

Listoe, Alana. "College Credit: Opportunity or Obstacle?" *Independent Record*, 20 Apr. 2008. Web. 20 Dec. 2008.

Metropolitan Community Colleges. *Dual-Credit Enrollment Handbook: High Schools, 2004–05.* Metropolitan Community Colleges, n.d. Web. 2 Apr. 2009.

Missouri Colloquium on Writing Assessment. *Guidelines for the Delivery of Dual-Credit Composition Courses.* Missouri Colloquium on Writing Assessment, 1995. Print.

National Alliance of Concurrent Enrollment Partnerships. *Statement of National Concurrent Enrollment Partnership Standards.* NACEP, 2002. Web. 20 Dec. 2008.

Palomba, Catherine A., and Trudy W. Banta. *Assessment Essentials: Planning, Implementing, and Improving Assessment in Higher Education.* San Francisco: Jossey-Bass, 1999. Print.

Schön, Donald A. *The Reflective Practitioner: How Professionals Think in Action.* London: Temple Smith, 1983. Print.

Schwalm, David E. "High School/College Dual Enrollment." *WPA: Writing Program Administration* 15.1–2 (1991): 51–54. Print.

Townsend, Barbara K., and Susan B. Twombly. *Community Colleges: Policy in the Future Context.* Westport: Ablex, 2001. Print.

Vivion, Michael J. "High School/College Dual Enrollment and the Composition Program." *WPA: Writing Program Administration* 15.1–2 (1991): 55–60. Print.

Wolf, Richard M. *Evaluation in Education: Foundations of Competency Assessment and Program Review*. 2nd ed. New York: Praeger, 1984. Print.

Yancey, Kathleen, ed. *Delivering College Composition: The Fifth Canon*. Portsmouth: Boynton/Cook, 2006. Print.

CHAPTER TWELVE

Minding the Gap and Learning the Game: Differences That Matter between High School and College Writing

CHRISTINE R. FARRIS
Indiana University

Since Kristine and I began this book project, I have been called upon in the span of a year to defend first-year college writing in three different venues, all new to my WPA experience of almost twenty years. One of these is a major overhaul of general education requirements mandated by my institution's board of trustees and set in motion by the faculty council. The second involves course articulation agreements among the flagship, branch, and two-year college campuses in the state university system. The third concerns the state legislators' decision to require all Indiana high schools to offer two AP and two concurrent enrollment courses. It is hard to take issue with the primary goal of all three of these initiatives: greater, quicker, and easier access to college, timely graduation, and employment for more Hoosiers, a high percentage of whom traditionally are not college bound. It is easy to see, though, in a market where producers and consumers are trying to do more with less, how composition becomes a commodity easily appropriated, sold, outsourced, and knocked off.

Despite my support for greater access to college and my history with both WAC and the university's concurrent enrollment program, I have found myself on various committees having to argue that English departments, courses, and instructors in research universities, two-year colleges, and high schools are not similarly rigorous (with good reason); that not all departments and disciplines in need of credit hours are equipped to deliver direct instruction in first-year composition; and that not all students are ready any time, anywhere, for college-level academic writing. Along with the differences in institutional missions, disciplinary expertise, and student needs and abilities, there is an issue that seldom gets acknowledged when advocates make articulation agreements and design so-called bridges between high school and college—and that is the differences in teachers working within different cultures of schooling.

Gerald Graff, in *Clueless in Academe,* maintains that what hampers the college preparation efforts in the secondary schools is our failure at the postsecondary level to clarify the "culture of ideas and arguments" that we take for granted (3). The academic culture at the top simply needs to demystify what Graff refers to as "the game" and clarify "how the argument world works" (11), so that high schools can prepare students to succeed in college. Certainly making visible to teachers and students the discursive moves characteristic of academic disciplines is a good thing. Joseph Harris, in his excellent book *Rewriting,* also aims to share with students how, as academic writers, they should go about not just arguing with but also "drawing from, commenting on, adding to—the work of others" (2). David Rosenwasser and Jill Stephen, in their textbook *Writing Analytically,* five editions of which I have used, introduce students to the "five analytical moves" as not so much "a set of skills" as a "frame of mind, an attitude toward experience" (4). I would argue that this broader objective of developing students' critical understanding, not just assigning writing that is practice for writing in situations yet to come, might best frame the college preparation shared by secondary and postsecondary teachers. Truly sharing this goal and changing practices in light of it, however, requires coming to an understanding of how our notions of good writing and our institutional constraints differ across the school culture divide.

These days, more than ever, high school teachers tell me of the pressure to teach accessible formats for writing-on-demand. "Success in college" starts with a high-enough test score. At the same time, however, most university faculty are concerned, not so much with format, as with students' engagement with the ideas in what they read for their courses. By "engage" they mean something more than just reacting or cutting and pasting the ideas of experts into a paper. Much of the time college writing assignments call for analysis, for understanding *how* something works or *why* it works the way it does. Often faculty report that students stop short of analysis when they merely ventriloquize the positions of authors, agree/disagree, or offer a personal response that ignores textual evidence or a significant larger context. Do these differences between high school and college thinking and writing constitute "a game"? If so, where are we likely to find the best coaches?

One of my favorite dramatizations of preparing students for the intellectual game of college is Alan Bennett's play and film *The History Boys*. In this British comic drama set in a 1980s Sheffield grammar school, Bennett contrasts the approaches of two instructors who, under the watchful eye of a headmaster seeking more prestigious college placements, are coaching a group of senior boys for the entrance exams to Oxford and Cambridge. The English teacher, Hector, is an old-school believer in learning for its own sake. His classes can best be described as E. D. Hirsch's *Cultural Literacy: The Musical*. Along with grammar rules, Hector's students recite lines from W. H. Auden and A. E. Housman, perform songs by Lorenz and Hart, and reenact Bette Davis's final scene from *Now, Voyager*.

Enter Irwin, a young history instructor hired to coach the students in writing strategies that will impress the university examiners. Hector values the eternal verities and close readings of poetry that function "as if a hand has come out and taken yours" (56). In sharp contrast, Irwin's tutorials in trickery push the boys' analyses of history beyond the predictable regurgitations of facts and received opinions toward more complicated theses that will get them noticed and admitted. "The wrong end of the stick is the right one," Irwin tells them. "A question has a front door and a back door. Go in the back, or, better still, the side" (35).

Ultimately, the play sides with Hector's more personal approach to lifelong learning—despite his, shall we say, hands-on excesses—and not with Irwin's more sophistical teaching-to-the-test. In one sense, *The History Boys* concerns the classic differences between high school and college thinking: the distinction made by Jack Meiland between high school–level learning of facts about what is currently believed and college-level investigation of the basis for those beliefs. Harvard's William G. Perry put it another way: "cow"—data without context or frame of reference—versus "bull"—discourse upon the context and frames of reference "which would determine the . . . meaning of data if one had any" (54–55). Deep down, the playwright Bennett seems less interested in cognitive or rhetorical differences than he is with the class difference laid bare by the two approaches. There are traces in the play of Bennett's fellow Brit Richard Hoggart (*The Uses of Literacy*) calling for and, at the same time, troubling the notion of access to college for the "scholarship boy."

The beloved Hector's aims for his students' democratic education are sincere: "Pass the parcel. Pass it on boys. That's the game I wanted you to learn" (Bennett 109). Irwin, who, it turns out, has been lying all along about his Oxford pedigree, merely equips the boys for what Hoggart calls "hurdle-jumps, the hurdles of scholarships which are won by learning how to amass and manipulate the new currency" (243), the strain of which may leave college students too jaded and exhausted for the actual college inquiry they have been "trying on," as David Bartholomae would say, before they own it (134). It was, of course, this "technique of apparent learning, of acquiring facts rather than handling and use of facts" (Hoggart 243) that resonated with essayist Richard Rodriguez, who recognized himself in that scholarship boy who sees "life as a ladder, as permanent examination with some praise and some exhortation at each stage" (Hoggart qtd. in Rodriguez 559).

To what extent, I wonder, is the increasing pressure to develop more AP and concurrent enrollment courses in high schools becoming the American version of Hoggart's "hurdle-jumping," a simulation of college that has more to do with padding applications and racking up credits for students (and ambitious headmasters) than with strengthening students' engagement with texts and ideas in ways that will sustain them in college and beyond? I like to think there is another way to mind the gap between high school and college that does not require choosing between sentimental recitation and superficial sophistry, a way that is not just all about mastering "the game."

A more nuanced reading of *The History Boys* might even lie with that which is made possible by, but which transcends, the headmaster's snobbish desperation. In one scene, English teacher Hector and history teacher Irwin collaborate in a class session, imagining an exam question on the Holocaust. The students apply what they've learned from both instructors as they consider the extent to which one can even teach the Holocaust: is it possible to achieve Irwin's brand of critical distance to analyze origins and consequences of the Holocaust within a framework of foreign policy, or is Hector's position of nonrepresentability and suggestion of silence more appropriate? By the end of the class period—the only one in which we have seen a line of thought pursued—the class raises more questions than it answers. The student most closely associated with Hector's recitations and song fests, Posner, a Jew, calls into question the contextualizing move as "a step toward saying it can be understood and that it can be explained. And if it can be explained that it can be explained away" (Bennett 74).

Later in the play, Dakin, the class star, also demonstrates what we know, but so often forget: while students often make less of what we teach them, they also can make more. Dakin muses that perhaps history involves chance, the what if's. . . . What if, he asks, in 1940, on the day that Chamberlain resigned, Halifax, the first choice for prime minister, hadn't had a toothache and gone to the dentist? Churchill might not have been appointed. "If Halifax had had better teeth, we might have lost the war." Dakin calls his "move" both "a good game" and "subjunctive history," melding concepts from across Hector's and Irwin's curricula (Bennett 90).

By the end of the play, all the boys eventually are admitted to either Oxford or Cambridge, having written exams that got them noticed by doing something more than following formulas or recycling received wisdom. Would that in real life disagreements about what should be taught could more often become the curriculum for students. I am reminded of Graff's earlier suggestion for how to make the moves of academic culture visible to students. His recommendation in the 1990s to "teach the conflicts" called for foregrounding rather than obscuring in separate courses our theoretical and ideological differences ("Teach the Conflicts" 62;

Clueless 12). Graff's goal, then as now—to help students develop habits of mind that encourage rather than reduce controversy—is laudable and relevant to considerations of how much we can do with college writing courses in high school.

While it is perhaps the AP courses designed to prepare students for exams, and not the full-blown concurrent-enrollment courses, that most resemble the sessions in *The History Boys,* I want to raise a question that applies to both: To what extent is it possible in high school to make visible, as Graff calls it, "this game that academia obscures" (*Clueless* 3)? I certainly believe that preparation for academic engagement takes time, that it involves, as with *The History Boys,* exposure to more than one teaching style and more than one expert on a subject, and that sometimes it takes collaboration. Such is the case with the concurrent enrollment program in which I serve as a faculty liaison.

In Indiana University's first-year composition course, one of the ways we work to instill new habits of mind is to use readings that provide "portable concepts"—DuBois's "double consciousness," Milgram's obedience to authority, or Foucault's panopticism—that can be used to analyze more than what an author is specifically writing about in his or her book or article. While some readings may model particular genres or rhetorical strategies, essays with portable concepts offer new lenses for understanding issues, phenomena, images, and events, some of which students may have taken for granted. As Harris suggests, this is how knowledge moves forward in many of the fields students plan to enter, and this is why college writing may differ a great deal from writing in high school.

Making visible the habits and moves that critical thinkers and successful academic writers may intuit on their own is thus central to the composition curriculum I introduce to new English department graduate TAs and to the high school instructors teaching our course for the Advance College Project (ACP), a twenty-seven-year-old cooperative program between Indiana University and more than 100 high schools in Indiana, Michigan, and Ohio. In seventeen years of working with the program as a faculty liaison, I have learned that sharing typical academic writing moves is not a simple matter. Often we risk turning those "moves" into formulas. When transported to the composition course in the high school culture, it is sometimes easy for heuristics or "templates" (Graff and Birkenstein xv), meant to encourage a more complex and contextualized argument, to become all about "the game" and not a part of the critical engagement with ideas that we expect in college. Eager to see their students succeed in a college course, some high school teachers still comfortable with the inoculation or admonition role, may, for instance, readily switch out the familiar five-paragraph essay for the "It seems to be about X, but it is also about Y" (Rosenwasser and Stephen 63) essay, rather than "move," perhaps informing their students that this is the paper format they'll be assigned at the university. Fostering genuine college-level inquiry in high school, out of which the writing should grow, involves more than sharing formulas, demystifying the rules, or passing an act of the state legislature.

With the help of Ted Leahey, current Advance College Project director and retired high school teacher, I conduct thirty-five-hour summer seminars that introduce the high school teachers (whose applications and credentials I have approved) to current methods in college composition and strategies for teaching the Indiana University English Department's first-year course emphasizing analytical reading and writing. While the teachers hold master's degrees and have experience teaching senior college prep English and, occasionally, composition at the college level, for the most part they work out of what compositionists would consider current-traditional and process writing lore. Typically, their identity and what power they have lies in encouraging self-discovery through reading and writing and, like Hector in *The History Boys*, a lifelong engagement with literature sprinkled with the maintenance of form and correctness.

While a week of "walking through" a standardized syllabus with a sequence of increasingly more complex academic writing tasks has been at the center of the concurrent-enrollment composition course training for many years, more often than not teachers would later implement that syllabus back in the high school through sets of rules and steps, more than through critical involvement with the ideas in the nonfiction readings from across the curriculum. After about a decade of disappointment in many of the student papers we saw on site visits to the high schools, I decided that our brand of demystification of what academic writing does (summary, critique, comparative critique, comparative analysis) was not enough to bring the high school course closer to the on-campus version.

While I stand by the quality of graduate instructors I prepare to teach composition on campus, I am also realistic about their delivery of instruction, especially those who are teaching for the first time. One advantage, though, is that the graduate student instructors are involved in those academic conversations, intellectual debates, and conflicts that Graff thinks we need to foreground, while the high school teachers are, most often, not. To prepare the first-time teacher, we have always been quick to simulate a real classroom in order to model on-the-spot rhetorical analysis of an essay, photograph, or film scene. I had been more likely to ask the new TAs to write the papers they would assign and share their drafts and concerns with one another. While they readily "get" what we are trying to accomplish in using essays by the likes of Foucault, Clifford Geertz, and Deborah Tannen for the keywords, portable concepts, and critical lenses they provide students in their analyses of issues and cultural phenomena, unlike the veteran high school teachers, the TAs need, at first, a weekly proseminar and peer mentors to guide them in matters of classroom management, leading discussion, and grading papers.

Eventually, I realized that if I wanted the otherwise experienced high school teachers to invite the sort of inquiry that their students' papers should reflect (and which the graduate student TAs were simultaneously experiencing in their graduate courses), I would need to model that inquiry with them also. I do more of this now in the summer seminar, not just by providing prompts or heuristics that take us beyond the five-paragraph essay, but by tracing the original impulses behind what it is in scholarly work across the curriculum that leads to an author's eventual claim. In explaining the final composition course assignment on researching a cultural trend, for instance, I now introduce them to sociologist Howard Becker's invention techniques that do not ask "What are the three causes of the trend?" (à la the five-paragraph essay), but what social, historical, and economic conditions would have to be in place for a particular trend to take hold? As a group, we explore possible avenues of inquiry on trends as diverse as weight loss reality shows and teenage chaste vampirism. The teachers are much more likely to view academic writing, then, not just as the problem/solution paper or the huge term paper with the requisite number of outside sources and proper citations, but as attempts to investigate a question that invites multiple disciplinary perspectives and further conversation and research.[1]

In an effort to continue high school teachers' own academic work in ways that will shape how they develop and teach the concurrent enrollment course, the Advance College Program offers fellowships for teachers to return for content-area graduate courses in rhetoric and composition as well as literature. This opportunity has made it possible for us to include those returning teachers in our graduate-level seminars, along with English graduate students/TAs, and to integrate graduate pedagogy courses with sections of advanced expository writing for preservice teachers, and occasionally with sections of first-year composition, making possible common assignments and discussion sessions, as well as teacher-researcher projects. In these two- and three-course clusters, we meet periodically as a whole group, read many of the same primary and secondary texts, write some of the same papers, exchange and respond to drafts, design and critique assignments and prompts, and sometimes conduct case study investigation in the first-year composition sections on pedagogical issues and problems in student writing. Naturally, our different practices and assumptions about literacy, interpretation, and what constitutes "good writing" come to light. The preservice teachers, especially, benefit from cross-talk among the high school teachers who will likely mentor their student teaching and the instructors on campus, reflecting on what they believe and practice in their respective classrooms.

Despite all the recent pressure to address the disconnect between high school and college curricula, increasing the number of AP and concurrent enrollment courses without consideration of the context for our pedagogical differences only ensures that precollege students will "hurdle-jump," not that they will learn to write, succeed in their course work, and graduate. It takes more than just sharing syllabi and credits to build a bridge across the high school–college gap. As concurrent enrollment moves from trend to business-as-usual, we must acknowledge that a growing number of high school teachers are now college teachers as well. Recently, on the reform front, there is pressure to replace methods courses in schools of education with a greater emphasis on disciplinary content. This need not be an either/or binary if English departments and concurrent enrollment programs are willing to embark on real disciplinary collaboration and professionalization that addresses, both theoretically and practically, the differences in our approaches to the use of texts and ideas in student writing. We can make more of the concurrent enrollment business than just the "taking care of" required courses.

Note

1. I also discuss these issues in my essay "Inventing the University in High School," part of a special symposium with Gerald Graff, Cathy Birkenstein-Graff, Doug Hesse, and Dennis Baron in *College Composition and Communication*. For a longer description of the Indiana University Advance College Project composition seminar, see my chapter "The Space Between: Dual-Credit Programs as Brokering, Community Building, and Professionalization."

Works Cited

Bartholomae, David. "Inventing the University." *When a Writer Can't Write: Studies in Writer's Block and Other Composing Problems.* Ed. Mike Rose. New York: Guilford, 1985. 134–65. Print.

Bennett, Alan. *The History Boys*. New York: Faber, 2004. Print.

Farris, Christine. "Inventing the University in High School." *College Composition and Communication* 61.1 (2009): W436–W443. Web. 29 Sept. 2009.

———. "The Space Between: Dual-Credit Programs as Brokering, Community Building, and Professionalization." *Delivering College Composition: The Fifth Canon.* Ed. Kathleen Blake Yancey. Portsmouth: Boynton/Cook, 2006. 104–14. Print.

Graff, Gerald. *Clueless in Academe: How Schooling Obscures the Life of the Mind.* New Haven: Yale UP, 2003. Print.

———. "Teach the Conflicts." *The Politics of Liberal Education*. Ed. Darryl J. Gless and Barbara Herrnstein Smith. Durham: Duke UP, 1992. 57–73. Print.

Graff, Gerald, and Cathy Birkenstein. *"They Say/I Say": The Moves That Matter in Academic Writing*. New York: Norton, 2006. Print.

Harris, Joseph. *Rewriting: How to Do Things with Texts*. Logan: Utah State UP, 2006. Print.

Hoggart, Richard. *The Uses of Literacy*. Boston: Beacon, 1961. Print.

Meiland, Jack W. "The Difference between High School and College." *College Thinking: How to Get the Best Out of College*. New York: New American Library, 1981. Print.

Perry, William. "Examsmanship and the Liberal Arts." *Examining in Harvard College: A Collection of Essays by Members of the Harvard Faculty*. Cambridge: Harvard U, 1963. Rpt. in *The Dolphin Reader*. 2nd ed. Ed. Douglas Hunt. Boston: Houghton, 1990. 48–59. Print.

Rodriguez, Richard. "The Achievement of Desire." *Ways of Reading: An Anthology for Writers*. Ed. David Bartholomae and Anthony Petrosky. 8th ed. Boston: Bedford/St. Martin's, 2008. 544–63. Print.

Rosenwasser, David, and Jill Stephen. *Writing Analytically*. 5th ed. Boston: Thomson, 2009. Print.

Afterword: Of Cellists and Writers, Getting Better and Getting On

DOUGLAS HESSE
University of Denver

My son is a professional cellist. He began taking lessons when he was five, spurred by a random comment from a grandmother that "it's too bad there isn't a cellist in the family to get my instrument when I retire." We convinced Dr. Rye, a retired music professor, to take on Andrew in the twilight of his career and began renting a series of quarter- and half-size cellos until the fateful day when we bought his first full-size cello.

I begin with this anecdote to stage the question, "Is learning to write like learning to play cello?" This isn't a frivolous question.

Consider that learning a musical instrument is largely decoupled from chronological age. One moves along through exercises, études, and the performance repertory according to one's skills and ability to perform the literature rather than by birthday. By the time that Andrew was in fourth grade, for example, he was playing in the junior high orchestra. As he became more accomplished, Andrew performed recitals, first on a program with others and later as solo events, so that by the time he completed his master's in cello performance, he played over an hour of memorized music, accompanied and not.

As is traditional, the program for that culminating recital listed his teachers: Howard Rye, Chris Frye, Greg Hamilton, Nina Gordon, and Hans Jensen. Learning a musical instrument happens largely through individual lessons with a single teacher over stretches of time lasting years. Each teacher may have a set "curriculum," but how quickly a student moves through it is a function of talent and application (or, in the case of Bill Murray's piano playing in the film *Groundog Day*, boredom). At some point a student has mastered what he or she can from a particular teacher and moves to another, in a succession of master/apprentice relationships.

Now, there are class-based counterparts to individual instruction—most famously, the Suzuki method. In the case of inexperienced college music majors, "class piano" is the most efficient way to get legions of students up to the rudimentary skills they'll need as band directors or singers. On the other end, as a fourth grader in small-town Iowa, I learned to play trombone with three other kids in a weekly lesson with a band director who was a clarinetist but who had taken a series of "methods" courses in college, giving him survival skills to teach any instrument in the band. Even though I went on to play in college and beyond, I never had the "private lessons" that were encouraged but unusual in that time and place for working-class kids like me.

However tempting it may be to reminisce about musical instruction, I've sketched enough of the process to make a few contrasts with writing. First, writing instruction nearly always takes place in a class setting rather than an individual one. We don't have a tradition of "writing lessons" in the same fashion as cello lessons and, in fact, one-on-one instruction is commonly associated with tutorial remediation. Second, except in the few remaining one-room school equivalents, home schools, or very small high schools with but one or two teachers per subject area, students have new teachers every year, perhaps even every semester. Third, the writing curriculum, such as it may be, is organized by grade level, with slight variations for electives or advanced placement in later years; in music, progress happens through mastery rather than by calendar or grade. Fourth, whereas writing—or English—is required, instrumental music is generally elective. Even schools that encourage or require all students to start an instrument eventually let them decide to opt out (though, in the case of parents obliging piano lessons, that point may not come soon enough). Fifth, although writing instruction is generally a class lesson rather than a private one, and although the goal is generally to bring students to some common standards, the performance of writing is almost exclusively individualistic. Most school music is performed socially, in groups; while there are solo and ensemble contests or performances, these generally exist outside of—and to supplement—the collective performances. School music is a communal activity with an important group identity mission.

What I've listed above are mainly structural and pedagogical differences in the relationships of music and writing to educational institutions. The distinctions are primarily social, sediments of long-accreting assumptions about what is "basic" and what is "elective" or ancillary. These social constructions have clear implications for how the respective arts of music and writing are taught and regarded, obviously. A thought experiment would be to reverse the polarity, teaching writing as an optional activity for interested and talented students who are largely expected to arrange and pay for their lessons on their own. Now, there are some relative counterparts to the band, orchestra, or chorus: the school literary magazine, yearbook, or newspaper, whether printed or pixeled. But there remains mainstream writing, required for all.

Beyond these structural differences are more complicated questions about the nature of learning to write versus learning to play. At first they may seem quite different acts, writing as primarily an act of socially mediated individual cognition and playing as primarily an act of muscular training and response. Mind/body. Certainly, there is a physical dimension to writing and a cognitive dimension to playing, so the break isn't clean. But let's take this a step further and wonder about the parallels between stages of development in these respective arts. We've seen plenty of musical prodigies with virtuoso technical abilities at very young ages. And yet, there are certain parts of the repertory closed off to young pianists, for example, whose hands can't span octaves or ninths. Even the most skilled cellist on a quarter-size instrument cannot produce the sounds possible through a full-sized one. To stretch this even further, regardless of one's individual abilities, certain areas of orchestral performance remain closed until one has access to others capable of that literature.

And writing? Is there a cognitive correlative to physical limitations on a young cellist? Can there be young writers capable of virtuosic grammar and syntax, capable of stunning compositions, who, nonetheless, necessarily lack the depth of knowledge and experience to do certain kinds of writing? Are there realms of writing experience parallel to orchestral performance that are closed to young virtuosos who have few peers with whom to write? Are there, further, topical realms closed to some "young" situations: the personal narrative of religious agnosticism, say, or the critique of school DARE programs? "Bong hits for Jesus," anyone?

Now, I've taxed you with this extended analogy in order to open two lines of thinking about college writing credit in high school courses: can the settings be equivalent (the answer depending on the nature of writing and learning) and what motivates the desire to earn credit in this fashion (the answer depending on who's doing the desiring)? I've taken this circuitous route because Kristine Hansen and Christine Farris have done such a masterful job introducing the many issues that their authors so expertly address in the chapters in this collection.

I recognize that people vary tremendously in their writing abilities, whether at ten, twenty, or fifty. In terms of developing both individual and society-wide writing talent, it makes sense to recognize and teach to those differences, especially challenging those students who, like cellists skilled at an early age, write well. There's a question, however, of whether selection and separation are good for writers, skilled and not. There are benefits, after all, of being among writers of different abilities; giving and receiving feedback serve not only the social good of collaborative learning but also an individual good, even for the skilled writer, of having to teach his or her craft to others. Returning to the music analogy, most college performance majors require studio classes in addition to private lessons. When my son was finishing his master's at Northwestern, for example, the cello studio gathered all cellists, freshmen to PhD players, for weekly meetings in which they played together and for each other. Proficiency varied tremendously, yet the logic of this tradition goes beyond the best musician acting out of noblesse oblige for the beginners.

If writing were taught through a combination of individual lessons and group sharing/performances, then the parallel to the music studio would apply. But writing mostly is not. This isn't to say it mightn't be. Still, tradition and the structure of schooling resist such revisions; there are the efficiencies of scheduling and planning from dealing with students in mass groups and a restricted number of levels.

Of course, one can imagine classes at the high school level precisely emulating those at the college level, with the same textbooks, assignments, grading standards, even teachers. The six months' difference between spring senior year and fall freshman, for example, can't reasonably be cited as profound, even when the rapid cognitive and emotional growth of adolescents parallels their shoe sizes. But even if the courses can be made the same, their surroundings at some level cannot. There are different mixes of other courses in the college and school settings. There are differences in the relative amount of unscheduled class time for college students (twelve to eighteen hours per week) versus high school (thirty or more). There are the different living arrangements: the residence hall versus the bedroom in Mom and Dad's house, for example; even college students living at home interact with students who aren't, not to mention with students of different ages. A profound question, then, is how much difference it makes for a student to take the identical course in two different circumstances.

The previous paragraphs explore the question of "can." Beyond it is the question of "should." If it is possible to reproduce in the high school setting all meaningful aspects of college, should we? One approach is to ask what's displaced. Are there kinds of writing that are developmentally, emotionally, and aesthetically appropriate at the high school level that would be detrimentally occluded by the college composition course? College composition generally focuses on argument, generally for academic situations that involve writing about readings. This is a narrower range than often pertains in high school. Each year at the University of Denver we ask first-year students about their high school writing experiences. Following are the most common types of writing experiences freshmen reported in 2009:

Selected "main types" of writing that 766 University of Denver first-year students did in high school. (Percentage of students reporting they did a type at least several times.)

"Five-paragraph" essays or themes   91.6%

Literary analyses/interpretations   91.5%

Argumentative or persuasive essays about an issue or event	85.3%
Research papers using library or other published sources	83.1%
Lab reports for science classes	73.7%
Creative writing (poems, short stories, plays, etc.)	69.1%
Personal responses to a nonfiction reading	64.6%
Analyses of a nonfiction reading (any kind)	55.2%
Autobiographical writings, such as a memoir or personal essay	49.1%
Research based on data that you generated	37.6%
Rhetorical analyses	34.1%

Now, I have reservations about some of these, especially the more fossilized forms of five-paragraph themism. And I'm frequently disheartened by students who come to college writing courses jaded about writing because they've been taught over and over again some fairly narrow versions of what college writing is. Please note that I'm not blaming high school English teachers, who are in incredibly tough and complicated situations. So, I'm all for the best practices of college writing instruction informing high school teaching.

Still, there's something to be said about the amount of creative writing and writing about literature in my list, imagining they're being taught well. Neither activity is particularly common in college composition; would it be better for seventeen-year-olds—or sixteen- or fourteen-year-olds—instead to be writing critical syntheses of argumentative essays? This is a complicated question whose answer I can't address in this space, but it's one worth asking, and it's one not much being asked. The question differs from those about developmental readiness or even the equivalence of instructional settings. It concerns the nature of experience and the value of doing some kinds of writing at particular times—or perhaps not at all. If we simply accept the logic that the kind of writing being assigned now should be determined by the kind a student will most likely be asked produce in the future, what trumps? For example, should first-year composition programs abandon traditional essayistic and academic forms because almost no college graduate will ever again need to use MLA citation? Should we instead teach the genres of workplace and professional writing that we know students will practice? And where does the chain end? If college freshmen should learn workplace writing, then why not high school freshmen, and so on down the line? My point is that while "because you have to do this in the future" is an important guideline for setting a curriculum, it's not the only one. We ought to pay as much attention to what is possible and desirable now, and we ought to imagine futures that have not only academic and vocational discourse but also civic, interpersonal, and personal.

The second large question above asked about the motivations to earn college credit in high school. Some students, having aspirations for themselves as writers, may truly want to advance as quickly as possible to levels of instruction and opportunity that challenge their talents, much like musicians. My twenty-five years of teaching and advising students, including several spent as director of a large university honors program, and my analysis of the national scene for writing suggest such students are uncommon. Considerably more frequent is the desire to "get it out of the way" (sometimes expressed more politely), where "it" is a writing requirement. Now, the desire to avoid requirements is hardly restricted to writing: calculus, chemistry, Spanish, and such all present annoying obstacles to students, and they all share degrees of demanding discomforting effort from students. But there's a difference with writing. Many students, complaining of college requirements, protest that they already learned to write in high school. Reading their writings, one often does see a high level of ingenuity, organization, and technical/stylistic proficiency, so that's not the concern. What concerns me is the assumption that writing is mastered once and for all, a complete and finite skill like bicycle riding. One clear conclusion of discourse community, genre, and activity theory and research over the past twenty-five years is that writing is not such a skill, either in terms of knowledge or performance. Hence, a prestigious university like Stanford, presumably admitting some of the best qualified students in the country, doesn't accept AP credit as exemption. There's more to learn among new peers and in a new setting.

To be fair to students wanting to "get it out of the way," academia has cued them, subtly and not, to adopt this goal. First-year writing courses remain staffed primarily by graduate teaching assistants, adjuncts, or junior faculty, and writing across the curriculum programs notwithstanding, there is precious little "vertical" component to the writing curriculum. Even when students write extensively after their first year of college, writing is more often assigned than taught or made an object of study. Further, to be completely fair to students, even placement tests and procedures that sort into two or three different levels are hardly fine-grained. A student may encounter "revision" or "peer response" in a writing class a second or third time since high school, the teacher or program little acknowledging previous experience, a shortcoming often compounded by the nature of course staffing and its support. Reading all of these signs, students might understandably have a skeptical view of writing, a view grounded rather in the structure of the academy than in the nature of writing and its learning.

Two other motivations for getting it over are as important: cost efficiency and prestige. If many students perceive writing as a finite skill whose teaching in college is an unfortunate sign of remediation, so doubly do any manner of parents, professors, pundits, and policymakers. "If the schools were doing their jobs," or "If the senior year of high school weren't such a waste," the thinking goes, then we could spare the expense of these relatively small college writing courses. And even if the money savings are scant to nil (as Chris Anson explains in his chapter in this volume), there's at least the freeing up of curricular space for more central course work. Few people besides writing professors and scattered colleagues want to get the required course out of the way in order to support a higher-level required course. David Jolliffe, former chief reader of the Advanced Placement Language and Composition exam, has emphasized the *placement* aspect of the program, as Hansen points out in her chapter in this volume, but the interest is far less in taking advanced writing than in earning credit and being done.

As enthralling as financial motivation is the affirmation of being better than average—as a student, a parent, a school, a politician. We tend to like quick indicators of educational quality: test scores, school grades, national report cards. For a high school, the number or percentage of students completing AP or concurrent college credit courses provides such an indicator, one that education writer Jay Mathews, among others, consistently heralds as the single best. It consoles students, too. While directing the honors program at a large midwestern state university, I helped recruit excellent students. Often adding even a small scholarship offer to an admitted student was enough to persuade him or her to attend. For them, it was less a case of meeting financial need (the awards were mostly paltry) than making them feel validated and recognized as better than their peers. They learn these expectations from how our society both prizes young achievement and expects everywhere and always the Lake Woebegone effect.

But why the hurry? In the case of college credit for writing courses taken in high school, I understand students' desires for flexibility in choosing courses and their (usually false) hope of knocking semesters off graduation time. I can't, however, quite fathom the societal desire. That is, while I can appreciate at some level the broad quest for "rigor," it's hard to see what we get from endorsing that many students' formal instruction in writing should end their junior or senior years of high school. That desire depends on a view of writing development that would be convenient but, alas, just isn't supported by research. To be fair, the case could be made for sophisticated writing across the curriculum and in the disciplines' programs to continue student development. But a crucial factor in such programs is a strong element of explicit and intentional focus on instruction in and about writing, not just the experience of writing. The difference is between writing ability imagined as a vaccine dosed once and for all in a course, perhaps measured by a test, and writing ability imagined as ongoing levels of fitness produced by skilled trainers. Or writing ability as akin to levels of musicianship.

But perhaps, to the same degree it needs skilled cellists, "society" needs only so many skilled writers. In weighing two different goals, "getting better" and "getting on," perhaps at some level we're happy enough with getting on. That is, instead of systematically devising levels of instruction to challenge the whole spectrum of writers' needs and talents, we find it easier to posit "college writing" at some basic level and consider every-thing beyond simply elective. Players in the orchestra of writing need competence only to perform a fairly basic repertory, and we simply need to establish what that is. Personally, I'd wish for more, for a writing curriculum that progressively develops the best of students at every level rather than a curriculum that sets some limited criteria and encourages students to stop when they get there, the sooner the better. But these are vexed issues wrapped in the complex intertwinings of what is possible and what is desirable to do in the name of teaching writing, when, and where. Fortunately, Kristine Hansen and Christine Farris have put together a book that explores these issues with fairness, completeness, integrity, and nuance.

Work Cited

Mathews, Jay. "Trends: Banging on the PK-16 Pipeline." *Washington Post.com*. Washington Post Company, 20 Feb. 2009. Web. 21 Feb. 2009.

INDEX

EDITORS

Kristine Hansen is professor of English at Brigham Young University, where she has directed the English composition program and served as associate dean of undergraduate education, overseeing the university's writing-across-the-curriculum program. She currently serves as director of the university's internship office. She teaches undergraduate courses in advanced writing, the history of rhetoric, and rhetorical style, as well as graduate courses on theory and research methods. She is author of *Writing in the Social Sciences: A Rhetoric with Readings*. With Joseph Janangelo, she coedited *Resituating Writing: Constructing and Administering Writing Programs*.

Christine R. Farris is professor of English and director of the composition program at Indiana University in Bloomington, where she teaches courses in rhetoric and composition theory, expository writing for teachers, and literature. A former secondary English teacher and university WAC consultant, she also coordinates the concurrent enrollment composition course for Indiana University's Advance College Project. She is the author of *Subject to Change: New Composition Instructors' Theory and Practice*; coeditor with Chris Anson of *Under Construction: Working at the Intersections of Composition Theory, Research, and Practice*; and coeditor with Judith H. Anderson of the MLA volume

EDITORS

Integrating Literature and Writing Instruction: First-Year English, Humanities Core Courses, Seminars.

CONTRIBUTORS

Chris M. Anson is University Distinguished Professor of English and director of the Campus Writing and Speaking program at North Carolina State University, where he helps faculty in nine colleges use writing and speaking in the service of students' learning and improved communication. Most of his scholarly work—fifteen books and more than eighty journal articles and book chapters—focuses on the development and teaching of writing abilities, particularly across the curriculum. He has spoken at conferences and universities across the United States and in twenty-one other countries. His latest project is a coauthored book on digital literacies in the teaching of writing.

Margaret D. Bonesteel recently retired from her position as administrator for the English and writing courses offered through Syracuse University's Project Advance. She has taught at both the secondary and collegiate levels. Her professional interests have included organizational culture and change, student development, and professional development for teachers. She currently lives in Austria, where she is tutoring for the American International School in Vienna.

Kevin Enerson has been an educator for twenty years and the principal at LeSueur-Henderson Middle/High School in Minnesota since 2000–01. He led his school in the offering of concurrent enrollment classes; LeSueur-Henderson High currently offers high school students fifteen credits through Minnesota State University, Mankato.

Douglas Hesse is professor and founding director of the writing program at the University of Denver. He is past chair of CCCC, past president of WPA, and past editor of *WPA: Writing Program Administration*. Among his books are *Creating Nonfiction* (with Becky Bradway) and *The Simon and Schuster Handbook for Writers* (with Lynn Troyka). Author of some fifty articles and chapters, Hesse previously taught at Illinois State University, directing the Honors Program and the Center for the Advancement of Teaching.

Jane Kepple Johnson, a high school English teacher for more than thirty years, has taught in rural Minnesota and Iowa. For the past ten years she has taught concurrent enrollment courses at United South Central High School in Wells, Minnesota. She is a Minnesota Writing Project Teacher-Consultant and Minnesota's Rural Sites representative to the National Writing Project.

David A. Jolliffe is professor of English and curriculum and instruction at the University of Arkansas, where he holds the Brown Chair in English Literacy. From 2002 to 2007, he was chief reader for the Advanced Placement English Language and Composition exam. With Hephzibah Roskelly, he is the author of *Everyday Use: Rhetoric at Work in Reading and Writing*. He now devotes most of his energies to developing community literacy programs throughout Arkansas.

Joseph Jones, a former high school AP English teacher in Arizona, currently teaches in the graduate concentration in composition and professional writing at the University of Memphis, where he has also directed the first-year composition program.

Patricia Lipetzky is currently dean of the College of Extended Learning at Minnesota State University, Mankato. In this position, she developed and implemented the university's concurrent enrollment program. Previously, she was dean of continuing education at Grand Valley State University and Southeast Missouri State University. She is an active member in the University Continuing Education Association.

Randall McClure is associate professor of English and chair of the Department of Writing and Linguistics at Georgia Southern University. He has authored several resources for composition teachers, including the *Longman Writer's Warehouse for Composition*. His articles have appeared in *Composition Studies, Computers and Composition Online*, portal: *Libraries and the Academy, Academic Exchange Quarterly*, and *Journal of Literacy and Technology*.

Miles McCrimmon has taught English at J. Sargeant Reynolds Community College since 1992. He has taught twenty-three sections of dual enrollment on-site at three high schools in the Reynolds service area. He has been English Program head and Community College System Chancellor's Commonwealth Professor. He has published articles in *Teaching English in the Two-Year College, College English*, and *Lesson Plans for Teaching Writing*.

Patricia A. Moody, associate professor of English at Syracuse University, has taught courses in composition, rhetoric, language, linguistics, literature, and literary theory. She is the editor of *Readings in Textual Studies* and the author of *Writing Today*. For almost twenty-five years, she has been faculty coordinator for writing and English courses taught through Project Advance, Syracuse University's concurrent enrollment program.

Deirdre Paulsen has taught composition, rhetoric, and folklore at Brigham Young University since 1968. She has also taught English in high school, where she established lay reader programs for all grade levels. She instituted the Writing Fellows program and became director of BYU's writing-across-the-curriculum program in 1993. In 2001 she became co-director and later director of BYU's Publication Lab, helping students publish in local and national venues. She publishes in both composition/rhetoric and folklore.

Cynthia Pope taught concurrent enrollment English composition and literature classes through Minnesota State University, Mankato for several years. She currently teaches language, composition, and literacy courses at South Central College in Minnesota. She is active in speech forensics at both the secondary and postsecondary levels and plans to pursue a PhD engaging rhetorical sensitivity theory.

Joanna Castner Post is assistant professor of writing and director of the writing center at the University of Central Arkansas. Her latest publications include *Compositions in the New Liberal Arts*, a collection coedited with James Inman; "Getting Real and Feeling in Control: Haptic Interfaces" in *Small Tech: The Culture of Digital Tools*, edited by Byron Hawk, David M. Rieder, and Ollie Oviedo; and an article in *Technology and English Studies: Innovative Professional Paths*, edited by James Inman and Beth Hewitt.

Kathleen M. Puhr taught English at Clayton High School in suburban St. Louis for twenty-two years, fifteen of those as department head. She currently teaches AP English Literature at Central Visual and Performing Arts High School in St. Louis. She has published articles in scholarly journals as well as the *AP English Language Teacher's Guide* and a teacher's guide to Robert DiYanni's *Literature*. Since 1991 she has served as a reader for the AP English Language exam and has worked part-time for Educational Testing Service.

Barbara Schneider is director of composition, director of the writing center, and associate professor of English at the University of Toledo. She teaches courses in writing theory, research methods, and composition. She has published work in *CCC, Pedagogy, RSQ, WPA: Writing Program Administration,* and several edited collections. She recently edited a special issue of *Pedagogy* and is currently at work on a book about the rhetoric of pregnancy.

Vicki Beard Simmons has taught university-level public speaking and interpersonal communication courses for more than fifteen years. She taught most recently at the University of Central Arkansas, where she also served as the concurrent enrollment coordinator, building the program from only forty-two students to more than a thousand.

Steve Thalheimer is assistant superintendent for Fairfield Community Schools in Goshen, Indiana. He previously served as district curriculum coordinator for Lawrenceburg Schools in southern Indiana. He has taught honors courses, served as department chair, and directed an at-risk freshmen academy. He also taught as an adjunct instructor for Indiana University on the Bloomington campus and through the Advance College Project.

Stephanie Vanderslice, associate professor of writing at the University of Central Arkansas, has published essays in books and journals, including *Creative Writing Studies; New Writing: An International Journal of Creative Writing Theory and Practice; Profession; Teaching Creative Writing;* and *The Creative Writing Handbook.* With Kelly Ritter, she edited *Can It Really Be Taught? Resisting Lore in the Teaching of Creative Writing* and authored *Teaching Creative Writing to Undergraduates: A Resource and Guide.*

Colleen Whitley is the author of five books and numerous articles, poems, and reviews. She has taught in public schools and the Job Corps. She retired after teaching for twenty years at Brigham Young University for the English department and honors program, where she advised the honors journal and directed the publication lab to help students move their work into local and national markets. She currently serves on the board of editors for *Utah Historical Quarterly*, the journal of the Utah State Historical Society.

This book was typeset in Sabon by Barbara Frazier.
The typefaces used on the cover are Garamond and
Formata Light, Medium, and Italic.
The book was printed on 50-lb. Williamsburg Offset paper
by Versa Press, Inc.